TRAILBLAZERS OF BLACK BRITISH THEATRE

Also by Stephen Bourne

Aunt Esther's Story (ECOHP, 1991)
Black in the British Frame: The Black Experience in British Film and Television (Cassell/Continuum, 2001)
Black Poppies: Britain's Black Community and the Great War (The History Press, 2014; 2nd edition 2019)
Brief Encounters: Lesbians and Gays in British Cinema 1930–1971 (Cassell, 1996)
Elisabeth Welch: Soft Lights and Sweet Music (Scarecrow Press, 2005)
Esther Bruce: A Black London Seamstress (History and Social Action Publications, 2012)
Evelyn Dove: Britain's Black Cabaret Queen (Jacaranda Books, 2016)
Fighting Proud: The Untold Story of the Gay Men Who Served in Two World Wars (I.B. Taurus, 2017)
Mother Country: Britain's Black Community on the Home Front 1939–1945 (The History Press, 2010)
The Motherland Calls: Britain's Black Servicemen and Women 1939–1945 (The History Press, 2012)
Playing Gay in the Golden Age of British Television (The History Press, 2019)
Under Fire: Black Britain in Wartime 1939–1945 (The History Press, 2020)
War to Windrush: Black Women in Britain 1939–1948 (Jacaranda Books, 2018)

Praise for *Trailblazers of Black British Theatre*

'An incredible starting point for any student or practitioner interested in exploring this area in more detail ... I particularly enjoyed the blending of the first-person narrative with the rigor of academic research, making this both an enjoyable and educational read.'

Erin Lee, Judge, 2022 Society for Theatre Research Book Prize

'Stephen Bourne is my go-to for the stories of Black British people that would otherwise be forgotten. [This book] is a history of trailblazing Black theatre-makers, exceptionally researched and brimming with detailed knowledge. It is also a love story and a tribute to the Black creatives that have shaped not only theatrical history but the way future generations view the world.'

Patrice Lawrence MBE, FRSL, author of *Orangeboy*

'I'm amazed by Stephen's extensive knowledge of the long history of Black theatre in Britain. This is an invaluable resource for anyone interested in Black British history, both on and off the stage.'

Kandace Chimbiri, author of *The Story of the Windrush* and *The Story of Afro Hair*

'Every young Black actor should read this book in recognition of the legacy of Black actors in the UK. Within it they will find inspiration, a sense of belonging and an understanding of the limitless possibilities that await them in the world of acting.'

Suzann McLean MBE, CEO/Artistic Director Theatre Peckham

TRAILBLAZERS OF BLACK BRITISH THEATRE

From Ira Aldridge to Cleo Laine

STEPHEN BOURNE

The History Press

Cover illustration: Cleo Laine and Pearl Prescod. (Author's collection, courtesy of Pearl Connor-Mogotsi)

First published as *Deep Are the Roots: Trailblazers Who Changed Black British Theatre* in 2021
This paperback edition first published 2025

The History Press
97 St George's Place, Cheltenham,
Gloucestershire, GL50 3QB
www.thehistorypress.co.uk

British Library Cataloguing in Publication Data.
A catalogue record for this book is available from the British Library.

ISBN 978 1 80399 923 4

Typesetting and origination by The History Press
Printed and bound in Great Britain by TJ Books Limited, Padstow, Cornwall

MIX
Paper | Supporting responsible forestry
FSC® C013056
FSC www.fsc.org

Trees for Life

Contents

Author's Note

Thanks go to David Hankin for digitally remastering some of the photographs; Keith Howes for his constructive comments on an early draft of the book; and Simon Wright, my editor at The History Press, who in the summer of 2020 asked me if I had an idea for a new book. This is the result.

I would like to recommend two online resources for further research: the University of Warwick's British Black and Asian Shakespeare Performance Database (bbashakespeare.warwick.ac.uk) and the National Theatre's Black Plays Archive (www.blackplaysarchive.org.uk).

In *Trailblazers of Black British Theatre*, the terms 'Black' and 'African Caribbean' refer to African, Caribbean and British people of African heritage. Other terms, such as 'West Indian', 'Negro' and 'coloured' are used in their historical contexts, usually before the 1960s and 1970s, the decades in which the term 'Black' came into popular use.

Though every care has been taken to trace or contact all copyright holders, I would be pleased to rectify at the earliest opportunity any errors or omissions brought to my attention.

Preface

Trailblazers of Black British Theatre evolved from the time I was invited by the Theatre Museum in London's Covent Garden to loan items from my collection to its *Let Paul Robeson Sing!* exhibition in 2001. Little did I realise that it would lead to me cataloguing its Black theatre collection. I drew the museum's attention to the fact that its vast archive included programmes, press cuttings, photographs, books and other material relating to Black theatre in Britain from as early as 1825, but that researchers who visited the museum's study room were not aware of the richness of what existed.

Funded by a small research grant from The Society for Theatre Research, I began by surveying the early years of Black British theatre from the 1820s to the 1970s under the supervision of Susan Croft, who was the museum's curator of contemporary performance. The stage careers of African American actors such as Ira Aldridge and Paul Robeson had already been well documented, and so it was not difficult to find material relating to them. It was fascinating to uncover the forgotten work of Black actors and writers from Africa, Britain and the Caribbean. Susan then put together the Theatre Museum's publication *Black and Asian Performance at the Theatre Museum: A User's Guide*, published in 2003, which included a database I had compiled of landmark Black British theatre productions from 1825 to 1975, while Dr Alda Terracciano compiled a similar database covering the period from 1975 to 2000.

Later on, I applied for and received a Wingate Scholarship in 2011 to further my research into early Black theatre in Britain. In 2012 I was interviewed for the documentary *Margins to Mainstream: The Story of Black Theatre in Britain*, and in July 2013 I participated in Warwick University's Shakespeare symposium with the presentation *Beyond Paul Robeson … Black British Actors and Shakespeare 1930–1965*.

And yet publishers repeatedly rejected my proposal for a book on the subject. 'Your book is too niche,' one of them said. Another told me that 'Black people do not buy books, so there is no market for them.' There was one exception: a young and enthusiastic editor did show an interest and he was keen to commission the book, but he was overruled by his editorial advisory board. Disheartened, I gave up and put the proposal away.

The landscape changed dramatically in 2020 with the Black Lives Matter movement, which drew attention to the Black presence in Britain both historically and in contemporary life. Almost immediately two of the publishers who had rejected my proposal contacted me and asked me if I had any ideas for Black history books, but they were too late. I had just been contacted by Simon Wright, my editor at The History Press, and I had sent him the proposal for this book. A contract was immediately negotiated. However, I decided to write *Trailblazers of Black British Theatre* in a different way to my previous books.

When I started out as a professional writer, I was always told to write objectively, not in the first person. I had never been encouraged to personalise my books. That is the academic way of writing history books; but with *Trailblazers of Black British*

Theatre, it was not going to be my way. For years I had enjoyed personal connections and friendships with many of the people I wanted to include in the book, so I wanted to avoid distancing myself from them by being 'objective'. This is why the reader will find *Trailblazers of Black British Theatre* a *personal* history and not an objective, academic one.

It is the personal relationships and anecdotes that are missing from so many books I have read on this subject – not that there have been very many. Two of my favourite academic works on the subject are Errol Hill's *Shakespeare in Sable: A History of Black Shakespearean Actors* (1984) and *The Cambridge Guide to African and Caribbean Theatre* (1994), co-edited by Hill. Colin Chambers's *Black and Asian Theatre in Britain: A History* (2011) is also recommended.

There have been several excellent autobiographies, including Norman Beaton's *Beaton But Unbowed* (1986), Gordon Heath's *Deep Are the Roots: Memoirs of a Black Expatriate* (1992), Yvonne Brewster's *The Undertaker's Daughter: The Colourful Life of a Theatre Director* (2004), Edric Connor's *Horizons: The Life and Times of Edric Connor* (published posthumously in 2007), Cy Grant's *Blackness and the Dreaming Soul* (2007) and Corinne Skinner-Carter's *Why Not Me?* (2011). I wish there had been more.

Trailblazers of Black British Theatre is not intended to be the definitive book on the subject. However, I have attempted to draw together the stories of some of the many personalities who created magic in British theatre from the 1820s to the 1970s, and to give them some context. I have also added many titles to my original 2003 database, in the hope that it will inspire others to embrace the breadth of the subject and undertake further research.

Carmen Munroe in James Baldwin's *The Amen Corner*, autographed at the Lyric Theatre, Shaftesbury Avenue, in 1987. (Author's collection)

Introduction

'The Women on Whose Shoulders We Now Stand'

On 2 December 2017 I had the pleasure of taking part in *Palimpsest Symposium: A Celebration of Black Women in Theatre* at the National Theatre. It was the actress Martina Laird who invited me to take part and celebrate the work of those she described as 'the women on whose shoulders we now stand'. I said I would be happy to start the event (which included two panel discussions) with an illustrated talk about early appearances of Black actresses in British theatre. I gave it the title 'Black Women in British Theatre: The Beginnings 1750s to 1950s' and I began by acknowledging the actress who had played Shakespeare's Juliet in Lancashire in the late 1700s. The attendees included many Black women who were drama students, actresses, playwrights and directors. I wasn't sure how many of them would have heard about the actresses I discussed. There is very little accessible information about the early years of Black British theatre and so the lives and achievements of many of these women have been lost to time.

The actress who played Juliet in the 1790s remains unidentified, but the reference to her ethnicity is clear. When John

Jackson published *The History of the Scottish Stage* in 1793, he noted the following:

> I had accidently seen the lady, as I was passing through Lancashire, in the part of Polly [in John Gay's *The Beggar's Opera*]. I could not help observing to my friend in the pit, when Macheath addressed her with 'Pretty Polly', that it would have been more germain to the matter, had he changed the phrase to 'SOOTY Polly.' I was informed, that a few nights before, she had enacted Juliet.[1]

Having begun my talk with this unidentified actress, I closed with Cleo Laine's dramatic debut in *Flesh to a Tiger* at the Royal Court in 1958. I also spoke about Emma Williams, the West African who acted in George Bernard Shaw's *Back to Methuselah* in the 1920s, sharing the stage of the Royal Court Theatre with Edith Evans and a young Laurence Olivier. After 1931, Emma vanishes, but other Black British actresses surface in the 1940s, including Ida Shepley and Pauline Henriques. I hoped that the talk would draw attention to the lives of these extraordinary women.

Afterwards, I took part in a panel discussion hosted by Martina Laird and Natasha Bonnelame, Archive Associate at the National Theatre. The panellists also included Yvonne Brewster and Angela Wynter. It was an enjoyable and inspiring morning session. In the afternoon, Martina and Natasha hosted another panel discussion, this time bringing Yvonne and Angela back together alongside the actresses Anni Domingo, Noma Dumezweni and Suzette Llewellyn.

In the 1980s and 1990s I had the pleasure of befriending some of the women who are featured in this book. They include Elisabeth Welch, Pauline Henriques, Carmen Munroe, Cleo Sylvestre, Pearl Connor-Mogotsi, Nadia Cattouse, Isabelle Lucas, Joan Hooley, Corinne Skinner-Carter and Anni Domingo. Over a long period of time, these personal friendships have given me insights into the work of Black women

Emma Williams as Doll in *And So to Bed* at the Queen's Theatre, 1926. (Author's collection)

whose lives intertwined with many aspects of Black British theatre. They have trusted me with their stories and, in some cases, shared their memorabilia. It has been a wonderful experience.

Sadly, I have never met the brilliant Mona Hammond. Somehow, I missed her. However, in 1989, I did see her wonderful performance as Lady Bracknell, directed by Yvonne Brewster, in the Black-cast version of Oscar Wilde's *The Importance of Being Earnest*. Shortly afterwards, when I was interviewed on BBC Radio, I met the actor Paul Barber at BBC Broadcasting House and we talked about Hammond. He told me that she is 'our Judi Dench'. Hammond had come to Britain from Jamaica in 1959 with a scholarship to the Royal Academy of Dramatic Art. It was her dream to play Shakespeare's Lady Macbeth, but such a plum role was unavailable to Hammond at the start of her career. However, in 1972, when she played her first leading role in the theatre at the Roundhouse Theatre, she was cast as the Wife of Mbeth (Lady Macbeth) in Peter Coe's innovative version of the

Shakespeare tragedy. Set in Africa, it was called *The Black Macbeth* and co-starred Oscar James as Mbeth. On 24 February 1972, Irving Wardle of *The Times* noted Hammond's 'reading of true passion and originality whose stone-faced exhaustion after the banquet and sleep-walk scene are as good as any I have seen'. In her biography for the programme, Hammond called the role 'a dream come true'. In the early 1970s, she followed her appearance in *The Black Macbeth* with parts in Mustapha Matura's *As Time Goes By*, Michael Abbensetts's *Sweet Talk* and Alfred Fagon's *11 Josephine House* and *The Death of a Black Man*. In 2005, Hammond received an OBE for her services to drama.

In 1987 I met Carmen Munroe for the first time when I interviewed her for the magazine *Plays and Players* in her dressing room at the Lyric Theatre in Shaftesbury Avenue. Munroe was taking it easy between the matinee and evening performances of James Baldwin's *The Amen Corner*, in which she played – brilliantly – the leading role of Sister Margaret. Carmen told me that her first professional appearance had been as a maid in Tennessee Williams's *Period of Adjustment* at the Royal Court in 1962, 'but I never played a maid again. I figured once you have played a maid, there didn't seem much point in playing another.'

Eventually some good theatre work came her way, including Alun Owen's *There'll Be Some Changes Made* (1969): 'I thought "Gosh, this is the opening that I've been dying for." We had wonderful reviews and I thought, "I hope this continues."' And it did, with a revival of Jean Genet's *The Blacks* (1970) at the Roundhouse: 'This gave Black actors and actresses a great opportunity to get together and really put on what turned out to be a wonderful production.' Then came George Bernard Shaw's *The Apple Cart* (1970) at the Mermaid. 'Following in Dame Edith Evans's footsteps,' wrote one reviewer. 'Why doesn't someone write something for this girl?' wrote B.A. Young in the *Financial Times*.

For Carmen, these years were particularly rewarding. But, in 1971, the work suddenly stopped: 'I did a lot of work.

Programme cover for *The Black Macbeth* at the Wyvern Theatre in Swindon, 1972. (Author's collection)

Mainly because directors wanted to use me. Then it changed. Suddenly Black artists became a "threat" to the establishment.' Carmen believes that Enoch Powell's inflammatory 'Rivers of Blood' speech in 1968 was partly responsible for this. In 1973, she seriously considered giving up her acting career: 'For almost a year I spent a depressing time believing that I was not going to realise my potential. This is a hard thing to take. But I hung on.'

In 1985, she played Lena Younger in Lorraine Hansberry's *A Raisin in the* Sun, directed by Yvonne Brewster, at the Tricycle

Theatre. And when *The Amen Corner* came along, she told me she found it:

> Amazing to be in a cast where people are doing something wonderful. It is fulfilling to be part of this. To experience this. I've been in the business a quarter of a century and I'm aiming to partake in the next quarter of a century too, and hope there will be more work like *The Amen Corner*.

There was, and Carmen continued to win critical acclaim for her leading roles in such plays as Alice Childress's *Trouble in Mind* at the Tricycle in 1992.

I met Isabelle Lucas in 1989 at her beautiful home in Kingston upon Thames. Isabelle had arrived here from Canada in 1954 with dreams of a career as an opera singer, but Covent Garden and Sadler's Wells turned her away. Penniless and desperate for work, Isabelle answered an advert in *The Stage* newspaper and successfully auditioned for *The Jazz Train* (1955), a Black-cast revue at the Piccadilly Theatre: 'I sang "Dat's Love" from *Carmen Jones* so my ambition to sing opera on the London stage was fulfilled, but not at Covent Garden!'

Isabelle then alternated between musicals and drama. Her stage work in the 1960s included *Ex-Africa* at the 1963 Edinburgh Festival, described as 'a Black odyssey in jazz, rhyme and calypso'; Brecht's *The Caucasian Chalk Circle* (1964), a Glasgow Citizens' production in which she was the first woman to play the Storyteller; the Negro Theatre Workshop's *Bethlehem Blues* (1964); and as Barbra Streisand's maid in the 1966 London production of the Broadway hit *Funny Girl*.

In 1968, two years after the release of the Oscar-winning film starring Elizabeth Taylor and Richard Burton, Isabelle and Thomas Baptiste were cast as the first Black Martha and George in Edward Albee's *Who's Afraid of Virginia Woolf?* at the

Connaught Theatre in Worthing. This was inspired casting, and it took a British production to make this breakthrough with a recent American stage classic. Isabelle proudly showed me photographs from this innovative production.

She then joined the National Theatre at the Old Vic in 1969 to appear in Peter Nichols's comedy *The National Health* and George Bernard Shaw's *Back to Methuselah*.

When Isabelle successfully auditioned for the role of Mammy in the stage musical version of *Gone with the Wind* (1972), she had reservations about taking the part:

> It was a good role and I had the Drury Lane stage to myself for a couple of solos ... But this was during the time of Black consciousness and I had doubts about wearing a bandanna and playing a mammy. Then I thought if I do it honestly it will be OK, and it was.

Isabelle concluded our interview by expressing disappointment that more had not been achieved in Britain for Black actors:

> In America they have pioneered integrated casting and there is work for mostly everybody, Black and white. Here, Black actors are kept in a ghetto ... I have worked in this country for nearly forty years and all we are left with is Notting Hill Carnival and a struggling Black theatre constantly under threat because of cuts in funding.

In 1993, Isabelle wrote to me to tell me how much she had enjoyed playing the Nurse in *Romeo and Juliet*, which Judi Dench directed at the Open Air Theatre in Regent's Park. It was to be her final stage appearance. Ill health forced her into semi-retirement, and she passed away on 24 February 1997.

I also met Nadia Cattouse for the first time in 1989, and she offered some fascinating insights into the problems Black actors faced in the 1950s and 1960s, especially if they came to Britain from the Caribbean:

> They had this fixed idea in their heads that, if you were American, you were streets better than anyone who came from the Caribbean. Our accent bothered them. They constantly told us to place our emphasis on a different syllable, and this would make us so self-conscious we could never think ourselves into a role because we were always conscious of the demand from the director, or whoever, that we speak in a different way. And so there was a kind of loss of control of the performance we would like to give. I had a lot of that. We did not want to rock the boat so usually we could use our intelligence to guide ourselves through, without upsetting the status quo, because time costs money in this business and we had to remember that too.

In 1991, Joan Hooley told me how the Royal Court Theatre was instrumental in helping to build the careers of Black playwrights and actors. In 1958, Joan had been an understudy in Errol John's *Moon on a Rainbow Shawl*. She was also in the cast of Jean Genet's *The Blacks*. She described this as:

> Great fun to do. To the best of my memory, it was the first stylised production of that type in England. It was around this time that theatres like the Royal Court started doing productions with Black casts. Well, I think there was a need for it, really, because there was so much Black talent around … Suddenly, these plays were being commissioned by people with insight into what needed to happen to the theatre. There was a general interest in seeing what Black writers had to offer, and what Black talent there was to perform these works. It was a very productive period between 1958 and 1962. I was constantly working – very little television, but a lot of theatre.

Corinne Skinner-Carter. (Author's collection, courtesy of Corinne Skinner-Carter)

I also enjoyed meeting Corinne Skinner-Carter in 1998 when I interviewed her for the *Black Film Bulletin*. Corinne had come to Britain from Trinidad in 1955. She worked as a dancer and actress but she also had teaching to fall back on when acting work became scarce. After her arrival, Corinne befriended Claudia Jones, a fellow Trinidadian who, like Edric and Pearl Connor (also Trinidadians) made things happen. Corinne said:

> Claudia had been persecuted in America for her political beliefs. After settling in England, she launched the *West Indian Gazette* in Brixton. This was Britain's first major newspaper for Black people. In 1958, Claudia decided to pull together a group of Black people from the arts, to show everybody that we were here to stay, that there was harmony between Blacks and whites, in spite of the Notting Hill riots. So, Claudia co-ordinated the first West Indian Carnival in Britain with the help of Edric and Pearl Connor, Cy Grant, Pearl Prescod, Nadia Cattouse and myself. The first Carnival took place in

> St Pancras Town Hall, and it was packed! It was not until 1965, the year after Claudia died, that Carnival took to the streets of Notting Hill.

Corinne also gave me an overview of her life and career: 'I have always been very selective. If I am not happy with a script, I turn it down. But I have been fortunate. On coming to England in 1955, I trained as a teacher, so I haven't always had to rely solely on acting for my bread and butter.'

In 1998, shortly before she passed away, Pauline Henriques wrote to me about my book *Black in the British Frame: The Black Experience in British Film and Television*, for which I had interviewed her. Pauline congratulated me on the publication, which she found intriguing:

> I find myself thrown back into a time that was a thrilling part of my young life … I can sink into the warm memories of my relationships to so many interesting Black people: Connie Smith, Edric and Pearl Connor, Errol John and Earl Cameron. I can't thank you enough. So, Stephen, you'll understand why I am filled with admiration for the time and effort you must have put into the book. I am also delighted at the threads of warmth throughout the text. With all good wishes to the successful author: Stephen Bourne.

A few weeks later, Nadia Cattouse also reacted positively to *Black in the British Frame* in a letter:

> I like the way you write. You are so deeply interested, never ever patronising the way one or two others can be, and full of insights. You hit the nail on the head when you mention 'the wall of silence that surrounds the history of our nation's Black people.' I have long come to the conclusion we will never be a society of real and not 'pretend' people … Some mean well and bless them for it. That is England.

Part 1

Beginnings

Sonia Pascal and Stephen Bourne in 1982. (Author's collection, courtesy of Linda Bourne Hull)

1

Sonia

In 1981, when I worked at the Peckham dole office, I took benefit claims from the unemployed and processed them. This was Maggie Thatcher's Britain and many people were out of work. Every day there were numerous claims to process. It was depressing, laborious work, but my days were brightened by a co-worker who became my best friend and soulmate.

Sonia Pascal and I immediately hit it off. We shared the frustration of the daily grind of our civil service office work. Sonia's background was a bit of a mystery. She was born in Grenada or Jamaica – I never did find out – but she was raised in Britain. She was a free spirit, but she was also down to earth. She loved acting and writing poetry. To relieve the boredom of our 'day jobs', we spent many happy lunch breaks in a local pub, putting the world to rights and sharing common interests in Black arts and theatre.

We giggled about the dole office gossips who were convinced we were an 'item'. This was not the case because I was gay. I had to keep it a secret from my colleagues because, when I joined the civil service, I signed the Official Secrets Act. In those days it included a paragraph which declared that I was not a homosexual. By signing my name to this document, I reassured the powers that be that I was not a 'security risk' to the United Kingdom. I told Sonia I was gay and she also kept it a secret; if senior staff at the dole office had found out, I would have risked being sacked. However, I had noticed that some of the male staff at the Peckham dole office were also 'musical' and, to please Mrs Thatcher, pretending to be straight. A couple of them were outrageously camp and obviously gay to members of staff who wished to acknowledge it but, as far as I can recall, no one was outed, sacked and forced to join the unemployed claimants. I was aware that gay liberation had happened in Britain in the 1970s, but it hadn't reached the civil service.

Just after I started working in the dole office, the Brixton uprisings began. From 10 to 12 April 1981 tensions between the police and Brixton's Black youth erupted into violence. It was inevitable that this would happen; the tensions had been building up for years.

We were living in the immediate aftermath of the tragic New Cross Fire on 18 January that year, in which thirteen Black British youths, all aged between 15 and 20, had lost their lives. People became angry and frustrated when they felt that the police were not taking seriously the investigation of the cause of the fire, which some suspected was racially motivated.

Consequently, the Black People's Day of Action was organised by activist John La Rose and others for 2 March 1981. With over 20,000 attendees, it was the largest demonstration of Black people and their allies in Britain to date. Sonia and I participated in the march. It started in New Cross and via Elephant and Castle it continued across Blackfriars Bridge. Here the police attempted to stop marchers going to Fleet Street, fearing there would be trouble in that area of London where right-wing journalists were based. The press had done much to fuel racism and negative media images of Britain's Black community. In spite of this interruption, and a confrontation with the police, the marchers eventually reached Hyde Park.

In 1981 Black youths felt alienated and victimised by the police. Margaret Thatcher and her Conservative government didn't help matters; their hostile language about the country being 'swamped' by immigrants inflamed the situation. The police used their repressive 'sus' (suspected person) stop-and-search law to openly bully and harass young Black men.

In south London our local police stations – Peckham, Brixton and Carter Street off Walworth Road – had terrible reputations in general. It was common knowledge that villains from all walks of life begged their arresting officers to take them anywhere except the cells at Brixton or Carter Street. As a kid growing up in the area, if we saw a policeman approaching us, we didn't stop and ask him the time. We ran for it.

By the early 1980s, Brixton was overrun by police officers who stopped and searched anything that moved. In 1980 my own fear and mistrust of the police was confirmed when I was stopped and searched by two officers opposite the council flat on Peckham Road where I lived with my parents. So I wasn't surprised when Black youths vented their anger and frustration with the authorities. They took to the streets and fought back. Other parts of the country followed, such as St Pauls (Bristol), Toxteth (Liverpool) and Handsworth (Birmingham).

Brixton became a 'no-go' area. Many shops and buildings were burnt out. The uprising spilled over into Peckham and we were in the thick of it. In Rye Lane, business owners were advised to close early and board up their windows. The dole office, situated off Rye Lane in Blenheim Grove, was advised to do the same. In the middle of the afternoon, I walked home, shocked by the sight of the boarded-up shop windows. For just one afternoon and evening, Peckham became a ghost town. The silence was eerie. Fortunately, the violence that Brixton had witnessed over several days and nights was not repeated in Peckham. However, from our living room window, we witnessed a number of police officers chasing Black youths along

Peckham Road or up Talfourd Road, which was directly opposite us.

Maggie Thatcher and the police made sure that the uprising was suppressed and eventually the tensions subsided. Commenting on Charles and Diana's marriage, which took place that July, Ray Gosling said wryly in *New Society* (1 December 1983): 'Oh happy day when Lady Diana became a Princess – because the riots were turned off like a tap by the royal wedding.'

Meanwhile, the unemployed continued to flood into our office to make claims, keeping Sonia and me extremely busy and stressed, though we still found time to share our interests.

Sonia's love of acting took her to the L'Ouverture Theatre Company, one of whose aims was to encourage young Black people into the world of theatre. In 1981, in her spare time, Sonia rehearsed their production of *Antigone* by Sophocles. It was translated by John Lavery and directed by the Jamaican-born theatre trailblazer Yvonne Brewster. At the dole office, Sonia described Yvonne to me as an inspiring director. The production was staged at Lambeth Town Hall from 19 to 22 October 1981.

In the programme I have kept all these years, Sonia is listed among the cast as 'Speaking Chorus'. I remember seeing her on stage and feeling proud that my friend and colleague was pursuing her dream. She was such an inspiration to me. In the programme her short biography reads: 'Searching for an identity may be an inappropriate starting point for some but Sonia feels this is paramount in her life. Excitement and a profound interest in people may be found in her satirical poetry. Her motto about life: Make it spicy!'

In 1981 Sonia took me to Peckham Odeon on the high street to see a double bill of Jamaican films then making the rounds. They were the classic reggae crime film *The Harder They Come*, starring Jimmy Cliff, and a hilarious comedy by Trevor Rhone called *Smile Orange*. Both of them had been made in the 1970s. Black youths packed into the Odeon to see Jimmy as a reggae singer forced into a life of crime, and then they screamed with

L'Ouverture Theatre Company's *Antigone* at Lambeth Town Hall in Brixton, 1981. (Author's collection)

laughter throughout *Smile Orange*. Unlike me, they understood the Jamaican patois and didn't need to read the subtitles. With the rise in unemployment, Peckham Odeon was demolished in 1983 to make way for a brand-new job centre.

The year 1982 was a landmark for me in terms of my developing interest in contemporary Black arts and culture. In February, Sonia and I went to the Festival of Black Independent Film Makers at the Commonwealth Institute in Kensington High Street. One of the Festival's highlights was Menelik Shabazz's acclaimed film *Burning an Illusion*. Its leading actor, Cassie McFarlane, gave a stunning performance as a young woman who becomes politicised in contemporary Britain. In her review of that evening's screening of the film, which was received with tremendous enthusiasm by a predominantly young Black audience, Isabel Appio commented in the *Caribbean Times* (26 February 1982):

> The most overwhelming audience turnout was for *Burning an Illusion* which had eager viewers spilling into the aisles.

> Females reacted openly: cheering Pat (Cassie McFarlane), through her journey as she confronts her troublesome boyfriend and discovers a more rewarding political identity. It was proved that night that there is a vast and receptive audience who at the moment is starved of films dealing with subjects with which they can identify.

In April, Sonia and I attended the first International Book Fair of Radical Black and Third World Books at Islington Town Hall. This had been founded by John La Rose and Jessica Huntley. In May, Sonia's love of poetry took us to the National Theatre in London's South Bank to see *Beyond the Blues*. This was a Jamaica National Theatre Trust presentation featuring the actor Lloyd Reckord reading poems from the Caribbean, USA and Africa. Poets represented included Louise Bennett, Evan Jones and Claude McKay. Some years later I befriended Lloyd and interviewed him about his acting career. In August, Sonia and I went to Notting Hill Carnival.

Black arts and culture were all around us to seek and find, but now and again Sonia and I went what we called 'up west' to London's West End in order to see a 'mainstream' film that appealed to us. As we sobbed through the tragic, emotionally charged climax of *Terms of Endearment*, when Shirley MacLaine faces the tragic death of her beloved daughter, we understood why she had won the Best Actress Oscar. We thought Barbra Streisand's *Yentl* was wonderful and failed to understand why some critics were harsh about her. Streisand wasn't even *nominated* for an Oscar, which we thought was a terrible oversight.

Sonia encouraged me to write poems, and one of them, 'Shadow', about the 1981 Brixton uprising, was published in a collection called *Dance to a Different Drum* (1983). The poems were selected by the celebrated Jamaican poet James Berry and published by the Brixton Festival. Other poets in the collection included the legendary Linton Kwesi Johnson and the playwright Alfred Fagon. Then Sonia introduced me to the playwright and director Don Kinch.

Don had come to London from Barbados in the 1960s and established the performing company Staunch Poets and Players in 1979. When Don planned to launch and edit a new Black monthly magazine called *Staunch*, Sonia gently encouraged me to offer my services as a feature writer, and so I began to contribute to the magazine. One of my first commissions, published in February 1983, was an interview with the actress Cassie McFarlane, on which I collaborated with Sonia.

Sonia also introduced me to the world of contemporary Black theatre. Immediately after the 1981 uprisings, the Greater London Council (GLC) began to fund some Black theatre companies. I remember Sonia taking me to the Albany Empire in Deptford in 1982 to see the Black Theatre Co-operative's presentation of Yemi Ajibade's *Fingers Only*. It was directed by Mustapha Matura, who had been a leading light in Britain's Black theatre movement since the 1970s.

In *The Struggle for Black Arts in Britain*, Kwesi Owusu described 1983 as a 'boom year' for Black theatre.[1] That year Sonia and I went to see some of the plays in the Black Theatre Season at the Arts Theatre in London's West End. They included Steve Carter's *Nevis Mountain Dew*, Trevor Rhone's *Two Can Play*, Michael Abbensetts's *The Outlaw* and Paulette Randall's *Fishing*, directed by Yvonne Brewster. In the 'boom year' we also went to see Cassie McFarlane in the stage version of *Smile Orange* at the Tricycle Theatre in Kilburn. The Ghana-born writer Kwesi Owusu commented, 'The use of Jamaican Creole was an unapologetic cultural statement to the play's British audiences. Not surprisingly, the play was perniciously attacked by some white media critics.'[2] McFarlane then played the lead in Don Kinch's play *The Balm Yard*, which toured many community theatres up and down the country. Sonia and I saw this production at a popular local fringe theatre, the Albany in Deptford.

In November 1983 we went to see the Theatre of Black Women at the Oval House Theatre, opposite the council flat where Sonia lived. One member of the company was Bernardine Evaristo, who went on to become a celebrated poet, novelist and Booker Prize winner. I still have the flyer with her photo on the cover.

I noticed that these productions brought together different generations of Black actors. Some came from African and Caribbean backgrounds; others were born in Britain. Some had been working here since the 1950s and 1960s, including Nadia Cattouse, Mona Hammond, Isabelle Lucas, T-Bone Wilson, Allister Bain, Corinne Skinner-Carter and Ena Cabayo; others were new faces such as Cassie McFarlane, Christopher Asante, Chris Tummings, Shope Shodeinde, Judith Jacob and Malcolm Frederick.

The February 1983 issue of *Staunch* included a long and detailed special report by Shirley Skerritt, the magazine's features editor, on Black theatre in Britain. She asked, 'Is there a Black renaissance?' and described the new Black theatre as 'community theatre':

> At a time when white establishment theatre is in decline … Black theatre is alive and well in community centres throughout London. Plays reflecting the Black experience are now being developed and presented by performers who are more concerned with the integrity of their material than in being stars. Playwrights like Edgar White, Don Kinch and Caryl Phillips to name but a few, are spearheading a movement which looks for its inspiration deep into the history and life-affirming struggles of the Black community. These writers have produced material which centres around Blacks themselves, with the involvement of the white world relegated to the fringes of Black life where it rightly belongs. They have transferred the preoccupation with actions which take place on the periphery, to a new focus on issues at the very heart of the Black experience.

Skerritt then explained how this 'uncoiled energy' boomeranged on James Fenton, the Oxford-educated white drama critic of *The Sunday Times* when, in November 1982, he 'presumptuously took the platform at the Battersea Arts Centre to discuss the future of Black theatre'. Skerritt described Fenton as 'still living in the colonial past':

> What was never understood by the colonialists was that art was never colonised – that the artist was never a slave … Black artistes have always been starved of resources, especially when they have adopted a Western philosophy towards art. Art must serve the interests of the people by whom and for whom it is created. The true critics of Black art are the Black masses who inspire it and who alone can judge its integrity.

Sonia and I remained friends forever. She eventually left the Peckham dole office to join a radio journalism course at the London College of Printing. From there she worked for BBC Radio London on the weekly magazine series *Black Londoners*, launched and presented by Alex Pascall in 1974. Sonia encouraged me to join a postgraduate course in journalism at the same college. It changed my life. There were times when our paths didn't cross, but we stayed in touch via Christmas cards and Sonia always remembered to send me postcards from her travels abroad. I have kept them all. In 2004 we spoke on the phone and she told me how excited she was about a landscape gardening course she was doing. A few months later she suffered a heart attack and passed away at the age of 45. Her passing was a shock to everyone who knew and loved her. She was always full of life and was a spiritual person. She never had a bad word to say about anyone. Sonia had gently given me the confidence to begin my career as a historian of Black Britain and to reach for the moon and the stars. I miss her and I will never forget her.

Jet magazine was critical of Laurence Olivier's portrayal of Othello: 'It is difficult to imagine a more vulgar, inept and, far more serious, racist interpretation of the role, denoting an almost complete lack of respect for black people on the part of Olivier.' (Author's collection)

2

Laughing at Larry

Critics said that Othello should be played by Laurence Olivier. I don't think it had anything to do with the standard of performance but it is one of the major parts in Shakespeare, and in the eyes of the critics the last great person to play Othello was Laurence Olivier. They measure all performances on that instead of taking it on an individual basis.

Rudolph Walker[1]

I was first asked to play Othello when I was fourteen, and still at school [in 1969 at Dean Close School in Cheltenham, Gloucestershire] ...Of course, I was not old enough, or experienced enough; nor, as it turned out, was I Black enough ... Accordingly, the make-up supervisor, the wife of the physics teacher, ruled that I should be 'blacked up', literally. But when I kissed Desdemona, the blackness rubbed off on her, and so this particular convention was short-lived. However, even without the aid of the black face, I attained a peak of grotesque absurdity with a faithful imitation of the accent Laurence Olivier used when he played Othello.

> As I recall, I was highly commended in school assembly. It was the theatrical equivalent of a Black man telling Rastus jokes. But, at the time, I was concerned to demonstrate how well I had assimilated the English theatrical tradition, and its conventions. Such naked idiocy is rare today; but my encounter with the physics teacher's wife sowed a seed of doubt about some of the conventions and tastes of the classical theatre.
>
> *Hugh Quarshie*[2]

My friend Sonia and I shared many things, including our sense of humour. When we were together, we always found something to laugh at. However, there was one afternoon in May 1983 when our laughter almost caused us to be thrown out of the National Film Theatre. We attended a screening of the 1965 film version of Laurence Olivier's National Theatre stage triumph *Othello*. As soon as Olivier appeared on screen we gasped and burst out laughing. We couldn't help ourselves. Having recently attended performances of several extraordinary and innovative Black theatre productions, we were left gasping for air at Lord Olivier's outrageous posturing in blackface. He even rolled his eyes while gently stroking the face of Iago (Frank Finlay) with a rose. I whispered to Sonia, 'When is he going to strum on a banjo and sing "oh, de doo-da day"?' She responded with more laughter. Later on, when Othello's jealousy turned into rage, Sonia and I were horrified at the way he distorted his blackened face and waved the palms of his hands in the air before crossing his eyes and falling to the floor. We burst out laughing again, but we didn't laugh because we thought he was funny. We laughed because this spectacle of 'great acting' was embarrassing and we were bemused at this insulting, furious betrayal.

It was a matinee aimed at senior citizens and our laughter irritated the older white, middle-class audience in the cinema. Every time someone turned round and shushed us we just giggled more and more. Somehow, we managed to contain ourselves after an usher crept silently towards us and whispered, 'Please could you refrain from laughing because it is upsetting others in the audience.' We restrained ourselves, for a little while, but when Larry as Othello lay across the dead body of his wife Desdemona, still rolling his eyes, shouting what sounded like 'Des-der-moan-ah! Des-der-moan-ah!', Sonia and I collapsed into gales of laughter and agreed that we'd seen enough. Much to the relief of the usher, we practically *fell* out of the cinema and into the foyer, laughing our heads off. We had *almost* made it to the end of the film.

We went straight to the bar and over drinks discussed what we had seen. In 1983 Lord Olivier was still alive and regarded as the greatest English actor of all time. Just a short walk from the National Film Theatre on the South Bank was the National Theatre. Olivier had been instrumental in setting it up at the Old Vic and he had worked as its artistic director from 1963 to 1973. When it relocated to its new base on the South Bank in 1976, one of its theatres was named in his honour. I had seen his magnificent film portrayals of other Shakespearean heroes – Henry V, Hamlet and Richard III – but his Othello was something else. I also greatly admired his superb performances in such films as *Wuthering Heights*, *Rebecca* and *The Entertainer*. His understated portrayal of George Hurstwood in William Wyler's *Carrie* (1952), opposite Jennifer Jones, is a masterclass of natural screen acting. In *Carrie* there are no histrionics and no showing off; instead, he gives us a spellbinding portrayal of a man whose degradation is emotionally charged and profoundly moving.

Sonia and I agreed that Olivier was one of the giants of British film and theatre, but he had made an error of judgement in blacking up as Othello. Nor was he the last to do so; it was a role that established white actors continued to play. In 1980, Paul Scofield had played Othello for Peter Hall at the Olivier Theatre, to be followed that same year by Donald Sinden at the Aldwych. There was also Anthony Hopkins's misguided portrayal in the BBC Television Shakespeare series, shown in

1981. Regarding Olivier in the film version of *Othello*, I could not bring myself to watch this travesty again until I prepared to write this book in the summer of 2020. The Black Lives Matter movement was building momentum. On this viewing, I didn't laugh once. In fact, I found it impossible to sit through without cringing and wondering what had motivated Olivier to take on this classic Shakespearean role and play it as a bizarre racist caricature.

It also brought back memories of listening to what the playwright Peter Nichols had said to the interviewer Sue Lawley in BBC Radio 4's *Desert Island Discs*, broadcast on 2 July 2000. Nichols had written the play *The National Health* for the National Theatre. It opened at the Old Vic on 16 October 1969 under the directorship of Olivier. However, early on, there were problems in the casting of two Black nurses, Nurse Norton and Nurse Lake. Nichols said that Olivier disliked the play, at which point Lawley enquired about the 'shades of racism' in his objections. Nichols explained that it was 'merely directed at the actors. When we were talking about casting the parts of the two Black nurses, he said "much as I love our coloured brethren, I am no great admirer of their histrionic ability. Do you think Joan could black up?" He actually wanted Joan Plowright to black up!' Plowright was a member of the National Theatre's first company and also Oliver's wife. In the end, two fine Black actresses, Cleo Sylvestre and Isabelle Lucas, were cast as the nurses.

For years Olivier had avoided playing Othello on stage. 'I've put it off because I think it's pretty well unplayable,' he said.[3] In 1950 he elaborated on why he had tackled all the great male Shakespearean roles except Othello: 'I have no burning desire to go into blackface and have the stage stolen from me by some young and brilliant Iago.'[4] However, in 1963, he decided to take on the role nonetheless.

He insisted that he had to *be* black. 'I had to feel Black down to my soul,' he said. 'I had to look out from a Black man's world.'[5] He made enquiries about the make-up used for BBC television's popular but racially offensive entertainment series *The Black and White Minstrel Show*. This had been running successfully since 1958. The BBC informed Olivier that the Minstrels used Max Factor's Negro No. 2. It was easy to apply and to take off and was guaranteed not to dry the skin. After applying Negro No. 2, Olivier polished his body with chiffon, until his skin gleamed a smooth ebony. 'I was so beautiful,' he said.[6]

Othello opened at the Old Vic on 21 April 1964 and Olivier made sure the actor playing Iago was not going to upstage him. He chose Frank Finlay, a highly competent but not particularly charismatic actor. There were stronger actors Olivier could have cast as Iago, but, 'He didn't want me or Albert Finney,' said fellow company member Robert Stephens. 'He wanted an ordinary actor … whom he could push out towards the corners, leaving the centre of the stage for him.'[7]

Almost without exception, the reviews were ecstatic. One of Olivier's biographers, Anthony Holden, claimed, 'There was a sense of theatrical history, of legend-making in the air,'[8] quoting several theatre critics as evidence. 'By heaven knows what witchcraft [Olivier has] managed to capture the very essence of what it must mean to be born with a dark skin,' wrote Herbert Kretzmer in the *Daily Express*. 'It is a performance full of grace, terror and insolence. I shall dream of its mysteries for years to come.' And Philip Hope-Wallace in *The Guardian* said, 'The inventiveness of it, the sheer variety and range of the actor's art … made it an experience in the theatre altogether unforgettable by anyone who saw it.'[9] Olivier's friend, the theatrical giant Noël Coward, was also captivated by his performance: 'I am so subjugated by Larry's dedicated talent that I would fly to see him if he elected to play Hamlet as a Chinaman.'[10] Anthony Holden noted that only Alan Brien of the *Sunday Telegraph* was critical: 'There is a kind of bad acting of which only a great actor is capable. I find Sir Laurence Olivier's Othello the most prodigious and perverse example of this in a decade … He begins to double and treble his vowels, to stretch his consonants, to stagger and shake, even to vomit, near the frontiers of self-parody.'[11]

Brien, though in a minority, was not the only critic or commentator who expressed reservations about Olivier's Othello. In 1973 Logan Gourlay interviewed many of Olivier's friends and associates for a tribute called *Olivier*. Titled theatrical luminaries such as Sir Noël Coward, Dame Sybil Thorndike, Sir John Gielgud, Sir Alec Guinness, Sir Michael Redgrave and Sir Terence Rattigan were among those who praised him, but there were two interviewees who were critical. Tony Richardson was one of them. He had directed two Black actors in the role, Gordon Heath on BBC Television in 1955 and Paul Robeson at the Stratford Memorial Theatre in 1959:

> His Othello ... was hailed by some of the critics and it could be called one of his successes, but for me it was a flop. I didn't like it at all. He based his performance entirely on an external image – an image of a NEGRO in capital letters that became a degrading image. He concentrated too much on all the external details and not on the feelings of the man, and the result in my view was a bad Othello.[12]

The dramatist John Osborne, who had collaborated with Olivier on the stage triumph *The Entertainer*, said:

> He can get away with almost anything. He can get away with being terribly vulgar. I thought, for example, he was unspeakably vulgar as Othello. At the same time he is the only actor who would have had the courage to do something as dreadful as his Othello. His courage is outstanding, though sometimes it's in danger of being wilful obstinacy. I don't think anyone could stop him doing something dreadful like Othello once he had made up his mind, just as I don't think anyone can really direct him. He will ultimately do what he wants to do. He has it all worked out in advance.[13]

By the time the film version was released in America at the end of 1965, the African American civil rights movement was making a great deal of progress. In March 1963, Dr Martin Luther King had given his famous 'I Have a Dream' speech at the Lincoln Memorial in Washington. It seemed incongruous that a great Shakespearean actor would be acceptable in blackface as Othello, but most white American critics applauded him. He was even nominated for the Best Actor Oscar. However, in *The New York Times* (2 February 1966), a notable but shocked film critic called Bosley Crowther described Olivier's performance as a 'Minstrel Show':

> He plays Othello in blackface! That's right, blackface … several times, in his rages or reflections, he rolls his eyes up into his head so that the whites gleam like small milk agates out of the inky face. The consequence is that he hits one – the sensitive American, anyhow - with the by-now outrageous impression of a theatrical Negro stereotype. He does not look like a Negro (if that's what he's aiming to make the Moor) – not even a West Indian … which some of the London critics likened him to. He looks like a Rastus or an end man in an American minstrel show. You almost wait for him to whip a banjo out from his flowing, white garments or start banging a tambourine.

In 1964–65, English theatre and film critics, those who reviewed Olivier's performances as Othello on stage and screen, were almost exclusively white, male and middle class. A white, middle-class *female* exception was Dilys Powell of the *Sunday Times*, known as the 'doyenne' of English film criticism. She also praised Olivier's screen interpretation. None of Olivier's biographers, including John Cottrell (1975), Donald Spoto (1991), Roger Lewis (1996), Anthony Holden (2007) and Philip Ziegler (2013), quote any *Black* critics or commentators about Olivier's Othello. Admittedly, finding examples of Black commentators on this portrayal is difficult, but some do exist and Olivier's biographers should have looked for and found them.

In 1964, Edric Connor was interviewed by the South African writer Lewis Nkosi for the quatercentenary of Shakespeare's birth. Connor, a popular Trinidadian actor and folk singer, was the first Black actor to be employed by the Shakespeare Memorial Theatre when he played Gower in Shakespeare's *Pericles* in 1958. Connor spoke favourably of Olivier's Othello which he had recently seen at the Old Vic:

> He's the seventh Othello I have seen on stage and I would say the greatest of them all. He called on all the technique within his powers to interpret the role without destroying the emotional aspect of it. In fact, my idea of Othello is the man who plays him to the full will not be able to take the curtain at the end because it might have pulled so much out of him … looking at him I saw my head. His colour, his makeup was perfect, except for the need of just a little bit of green mascara as eye shadow.[14]

In 1992 the African American actor Gordon Heath, who had played Othello for BBC Television in 1955, recalled Olivier as Othello:

> His first appearance: coal-black, red-lipped, fuzzy short-haired wig, dressed in a white wraparound robe, sniffing at the reddest rose this side of Picardy … and all this with a swaying, arrogant, calypso walk – a picturesque and beautiful apparition. Joan Plowright, his wife, said to me wistfully, 'it's very disappointing when he washes it all off at night.' Sir Laurence … played him as a contemporary Black, letting the poetry fall where it might. He chose, I thought the wrong kind of Negro(es) to impersonate and his rightly celebrated 'technique' showed through the burnt cork. I admired the virtuosity but felt nothing for the man … one watched the

> wheels turning and never became involved. Frank Finlay's Iago was never allowed to be the mainspring of the action and Maggie Smith's Desdemona was a trifle nasal and hostessy, but wonderfully touching at the end … the tale unfolded excitingly, but we did not weep. Mine is a minority opinion but not a unique one.[15]

Born in Guyana, Cy Grant was the most critical of the Black British actors who saw Olivier's Othello. Grant played the role at the Phoenix Theatre in Leicester in 1965. Later, in his memoir *Blackness and the Dreaming Soul*, he didn't hold back:

> To say that I did not like Olivier's portrayal of Othello would be an understatement. If Orson Welles at the St James's a decade earlier made him into a gorilla, Olivier's was a white man's ignoble caricature of a Moor. How could such a great actor and warm human being be so misguided? I had watched the production from the gods at the Old Vic. It was the only seat I could get. I dread to think what my reaction would have been if I had been sitting in the stalls to observe it in close up! I was, of course, to have all my fears confirmed when I later saw the screen version … I hated his portrayal of Shakespeare's 'Noble Moor'.[16]

Cy Grant also acknowledged that Olivier's Othello took place against a notable political backdrop in the United Kingdom regarding race relations. In 1968, Enoch Powell made his deeply racist anti-immigration 'Rivers of Blood' speech. Grant commented, 'Although he was consequently dismissed from Edward Heath's shadow cabinet, the era ushered in by Powell simmered on for many years. It brought into the open the full extent of British racism.'[17]

In America, in the weekly Black magazine *Jet* (17 March 1966), Chester Higgins acknowledged several outstanding African American actors who had played Othello, singling out Paul

Robeson, William Marshall, James Earl Jones and Earle Hyman for praise. Higgins criticised Olivier's film performance:

> it is difficult to imagine a more vulgar, inept and, far more serious, racist interpretation of the role, denoting an almost complete lack of respect for Black people on the part of Olivier, indeed a lack of respect perhaps even for himself. If Othello were the mawkish, servile, black face minstrel-like character that Olivier sees him to have been, it is difficult to imagine the proud Venetian people falling at his feet, extolling his virtues, inviting him into their homes and more, investing him the honor and responsibility of heading up their most vital armed forces ... Most of the other [Black] actors, especially Marshall and Robeson, brought empathy to their portrayals of this tragic giant of a man. The resonance and timbre of their voices admirably reflected his inner torment ... 'Olivier, in the face of the rising tide of nationalism among the underprivileged dark countries of the world, should get down on his knees, and ask the forgiveness of every Black man in the world,' said one critic.

In 1986, Kwesi Owusu reflected in *The Struggle for Black Arts in Britain*:

> The rather grotesque spectacle of white actors with painted Black faces produced caricatures and devalued Black experience, stripping it of its authenticity and realism. And such grotesquery is still alive both in the theatre and film: despite their quality as actors, Laurence Olivier as Othello or Alec Guinness as Godbole in *A Passage to India* succeed only in producing unrealistic caricatures of the characters they play.[18]

In 1950 the State Department of the United States withdrew Paul Robeson's passport. They considered his politics and left-wing sympathies a threat to national security. He was a victim of McCarthyism. For eight years he was unable to continue with his career or travel outside his homeland. He became a prisoner in his own country. Campaigns and petitions were organised all over the world to try to persuade the State Department to reinstate Robeson's passport. London County Council's Paul Robeson Committee gained the support of many of Robeson's friends and colleagues, who readily signed their petition. But when they asked Sir Laurence Olivier to do so, he refused.[19]

Olivier was aware that Robeson had accepted an invitation to play Othello at the Shakespeare Memorial Theatre's 100th season in Stratford-upon-Avon in 1959. However, in spite of his earlier reservations, Olivier wished to 'have a bash' at the role himself. Could jealousy have been the motive for Olivier's refusal to sign the petition? Throughout his career, Olivier was known in theatrical circles for being competitive, his jealousy of other actors, including Sir John Gielgud, 'being the more frequent and the more consuming', according to Ziegler.[20]

Did Olivier look upon Robeson as a threat? In 1958, when Robeson's passport was reinstated, he was finally allowed to travel abroad. When he arrived in London that July he was greeted with overwhelming love and affection by his fans. Says Lindsey R. Swindall in *The Politics of Paul Robeson's Othello*:

> Robeson's performance at St. Paul's Cathedral in London in October 1958 was indicative of the tremendous outpouring of goodwill that he received in Britain. Eslanda Robeson, in a press release for the Associated Negro Press, noted that the only other time St. Paul's had been filled to capacity was for Victory in Japan Day in 1945. Four thousand people crowded into the pews to hear Robeson sing at evensong, following the service, police had to 'rescue' him from the throngs of admirers. Robeson commented to a reporter, 'This is an historic moment in my life. I am terribly moved by this tremendous demonstration for me. I am close to tears about it.' This

> foreshadowed the prodigious reception Robeson received at the Memorial Theatre for the *Othello* opening.[21]

Robeson filled St Paul's Cathedral to overflowing, with 4,000 inside and more than 5,000 outside listening to him through loudspeakers. Unlike Olivier, Robeson was loved and respected by the masses, of all social classes. He had the 'common touch', something Olivier could only dream about. Also, Robeson's audiences were culturally diverse, which certainly did not apply to Olivier. When Robeson's *Othello* opened on 7 April 1959, Olivier was in Hollywood filming Stanley Kubrick's *Spartacus*. When he arrived at Stratford to take on the role of Coriolanus, which opened on 7 July, Olivier discovered that Robeson had stolen his thunder. He would continue to do so until *Othello* ended its seven-month run in November. When Olivier and other theatrical giants performed at Stratford that centenary year, including Charles Laughton and Edith Evans, Robeson drew the most attention from the media. Every performance of *Othello* sold out.

Some truths came to light in 2001 when Robeson's son, Paul Robeson Jr, visited London to open the exhibition *Let Paul Robeson Sing!* at the Theatre Museum. In a revealing interview with Maureen Paton in the *Evening Standard* ('The First Black Superstar', 20 September 2001), Robeson Jr recalled his visit to Stratford in 1959 to see his father as Othello. He also discovered that Robeson, not Olivier, was dominating the season:

> When Dad introduced me to Olivier, he looked at me like I was a piece of dirt and cut me dead. Afterwards, I asked Dad why Olivier had done that. He laughed and said, 'He's never gotten over the fact that the most popular performance in the repertoire is not his Coriolanus but my Othello. So, he takes it out on you.' I said, 'Wow, a guy that great is that petty?' and Dad said, 'I've known heads of state like that.'

When Paton asked Robeson Jr what his father had thought of Olivier's Othello, he replied:

> Dad always refused to be quoted on Olivier's performance as Othello, but I can say this: it was absurd. What Olivier did was to hang around the Caribbean community in London and imitate their ways. Only somebody with a huge cultural insensitivity would figure, 'Well, the guy's Black, so I'll watch the Blacks round here and then impose that on a Shakespearean role.' That reflects a man who is narrow-minded and racist.

Cleo Sylvestre, autographed in the 1990s. (Author's collection)

3

Cleo and Tommy

I first met Cleo Sylvestre in January 1976 when I was a student in the sixth form of a comprehensive school. I was researching a project for an exam about Black actors on British television. My teacher suggested that I undertake an interview for the project and I thought about Cleo. I remembered her continuing role as Melanie (Meg Richardson's foster daughter) in the soap opera *Crossroads*, and I had recently seen her on stage while on a school trip to the Young Vic to see *Othello*. Cleo played Bianca. I had seen many Black actors in films and on television, but this was the first time I had seen a Black stage actor. I wrote to her at the Young Vic and she kindly invited me to meet her there in the coffee bar. It was the beginning of a friendship that has lasted to this day. In 2017, Cleo attended my graduation at the Royal Festival Hall when I received an Honorary Fellowship from London South Bank University.

The 2019 Booker Prize winner Bernardine Evaristo has also recalled Cleo being the first Black actor she saw in a stage production. For Evaristo it was in a Bubble Theatre (tent) production on Blackheath Common around 1972. Evaristo, then aged 12, was a member of the Greenwich Young People's Theatre. It was an outing she never forgot:

> Two years later I decided to become an actor myself. Cleo was the role model. I didn't see any other Black actors perform on stage until the musical *Two Gentlemen of Verona* at the Phoenix in 1973 [Brenda Arnau and Derek Griffiths] and Peter Brook's *The Ik* at the Roundhouse in 1976 [Miriam Goldschmidt]. I finally met Cleo in 2012 and told her how important it had been for me to see her perform when I was so young and dipping my toes into acting. She's still acting in plays and on the screen and is one of our sheroes who deserve to be better known.[1]

Raised in north London, Cleo's mother, Laureen, was mixed-race and had been in show business in the 1930s as a tap dancer in cabaret shows at the popular Shim Sham Club in London's West End. Interviewed in the *Express* in 2020, Cleo recalled, 'Being an only child you invent friends and I used to play little scenarios with my mum under our kitchen table, pretending we were lost and couldn't find our way home.'[2]

In the early 1950s Laureen enrolled young Cleo into the Italia Conti Academy of Theatre Arts on Saturdays. Attending this well-known stage school for children led Cleo to her debut as an actor at the age of 7 in *Johnny on the Run* (1953), produced by the Children's Film Foundation. 'That was my first real acting job,' recalled Cleo, when I interviewed her in 1976, 'and the bug just stayed with me. I went to grammar school and my headmistress was appalled when we started discussing careers and I told her what I wanted to do.'[3]

Cleo had kept it a secret that she wanted to be an actress. She told her mother, but at the grammar school her headmistress expected her to go to a teachers' training college. 'I really wanted to go somewhere to study drama,' she said. 'My headmistress was horrified when I told her I wanted to become an actress.

She said there were no parts for coloured actresses. In those days we were called "coloured". So, I went off to a teachers' training college but I soon left because I didn't want to teach.'[4]

Cleo's early stage experiences included an appearance with George Browne and Tommy Eytle in a Negro Theatre Workshop production called *The Prodigal Son* at St Martin-in-the-Fields in 1965. Simon Gray's *Wise Child* (1967) was her first big break in the theatre. This was a West End production with Alec Guinness at the Wyndham's Theatre. For Cleo, Guinness was 'charming and solicitous. I used to watch him like a hawk in rehearsals and I picked up so much from him'.[5] Cleo was also successful in television, playing roles in *Up the Junction* (1965) and *Cathy Come Home* (1966), two groundbreaking social realist dramas directed by Ken Loach. A few years later she was cast as Melanie in *Crossroads*, a rare occasion when a Black actor appeared regularly in a popular soap opera. But theatre was Cleo's first love:

> I enjoy working in television, but I like the immediacy of the theatre. You walk on stage and you go through the play and hopefully you can sense what the audience is feeling, particularly in comedy, which I love doing. I feel perfectly at home on the stage. When I was appearing in *Crossroads* the producer, Reg Watson, came up to me one day in the spring and said, 'Cleo, we've got a storyline for you in November,' and I suddenly thought, 'no, I'm not going to stay.' Reg wanted me to stay and it was very tempting. But I wanted to get out there and my first love was, and still is, the theatre. I could have stayed in *Crossroads* for a very long time, but I chose not to.[6]

Following her appearance in *Wise Child*, Cleo was offered another important stage role in Peter Nichols's satire *The National Health* (1969). This was the first time a Black actress had been given an opportunity to play a leading role for the National Theatre. The only other Black actress to work for the National had been Pearl Prescod, a Trinidadian who had a supporting role as the slave Tituba in *The Crucible* (1965). In 2020, Cleo told Lanre Bakare in an interview in *The Guardian*, 'Being an actor then for me was like being a hamster on a wheel. You'd do a show and get great reviews, but then you'd have to start all over again. Being at the National Theatre didn't then lead to a West End play. Nothing led anywhere.'[7]

Following *Wise Child* and *The National Health*, Cleo wrote to every repertory theatre company in Britain. Only three replied. 'If we're doing Arthur Miller's *The Crucible*, we'll keep you in mind,' they said. It was clear that they would only consider Cleo for the role of the slave Tituba in Miller's play. However, Cleo's persistence did lead to some interesting opportunities. She credits Frank Dunlop for opening doors to actors regardless of their background or race. Dunlop was a British director and manager, best known for founding the Young Vic in London in 1970. It was initially part of the National Theatre, but in 1975 it became independent with Dunlop in charge. He succeeded in bringing accessible classical plays to wide – especially young – audiences. He cast Cleo as Hecate in the Young Vic's first independent production, *Macbeth*, which opened on 15 January 1975. In an interview for the British Library's Theatre Archive Project, Cleo described Dunlop as 'amazing' and she said that her association with him and the Young Vic was the real turning point in her stage career:

> Frank didn't allow any sort of restrictions on his actors. He just chose the actors he thought were best for the play because, to him, theatre represented life and it's made for all sorts of people. Frank let me play roles which I probably wouldn't have been considered for by any other director. Frank gave me that chance.[8]

Cleo took part in several Young Vic seasons from 1974–77. In addition to *Macbeth*, she was seen in *Scapino*, a Young Vic production starring Jim Dale which was presented on Broadway,

The Fantastic Fairground, *Othello* (as Bianca), *Dream People*, *All Walks of Leg* and *Wild Wild West*. Cleo said:

> I loved Frank's whole vision for the theatre and the way that he brought theatre to people who weren't traditionally used to going to see theatre. And as an actor, I just loved rehearsals with him. He always assembled a company that got on well with each other. We went on tours. We went to America. We went to Mexico. I don't think we ever had any problem and that, I think, was due to the way that he picked everybody.[9]

At the Young Vic, Cleo played a range of parts in integrated casts, but in 1975 she ventured into Black British theatre with a production of Michael Abbensetts's *Sweet Talk* at the King's Head in Islington and then at the Institute of Contemporary Arts (ICA). The cast also included Stefan Kalipha and T-Bone Wilson. The theatre critic for *The Stage* (3 July 1975) noted that Cleo gave a study of 'unobtrusive dignity as Rita, bringing out the pain in the woman's heart with great poignancy'.

In addition to her acting career, in the 1970s Cleo joined the Afro-Asian Artists' Committee of Equity, the actors' union, and assisted with the campaign for better treatment of Black and minority ethnic (BAME) actors. They wanted casting directors to offer them more opportunities, particularly by embracing integrated casting, which would enable a Black actor to be cast in any role, regardless of their race.

It was around this time that Cleo befriended another member, Thomas ('Tommy') Baptiste, who had travelled to Britain from Guyana in 1950 to begin a long and successful acting career. His early London stage appearances included Noël Coward's comedy of manners *Nude with Violin* (Globe, 1956) alongside John Gielgud. In 1960 Harold Pinter cast him as Riley, the blind Black man in *The Room*, which transferred from the Hampstead Theatre to the Royal Court. He also worked with Joan Littlewood's revolutionary Theatre Workshop company. In the 1960s he worked at the

Bristol Old Vic, Liverpool Playhouse and the Connaught Theatre in Worthing. In 1968, at the Connaught, Baptiste played George in the innovative production of Edward Albee's *Who's Afraid of Virginia Woolf?* and Isabelle Lucas played Martha. This was the first time Black actors had taken the lead roles in this classic play, and it was an outstanding example of 'colour-blind' casting.

In the same year, Equity published a report from the Afro-Asian Artists' Committee. Among its recommendations was a call to theatre managements and casting directors to embrace integrated casting. One of the responses came from the Hampstead Theatre Club, which supported the recommendation. They gave the example of the West African actor Johnny Sekka, who had been cast in their production of John McGrath's *Bakke's Night of Fame*. McGrath considered Sekka the best actor for the lead, even though he hadn't written the part for a Black actor. However, an editorial in *The Stage* (1 February 1968), though generally supportive of the recommendations, stated that producers and casting directors would:

> Find it practically impossible in nine cases out of ten to cast Negro artists in non-coloured parts. The relationship with the other characters in the play will make coloured casting impossible in scores of instances. If the Negro actor has brothers and sisters in the play, he would have to make up as a white man and in most instances the cast of his features and the richness of his voice would suggest that he came from a totally different world. How could a Negro actor be slipped into a Chekhov cast without affecting the delicate balance and nuance of the production?

By 1968, Thomas Baptiste's stage career had been varied. He had been successful in securing interesting, non-stereotypical roles. However, he wasn't prepared to remain silent when *The Stage* newspaper published this editorial. In a letter to *The Stage* (8 February 1968), he said:

> For the life of me I don't understand the point or logic of your editorial. Are you or aren't you in complete support of Equity's belated stand apropos the casting of coloured artists in theatrical productions? If the purpose of your Leader is meant to support Equity's stand, then you have certainly not done so honestly. Your article, because of its reticence to quote, 'With all the goodwill in the world, producers will find it practically impossible in nine cases out of ten, to cast Negro artists in non-coloured parts' seems to me, not only obstructive but really most unhelpful in this matter. A genuinely sympathetic attitude would have compelled you not to write such fallacious platitudes about 'the richness of his voice' etc. Do not white people have this blessing also; or is it akin exclusively to the Negro? ... Your conservative attitude is in complete contrast to that of many responsible people who can influence progressive attitudes … There aren't that many Negro actors in England, hence any likely competition is almost nil if Equity's plea is fostered. There are always snags in casting plays, but unless a character specifically in dialogue identifies another character's racial origin, then there is no good reason why the Venetian Cassio in *Othello* shouldn't be played by a Negro, or Prospero and Miranda in *The Tempest*. Negroes have always been around in every strata of society; that's why Shakespeare was able to write *Othello* … it would be better and more in line with the very sensible attitude pros have in the theatre if your writer can stop 'seeing' people as coloured and white actors, but as actors who in most cases have formally prepared themselves for their profession and are thus equipped to make an audience accept their work on an equal critical level, as either good or bad, instead of on a racial basis. If not, I'm afraid we'll never get beyond the eternal racial plays.

After this letter was published, Thomas lobbied Equity, the actors' union, to protect minority actors and urge casting directors to use Black and minority ethnic actors as actors, regardless of their race and based purely upon their talent. When I first met Tommy in 1991, he told me:

> A number of us were involved in that, including a few white actors like Paul Eddington who was very active. We were an advisory committee and the first thing we accomplished was for Equity to support integrated casting. This meant that Black actors would be cast on their merit and not for their skin colour. But there came a time when we had to back off because we were saying the same thing over and over again, and not making any headway. The writers would excuse themselves by saying things like, 'We don't know anything about the Black experience.' And nothing happened. Sometime later a producer told me he had been advised not to use me because I was a troublemaker. Equity had a Blacklist. When I stopped lobbying and being involved in Equity affairs, I began working regularly again.[10]

In spite of being labelled a troublemaker, Tommy continued to work in the theatre in the 1970s. In 1973 he played Brutus Jones in Eugene O'Neill's *The Emperor Jones* for the Dark and Light Theatre, and in 1976 he played one of his heroes, Paul Robeson, in the British premiere of Eric Bentley's *Are You Now or Have You Ever Been?* at the Brum Studio in Birmingham. This was described as a 'documentary with a difference' that looked back at some of the victims of the 1950s McCarthy witch hunt in America.

Tommy had a great sense of humour and when we met for the first time at his beautiful home in north London, full of oil paintings and antiques, and a fountain in the garden, he 'tested' me before we started talking. 'I have a question for you,' he said. 'Name all of the Goons.' I looked at Tommy and I knew straight away what he was *really* asking me. I replied, without any hesitation, 'Peter Sellers, Spike Milligan, Harry Secombe and Ray

Poster for Eugene O'Neill's *The Emperor Jones*, starring Thomas Baptiste. (Courtesy of Longfield Hall Trust, with thanks to Ian Wooldridge)

Ellington.' Ellington, a Black British bandleader, had been an integral part of the popular *Goon Show* on BBC Radio and Television, but he had never been recognised for this. Tommy's broad smile turned into a loud laugh and he shook my hand, saying, 'You've passed! Now you can proceed with the interview.'

Other interviews followed, including one about Edric Connor for BBC Radio 2 in 1993, and we remained friends. The last time I saw Tommy was at a performance of Cleo's one-woman play about the Crimean War nurse Mary Seacole in July 2016. He passed away, aged 89, on 6 December 2018. One time, in the 1990s, Tommy invited me to lunch. He said he had something important to discuss. When we met, he asked me if I would write his obituary when he passed away, 'because you are the only one who has taken the trouble to find out the facts about my career'. When Tommy passed, I didn't *write* an obituary, but I was interviewed about him for BBC Radio 4's obituary series *Last Word*. It was an honour.

Tommy struck me as someone who was extremely proud of his achievements, especially with integrated casting. His many stage roles included the dustman Alfred P. Doolittle in George Bernard Shaw's *Pygmalion*, Caliban in *The Tempest*, the title role in *Othello* and Duke Orsino in *Twelfth Night*, but Tommy was sad that he wasn't recognised for his pioneering work, especially among the younger generation of Black actors. He said:

> What I want to say now may sound bitter but it isn't, it's just realising the way the dice is loaded. If I were a white actor, with the plays I have done, and the fact that I haven't had a bad review, I would have been asked to work for the Royal Shakespeare Company and the National Theatre. I have always tried to avoid playing stereotypes, and with parts I have felt I have scored a bullseye with, I have had to wait for long periods for another interesting role. Shakespeare and Chekhov wrote plays for people, not for racial groups. The casting of an actor shouldn't be based on race but on talent. Why should it be difficult to accept a Black actor as King Lear on stage when it might be perfectly acceptable on radio? The answer, of course, is because you can't *see* the person on radio. Well, that shows some basic racism.[11]

When Cleo Sylvestre was interviewed by Lanre Bakare in *The Guardian* she mentioned Tommy and Louis Mahoney, another actor who had recently passed away. She said they were never recognised in their lifetimes despite their work on- and offstage to pave the way for younger Black actors:

> Sylvestre says that, before his death in 2018, Baptiste would ring her up each year and ask who had been given an honour by the queen. She would go through a list of younger Black actors who had been given MBEs and OBEs, and invariably he would say: 'Oh, and I haven't even been given a F.U.C.K.'[12]

Cleo passed away 20 September 2024.

Part 2

The First Trailblazers

Ira Aldridge as Aaron the Moor in *Titus Andronicus*, 1852. (Courtesy of the Library of Congress, Washington DC)

4

Ira Aldridge

Ira Aldridge was one of the most accomplished and celebrated actors of the Victorian era. He was often advertised on posters and playbills as 'the African Roscius', a reference to Quintus Roscius Gallus, who was considered the great actor of Roman times. In *Ira Aldridge: The Negro Tragedian*, Herbert Marshall and Mildred Stock described him as the first to show that a Black man could scale any heights in theatrical art reached by a white man:

> And recreate with equal artistry the greatest characters in world drama. He did this alone, without the aid of any social or political organisations … without any subsidies or scholarships, on his own two feet, with his own skill, versatility and talent. He did this in a white world, and showed that if a white can Blacken his skin to represent Othello, then a Black man can … represent Lear, Macbeth, or Shylock with equal artistry.[1]

Unable to pursue a career as an actor in the United States, Aldridge left New York City, where he had been born in 1807, and relocated to Britain, where he successfully established himself. Best known for playing tragic roles, such as Shakespeare's *Othello*, he was also popular in a range of comedy parts.

Ira's father, Daniel, a clerk and a lay preacher who became a minister, sent him to New York's African Free School to be educated, hoping that his son would also become a preacher. However, young Ira had other plans. He was inspired to become an actor by the African Grove Theatre, which had been founded in New York in 1821. Ira was greatly assisted by its leading player, James Hewlett, who is considered to be the first African American to scale the heights as a Shakespearean actor. However, the ambitious Aldridge realised he could not achieve the success he craved in his homeland, and looked to Britain to establish himself.

In 1824 he worked his passage to Liverpool as a ship's steward and it is generally accepted that he made one of his first appearances in Britain on 10 October 1825 in the role of Oroonoko in *The Revolt of Surinam; or, A Slave's Revenge* at London's Royal Coburg Theatre (later renamed the Old Vic). Reviews were mixed. *The Times* dismissed Aldridge's acting abilities, but other critics applauded him. *The Morning Advertiser* reported that he gave a 'very novel performance … [Aldridge was] evidently a man of much observation, and had a very excellent conception of the character, which he performed in a manner so as to receive the approbation of a numerous audience.' The managers of the Coburg were impressed and extended his engagement to seven weeks. During his time there he was seen in five plays, three of which were set in the Caribbean. These included *The Slave* and *The Death of Christophe, King of Haiti*. Audiences loved him and gave him a rousing reception.[2]

While appearing at the Royal Coburg he met and married Margaret Gill, who was white, and this angered many pro-slavery activists. They were hostile towards him and his interracial marriage in the midst of the controversy over the abolition of slavery. The British Parliament had already abolished the slave trade in 1807, and the liberation of all slaves in countries under British rule would eventually take place in 1833. This political climate made it difficult for Aldridge to establish himself in London, for his appearances on stage demonstrated that the Black man could rise above slavery and express himself on an equal footing with the white race. In *Black People in Britain 1555–1833*, Folarin Shyllon said that Aldridge was shunned for one whole year by London theatres: 'Many pro-slavery newspaper and journals, which were mouthpieces for the powerful sugar, coffee, tobacco, and cotton barons, the estate and plantation owners, and slave traders of the West Indies, organised vile smear campaigns against him.'[3]

Forced to give up his ambition of a career on the London stage, Aldridge began to accept offers of acting work in the provinces. His repertoire included *Othello*, *Oroonoko*, *The Slave*, *The Castle Spectre* and *The Revenge*. 'When these Black roles became monotonous,' wrote Shyllon, 'he expanded his repertoire to include roles specifically written for white actors – Macbeth, Shylock, King Lear, Richard III, Titus Andronicus.'[4]

His first tour commenced in Brighton at their popular Theatre Royal, and he made regular appearances there during his career. It was in Brighton that he played Othello for the first time in 1825. For many years he toured extensively and successfully, giving acclaimed performances in such towns and cities as Wolverhampton, Northampton, Derby, Liverpool, Lancaster, Hull, Manchester, Newcastle, Sunderland, Aberdeen and Edinburgh. He also travelled to Ireland, and in 1831 he reached a high point when his performance as Othello at the Theatre Royal in Dublin was seen by the celebrated actor Edmund Kean. It led to a letter of introduction to the manager of the Theatre Royal in Bath. Aldridge's appearance there as Othello was enthusiastically reviewed in the *Bath Journal* (26 January 1832):

> The African Roscius ... gave freshness of novelty and throughout his performance, evinced nothing but the

> emanations of sterling self-thinking treasures from his own laboratory. In pronunciation, he is exceedingly correct, and in his reading most clear and distinct, in his countenance animated, in expression forcible, in deportment graceful. The whole of the part was exceedingly well executed and our admiration of the actor was felt by all who witnessed him.

On 10 April 1833, Aldridge, just 26 years old, made his official West End debut when he played Othello at the Theatre Royal, Covent Garden. It was the first time a Black actor had appeared in a Shakespeare tragedy in a first-rate London theatre. Ellen Tree co-starred as Desdemona, and she would later marry Charles Kean, who played Iago. Once again, the press did everything they could to destroy Aldridge. One newspaper warned that 'Aldridge shall be jammed to atoms by the relentless power of our critical "BATTERING RAM" if his name is not immediately withdrawn from the Bills!!!'[5]

Actor friends of Aldridge, angry with the press, printed and distributed handbills that pleaded, 'We beg of a London audience "fair play" on his behalf,' but it was to no avail. *The Times* (11 April 1833) commented: 'Mr. Aldridge's Othello … wanted spirit and feeling. His accent is unpleasantly, and we would say, vulgarly foreign; his manner, drawling and unimpressive.' *The Times* also protested against a white 'lady-like girl' (Ellen Tree) being subjected to being 'pawed' by Aldridge. On the other hand, some reviewers were unbiased. *The Globe* (11 April 1833) praised him: 'He possesses a good figure and a speaking, intelligent countenance … there are beauties throughout his performance … and those who go to see the mere novelty of an African Othello will find more than mere curiosity gratified.'

Despite a masterly performance, the theatre's leaseholder, Pierre François Laporte, was forced to cut short Aldridge's engagement. Said Shyllon, 'Aldridge spent the next nineteen years playing in minor London theatres and provincial theatres … he became convinced that his colour and his marriage

Ira Aldridge poster, 1856. (Author's collection)

to a white woman were viewed with disfavour among the impresarios of the English theatre.'[6] Aldridge wrote in his diary, 'Bigotry and fanaticism have excited themselves in all possible shapes to annoy the profession of dramatic art, but I have been very successful, indeed, thank God.'[7]

Frustrated by the hostility shown towards him in London, Aldridge sought recognition abroad. His first Continental tour in 1852 was a success: 'Appearances in Switzerland and Germany, where he played *Othello*, *The Padlock* and *Macbeth*, were met with great acclaim … On his visits to Russia in 1858 and 1862 he was credited with introducing a more naturalistic acting style and encouraging the production of Shakespeare's plays.'[8]

In *Staying Power*, the historian Peter Fryer said that Aldridge was 'lionized' in Russia: 'Though he was playing in English with a German company, the controlled passion of his performances stirred Russian audiences as they had never been stirred before.'[9] One Russian critic, after seeing him as Othello, Lear, Shylock and Macbeth at St Petersburg's Imperial Theatre, described those evenings as 'undoubtedly the best that I have ever spent in the theatre'.[10] Another wrote, 'After Aldridge it is impossible to see Othello performed by a white actor.'[11]

According to Corporal John Lovell Jr, in *Theatre Arts*, Aldridge's tour of Russia in 1863 received a favourable press because Theophile Gautier, an influential French poet and literary critic, was in St Petersburg when Aldridge played there:

> Gautier says he was the lion of the town. Seats for his plays had to be taken days ahead, and audiences sat enthralled from the moment of his magnificent entrance. He was, reports Gautier, 'Othello himself, as Shakespeare has created him, with eyes half-closed as if dazzled from the African suns, his nonchalant, oriental attitude, and that Negro free-and-easy air that no European can imitate.' Gautier also reports that Aldridge recited in English but the Iago, Cassio and

> Desdemona of the play recited in German. In spite of these apparent barriers, the audiences were indelibly impressed and rewarded Aldridge 'with boundless applause'.[12]

Gautier added that he expected from Aldridge the 'energetic disordered, fiery, rather barbaric' style of Edmund Kean; actually, he found Aldridge 'quiet, reserved, classic, majestic', depending on science rather than on inspiration. 'There is no question that the American theatre was greatly the loser by its exclusion of Ira Aldridge.'[13]

An estimated 3 million African Americans were enslaved in the United States until the end of the Civil War in 1865. England's Anti-Slavery Society referred to Aldridge's triumphant appearances on stage as significant contributions to the struggle for abolition. With his wealth he contributed to many fundraising campaigns to end slavery in America.

Following a return visit to Brighton's Theatre Royal in 1858, Aldridge responded to a critic who had questioned why the audience had been so appreciative of his acting:

> It may be that they tolerate in the African what they would not submit to in the European; but then that is indicative of their sympathy for the coloured race rather than significant of a want of artistic appreciation. I have struggled hard, encountering almost insurmountable difficulties, to make not only for myself, a name, but to refute the assertions made by the enemies of my race and colour, that we Blacks are incapable of mental cultivation. I did not come to Brighton unsolicited. Mr N Chart, a friend of long standing, gave me an invitation, which I accepted … When such an assertion is made in my presence, I unhesitatingly class the speaker as a false-speaking knave or fool.[14]

On 3 November 1863, Aldridge was granted British citizenship. Two years later he played Othello to great acclaim at London's Theatre Royal Haymarket with Madge Kendal as Desdemona.

Reviews were favourable and these included the *Athenaeum* (26 August 1865) which had, in 1833, attacked his portrayal of Othello: 'He plays with feeling, intelligence, and finish. We were glad that he was well received on Monday, and that his merits were acknowledged by a numerous audience … The tragedy was well performed … Altogether we have seldom witnessed a representation of this great tragedy which pleases us more.'

Aldridge died on 7 August 1867, while on tour in the Polish city of Lodz. He was 60. His career had spanned four decades and in that time he had performed over forty roles, including Shakespeare's Othello, Aaron the Moor, Richard III, Shylock, Hamlet, Macbeth and King Lear. 'He played in towns and cities throughout England, Scotland, Wales, and Ireland,' wrote Errol Hill in *Shakespeare in Sable: A History of Black Shakespearean Actors*. 'He appeared in some thirty cities of Europe and Russia … He performed in many towns that had never before seen Shakespeare on stage. He played the great tragic roles in bilingual productions, speaking English himself with foreign companies who spoke their native language.'[15]

Throughout his life, Aldridge was showered with honours, including the first-class Medal of Arts and Sciences from the King of Prussia (1853). The name of Ira Aldridge has been inscribed on a chair at the Shakespeare Memorial Theatre in Stratford-upon-Avon. In 2004, Oku Ekpenyon, with the support of the Black and Asian Studies Association, succeeded in her campaign for Aldridge to be honoured at the Old Vic theatre. The unveiling of a print of Aldridge as Aaron the Moor in Shakespeare's *Titus Andronicus*, donated by the National Portrait Gallery, took place on 24 September that year. It was unveiled by the actor Earl Cameron who, in the 1940s, had been given elocution lessons by Aldridge's daughter Amanda Ira Aldridge, then in her 80s. In 2007, to commemorate the 200th anniversary of Aldridge's birth, English Heritage placed a blue plaque on his former home in Hamlet Road, Upper Norwood in the London Borough of

Bromley. In the 1860s Aldridge named the house Luranah Villa, in memory of his mother.

A BBC documentary about Aldridge called *The Black Othello* was broadcast on Radio 4 in 1986. It featured interviews with Aldridge's first biographer, Herbert Marshall, and the actors Hugh Quarshie and Joseph Marcell. In 2009, Radio 4 broadcast a second documentary, *The Negro Tragedian*, presented by Kwame Kwei-Armah. Several American and British stage productions have been based on the life of Ira Aldridge, including Lonne Elder III's *Splendid Mummer.* One of the most successful was *Red Velvet*, starring Adrian Lester. It was written by Lester's wife, Lolita Chakrabarti, and opened at the Tricycle Theatre in London in 2012. There have also been several biographies, including three volumes by Bernth Lindfors, without doubt the world's leading expert on Aldridge: *The Early Years 1807–1833* (2011), *The Vagabond Years 1833–1852* (2011) and *Performing Shakespeare in Europe 1852–1855* (2013). Aldridge has not been forgotten.

KILBURN TOWN HALL.

GREAT ATTRACTION!

For Two Nights Only.

MR. PAUL MOLYNEAUX,

The Great American CREOLE TRAGEDIAN, so justly styled the

"BLACK ROSCIUS,"

THE "NATURAL MOOR."

FRIDAY, JAN. 26th,

OTHELLO!

SATURDAY, JAN. 27th,

RICHARD III.

Grand Orchestra, Splendid Costumes, and Beautiful Scenery. Doors open 7.15; Farce 7.30; Tragedy 8. Carriages may be ordered for 10.30.

Paul Molyneaux advert from the *Kilburn Times* on 26 January 1883.

5

Paul Molyneaux: The Forgotten Othello

Some sources claim that Ira Aldridge was the last Black actor to play Othello in Britain until Paul Robeson took the role in 1930. However, further investigation reveals that there were others from the late Victorian era. The most prominent was S. Morgan Smith, who is mentioned in Herbert Marshall and Mildred Stock's 1958 biography of Aldridge. Smith was born in Philadelphia in 1832 and moved to England in 1866, where, one year before Aldridge's death, he appeared as Othello in Gravesend before taking the production to Birmingham and then London, opening on 29 August at the Royal Olympic Theatre off the Strand. He played a wide range of other roles throughout his career, including Shakespeare's Hamlet, Macbeth and Romeo. Smith died in Sheffield on 22 March 1882. He was recently the subject of a full-length biography by Bernth Lindfors.

Paul Molyneaux is the 'forgotten' Othello. Information about his theatrical career is scarce. He used the stage name Paul Molyneaux, but he was born Paul Molyneaux Hewlett in Cambridge, Massachusetts, in 1854. His father, Aaron Molyneaux Hewlett, was the first African American on the

Harvard University staff, so Hewlett's children had the advantage of a good education. Paul's brother Emanuel D. Molyneaux Hewlett (1850–1929) was among the first African Americans to be admitted to the bar of the United States Supreme Court in 1883. He served as a Justice of the Peace in Washington DC from 1890 to 1906. Their sister Virginia married Frederick Douglass Junior, the son of the escaped slave who became a renowned social reformer, abolitionist, orator, writer and statesman.

Paul was given a good start in life. He loved going to the theatre, but his father disapproved of his plans to become an actor. Nonetheless, perhaps inspired by the success of Ira Aldridge, Molyneaux pursued a stage career in England. Within a few years of his arrival, Molyneaux had acted several times in the provincial theatres and occasionally in London, but, according to the historian Errol Hill, 'The novelty of another authentic Black like Aldridge or Morgan Smith was apparently wearing thin … Molyneaux found life very difficult indeed.'[1]

Though information about his stage work is hard to find, there is an advertisement in the *Kilburn Times* confirming that Molyneaux played *Othello* and *Richard III* at Kilburn Town Hall in January 1883. He advertised himself as 'The Great American Creole Tragedian'. A review of *Richard III* has also been found in *The Era* (3 February 1883), but the critic was unimpressed and described Molyneaux's supporting cast as 'incompetent'. In a letter to *The Era* (10 February 1883), sent from his south London home in Fearnley Road, Camberwell Grove, Molyneux defended his production:

> I need not tell you that I was endeavoring to get a start in England. With an empty pocket I had to rely almost entirely on amateurs. The night previous *Othello* was performed to the entire satisfaction of the audience, who, though few, were lavish with their rounds of applause, and at the close we had again to raise the curtain. But even on this occasion the performance was not what it should have been – not one half

> what I have done and can do under more favourable circumstances … I only state this in order that you may deal justly with me. I crave no favours. I simply wish you to speak of me as I am. As for the company, I acknowledge they were inexperienced in the play. I trust you will read this carefully and deal as you think best.

In 1886, when Molyneaux was residing at 141 Chatham Street in Reading, he wrote a letter to Frederick Douglass in the United States. It has survived and reveals something about his views on racial equality:

> The Bible strictly calls upon us to love our neighbors as ourselves. At another time I saw an account where the Indians in a certain state or Territory had been openly defrauded of a large sum of money by Government officials. The Supreme Court claimed that they were foreigners, and therefore refused to act … But if the American Indians are foreigners, I am at a loss to know who are real Americans. If they are foreigners what are the white people? … I am not much of a Politician myself, but on my return to America I shall certainly devote some of my time and energy to arousing our people to a proper sense of duty. I have been in England too long, and enjoyed equal rights too long, to lamely yield to whims and prejudices of our white countrymen at home. I did not intend to stay so long when I started for these shores. But circumstances have compelled me to do so.

In 1888 the *Ayr Advertiser, or, West Country Journal* (25 May 1888) described how the Good Templar's Hall was occupied by Uncle Tom's Jubilee Singers, said to be native Blacks from America, who gave a grand concert of plantation songs and, in addition to the concert, Molyneaux gave an interesting address on slavery and appeared in the following recitations: 'Fate of Virginia', 'Rejected Lover' and 'Othello's address to the Senate'.

In an undated letter sent to America from 52 Bromar Road, Camberwell, Molyneaux made a reference to a contract he had just signed to join a theatrical company and the support he had received from two well-known actor-managers. He also mentioned his relationship with a 'fine young lady':

> This will be the first regular engagement I have had. I have played two or three times at my own expense, but playing in Halls generally proves fatal. Henry Irving [actor-manager], Wilson Barrett [actor-manager], and the U.S. Minister all patronised me. There is no doubt as to future success. The papers gave me good criticisms. I shall not have a large salary in this company, but it is a good reliable company … I should have been starved but I was fortunate in forming the acquaintance of a very fine young lady, to whom I have been engaged a long time, and she has been as generous as she has been good. Her father was a wholesale hatter in London but he has been dead fifteen years … she is no hum-bug. I have been stopping at Reading about three months, just doing a little something to help along until my theatrical engagement commences. It is 42 miles from Reading to my young ladies' [*sic*] home in London. I start every Friday evening at 9 and walk to her home, arriving 7.30 the next morning. By this arrangement I have managed to get along as it costs me nothing while staying in London. The walk does not affect me in the least as I am not delicate. Being a strict teetotaler.

Molyneaux then mentioned joining the theatrical company in Glasgow, and it was in Glasgow in 1887 that he married his 'fine young lady', Amy Joyce, a stationer's assistant. Their daughter Amy Virginia Douglas Molyneaux Hewlett was born on 26 November 1889 in Bishop Auckland, Durham. For most of her life she was known to her family and friends as Molly. Paul Molyneaux then returned to America with his wife and child, but he was taken ill and died on 24 June 1891. The cause of his death was probably a brain tumour. He was buried in Boston, Massachusetts. His widow and child returned to England. Amy Hewlett became a nurse, and so did their daughter, who married and had four children. One of them, a daughter called Patricia, followed in both her mother's and grandmother's footsteps by training as a nurse. She died on New Year's Day 2021, while I was writing this book.

Molyneaux's British descendants only recently found out about him. At the time of writing, his grandson Douglas lives in Wales with his wife Susie, and his great-granddaughter Tamara lives with her family in Devon. They have kindly shared some of the information I have included in this chapter, including the letters, which, to my knowledge, have not been previously published. This information gives only a fragmented but nonetheless fascinating insight into this forgotten Othello of the 1880s. Regrettably, no photographs of Molyneux have come to light.

Tamara told me: 'My son Olly performed in his first ever Shakespeare performance at Dartmouth Castle at the age of 10, just a few years ago, and I mentioned my great-grandfather's achievements and how difficult it was for him back then.' So, the acting tradition continues with one of Paul Molyneaux's British descendants. He would surely be proud.

On 17 January 2021, after sending this chapter to them, I received a message from the family:

> It has given us great pleasure to know that Paul's achievements are not forgotten and that his life and experiences will inspire other young actors to keep battling against disadvantage and discrimination. As a family we are all very proud to have had such brave and inspiring ancestors.

Bert Williams and George Walker in 1903. (Author's collection/Mary Evans Picture Library)

6

Victorian and Edwardian Music Halls

During the reigns of Queen Victoria and her son Edward VII, the main contact white Britons had with people of African descent was either in sport (primarily boxing) or in entertainment. Before the existence of cinema, radio and television, the British public from all social classes flocked to music halls to be entertained. Black artistes who made careers as stars of music-hall theatres up and down the country included comedians, dancers and singers, and they coexisted with white players. The historian Ziggi Alexander has commented that seeing fellow Black people on the stage gave Black audiences a sense of race pride, but they were also aware that harmful racial stereotypes were continually reinforced. This could happen by Black artistes themselves, or by the white performers who blacked up as minstrels. Although white professionals dominated minstrelsy, there was interest in seeing Black performers on stage: 'Whilst music halls provided work for the vast majority of Black performers, others succeeded by different means.'[1]

The Bohee Brothers were among the most popular stars of Victorian music halls. James Bohee (1844–97) and his younger brother George (1857–1930) were Canadian-born banjo players who toured the United States from 1876. In 1878 they joined the all-Black Haverley's Minstrels troupe. Travelling to Britain, the troupe opened at Her Majesty's Theatre in London in 1881 with sixty-five Black performers. They made a successful tour of Britain before returning to America in 1882, but James and George remained. 'Their clever banjo playing popularised this instrument to such an extent,' wrote historian Henry T. Sampson, 'that they began to give lessons, and learning the banjo became a popular craze among London society folk.'[2] In 1883 they opened a banjo studio in London where they famously taught the Prince of Wales, the future King Edward VII, how to play the instrument. After the brothers assembled their own troupe of Black artistes, they toured all over Britain. Their encounter with the Prince of Wales enabled them to bill themselves as 'the Royal Bohee Brothers'. Everywhere they went, audiences and critics loved them. By 1890 they were a London institution, appearing regularly at the London Pavilion, the crème de la crème of music-hall venues at the time. 'The Bohees presented a highly musical act, visually attractive, for they played and danced at the same time,' wrote Jeffrey Green and Rainer E. Lotz. '"Home Sweet Home" and "A Boy's Best Friend is his Mother" are examples of the sentimental compositions that made them famous.'[3] After James died of pneumonia in Ebbw Vale, South Wales, in 1897, George Bohee continued working as a solo artiste.

Amy Height was one of the many African American music-hall entertainers who worked with the Bohee Brothers. She arrived in Britain in the early 1880s when she was still a teenager. Her name first appeared in *The Stage* newspaper in July 1883, credited as a member of a variety show at the Surrey Music Hall in Barnsley. Theatre critics often singled her out for praise. When she appeared as Friday's Squaw in the pantomime *Robinson Crusoe* at the Grand Theatre in Islington in 1886, *The Stage* (31 December 1886) noted that she 'displays considerable humorous power and command of expression, whilst in the vocalisation of her songs she uses a clear and musical organ with considerable skill and effect'.

In 1888, Height joined the first provincial tour of the Bohee Brothers. When she appeared on the London variety stage in Hoxton three years later, *The Stage* (8 October 1891) noted that she put 'much vitality and go into her songs and actions, and scored a distinct success'. In 1894, at Hammersmith's Lyric Opera House, she made the first of several appearances as the slave Aunt Chloe in the melodrama *Uncle Tom's Cabin*. Later that year she was praised for her role as the Princess in another pantomime, *Dick Whittington and His Cat*, staged at the Elephant and Castle in London. In 1895 she shared the bill with the popular music-hall comedian George Robey, and four years later she enjoyed one of her biggest successes as Princess Lulu in a 'bright and tuneful musical farce' called *The Gay Grisette* in London and then on tour. *The Stage* (17 August 1899) described her as, 'the cleverest coloured lady we have seen. She is a born comedienne, can sing, and introduce patter and gag, and makes herself a general favourite on her first entrance.' In 1900 the *New York*

Amy Height. (Author's collection)

Times (22 July 1900) reported on Height's successful transition from singer to 'straight' actress when she appeared in London in *Madame Delphine*. The newspaper noted that Height, whom they described as 'a coloured actress from Boston', had made a 'hit' with Londoners as 'a negro mammy, which is quite new to the English stage, and proved the chief artistic success of the play'. An appearance at the Tivoli Theatre in London in 1901 received this enthusiastic acknowledgement from the *Music Hall and Theatre Review* (16 August 1901):

> Such cheery good-humour has Miss Amy Height, and such an infectious laugh, that her audience find her quite irresistible. She is described as a Princess of Ethiopian Comedy. She chatters to the house in the most delightful manner, and arouses roars of laughter with her quaint remarks. Her second song is a very amusing account of a christening, given with much spirit.

Height's last recorded appearance in *The Stage* (16 January 1913) was a role in the pantomime *Aladdin* at the Royal Theatre in Smethwick. While living at 90 St George's Road, Southwark, Amy died from pneumonia on 21 March 1913. She was buried in an unmarked grave in Streatham Park Cemetery, which has had a long connection with the Variety Artistes' Benevolent Fund. Hundreds of variety artistes and music-hall performers have been buried there.

Amy Height's success in music halls and pantomime, let alone her transition to 'straight' theatre, was unusual for a Black woman in Britain at that time. The public's contact with Black women in the world of theatre was minimal in the Victorian and Edwardian era, but the versatile and popular Height helped open the doors for others.[4]

In America, a comedian and singer called Eddie Whaley teamed up with another African American, Harry Scott, and together they formed a cross-talking double act. They called themselves Cuthbert and Pussyfoot. Whaley was the straight man, intelligent and smartly dressed, and Scott the comedy half, appearing in blackface as the lugubrious country bumpkin. Accepting an invitation to tour England, Scott and Whaley made their first British appearance at the Hippodrome, Sheffield, in November 1909. They arrived with bookings for only eight weeks but they were so successful that they never returned to the United States and became British subjects. Apart from their successful cross-talking routine, they also worked a songs-at-the-piano act. Whaley was the vocalist and Scott a jazz pianist.

They made their London debut in January 1910 at the Empire, Leicester Square, in the revue *Hullo – London!* In 1913 they starred at the London Palladium. They were a successful variety act during the First World War and for more than thirty years they were music-hall headliners all over the country. They were also popular in West End revues including *Johnny Jones* (Alhambra, Leicester Square, 1920) starring George Robey. They headlined the Victoria Palace (1923) and Holborn Empire (1926), and were equally popular abroad. During the Second World War, Scott and Whaley continued to work in variety. In 1941 they headlined at the Stoll, Kingsway, in a revue called *Broadway to Blighty*, and they often entertained the troops in concerts. The partnership finally ended in 1946 and Scott died in 1947. Whaley made Brighton his family home in the 1930s and purchased 124 Marine Parade. He named it Whaley House and, after Scott's death, he gave up show business to run his home as a hotel. It became a popular holiday home for entertainers in Britain, and among the many Black stars who visited were Turner Layton, Leslie 'Hutch' Hutchinson, Ellis Jackson, Ray Ellington, Ike Hatch and Adelaide Hall. Whaley died in 1960.[5]

Harry Scott was not the only Black entertainer to use blackface make-up. One of the most famous was Bert Williams, of Williams and Walker fame. They were the stars of *In Dahomey*, the first full-length musical comedy to be written, performed and staged by Black artistes. Bert Williams (1874–1922) and George Walker (1873–1911) were already big names in American vaudeville when they came to London. In 1903 the *In Dahomey* company, which also included Walker's wife Aida Overton Walker, came from a successful run in New York to the Shaftesbury Theatre in London's West End and after its premiere on 16 May the show became the 'in' thing to see. Music historian Jeffrey Green certainly attributes its success to:

> Word of mouth recommendation. Curiosity, because it was an all-Black show, leading to people saying 'You must go and see Williams and Walker, you must go and see *In Dahomey*, it's so funny, so lively.' That led to the contract being extended. It played from May into Christmas of 1903. Then it toured all over England into Scotland. So, it was in Britain for well over a year.[6]

Reviews were enthusiastic, with the *Daily Mail* (18 May) reporting, 'a welcome sensation of surprise was afforded visitors to the Shaftesbury Theatre ... those who had come to scoff remained to laugh.' One of the most outstanding notices appeared in the *Sunday Dispatch* (20 May), in which the reviewer singled out Bert Williams and his co-stars, George and Aida, for praise:

> Mr. Williams facial expression can only be described as marvellous. Even when he allows himself to dance, it is executed with quaint restraint which takes it entirely out of the category of anything ordinary. In a word, Mr. Williams must be seen to be appreciated. There is not a white comedian on our stage who could not profit by watching his methods. His singing of 'Jonah Man' is the quintessence of art. His side partner, Mr. Walker, is equally gifted. Natural grace and refinement are his attributes. His cakewalk is absolutely irresistible. Aida Overton Walker's singing and dancing were a revelation, as was the melodious chorus. The music of Will Marion Cook, the Negro musician, was of the very highest class.

The demand for tickets meant that extra performances had to be added for the Christmas period and the show reached its 250th performance on 26 December. In the new year, *In Dahomey* toured a number of British cities, including Manchester, Newcastle and Glasgow.

In Dahomey was so popular with the British public that the cast were invited to give a command performance at Buckingham Palace on 23 June 1903. The royal family were celebrating the 9th birthday of King Edward VII's favourite grandson, David (the future Edward VIII and Duke of Windsor). He and his brother (later King George VI) were there for the party with 150 other children, and the cast of *In Dahomey*, led by Williams, Walker and Overton Walker, entertained them.

Before the performance could take place, all the scenery and costumes for the cast had to be transported from the Shaftesbury Theatre to Buckingham Palace. They travelled from Shaftesbury Avenue, through Piccadilly, and via parks to the palace. Although this distance was only a brisk ten-minute walk, *The Era* (27 June 1903) noted that 'to transport some eighty coloured comedians, together with the scenery belonging to their show, is not an easy matter; but, then, it was the command of the King.'

Williams fondly recalled the historic occasion:

> I had just finished dressing and was standing in the wings ... The curtain was down. Suddenly, the strains of that inspiring anthem, 'God Save the King' filled the air. The King and Queen and the young Prince of Wales walked down the palace steps and terrace to the lawn chairs reserved for the King and Queen. The other members of the royal party found places on the grass ... I looked through the [theatre] curtain and saw the royal family ... There were several peepholes in the curtain; my company made several more! It was, actually, the time of our lives.[7]

That afternoon, Williams had a bad case of stage fright, but he later explained in an interview in *American Magazine*

(January 1918), that the King put him at ease. He was 'the kindest, most courteous, most democratic man I ever met'. Williams's biographer Eric Ledell Smith noted the following:

> After the performance, there was a reception for the company. The King asked Williams and Walker and Aida Overton Walker to show him how to cakewalk. Walker reminisced: 'We were treated royally. That is the only word for it. We had champagne from the Royal cellar and strawberries and cream from the Royal garden. The Queen was perfectly lovely, and the King was as jolly as he could be.'[8]

The African American cast of *In Dahomey*, within five weeks of their arrival in London, were playing before the royal family. This was, of course, reported in the Black and white American newspapers and gave the show and its artistes an enormous amount of prestige.

Williams had been born in Nassau, the capital of the Bahamas in the Caribbean (then known as the British West Indies), and he remained there until he migrated with his family to Florida in around 1885. He met George Walker in 1893 and they formed a double act which helped to change the face of American entertainment. Vaudeville had been seen as a solely white tradition before they burst onto the scene. Following his break-up with Walker in 1909, Williams continued as a solo act. He wrote over seventy songs, made gramophone recordings from 1901, and directed and starred in the film *A Natural Born Gambler* (1916). America's top showman, Florenz Ziegfeld, featured him in his popular *Follies* revues on Broadway from 1910 to 1919. Williams was famous for playing an amiable character who was down on his luck, in which he wore a shabby dress suit and shoes three sizes too big. He had a theme song called 'Nobody' that audiences demanded to hear whenever he appeared. He died in 1922.

Williams's stage character was complex. In 2020, when Colin Grant assessed Williams for BBC Radio 3's *The Essay*, he drew attention to the man behind the mask:

> Off-stage he was a tall, light-skinned, mixed race man with marked poise and dignity. On stage Williams became shuffling and inept. He pulled on a wig of kinky hair over his head, applied blackface make-up and concealed his hands in gloves. Usually, his characters wore a shabby dress-suit and over-sized battered shoes. The idea of a Black man blacking up seems problematic today but Bert Williams was no theatrical Uncle Tom either … every night, Williams disappeared behind the mask.[9]

Some Black entertainers who found fame in the Victorian and Edwardian eras enjoyed not only acclaim and popularity but also positions in high society. The association of Black entertainers with Britain's upper classes and Royal family can be traced back to the African American concert singer Elizabeth Taylor Greenfield, who performed for Queen Victoria in 1854. The Fisk Jubilee Singers followed her in the 1870s. The cast of *In Dahomey* attracted a great deal of attention in the newspapers. But while such contacts suggest a level of social acceptance, Jeffrey Green has revealed that:

> Further investigation shows that to be a superficial view, for Black entertainers were seldom truly accepted as individuals, but in general only as symbols. This led to a paradox, since the association of Black people with the aristocratic and ruling elite of Britain was seen in America as a social triumph, and was reported as such in the press, biographies, and autobiographies … If the Americans saw the association of Black entertainers and Britain's high society as a Black success, it would seem likely that a number of Britons, Black and white, would conclude the same. British liberals, aghast at lynching, Jim Crow, and other manifestations of racism in America, could show that the mingling of Black people in British high society proved how different life was in Britain. The reality was that Black access to high society was as volatile as show business, and friends were as fickle as audiences.[10]

Connie Smith, Norris Smith and Ed Wallace at Ed's home in Lambeth's Kennington Lane, 1956. (Author's collection, courtesy of Edward Scobie)

7

Sentimental Journey

The story of Connie Smith began to emerge when, in 1983, I attended a special screening of the film *Song of Freedom* at the British Film Institute (BFI). It had been organised in honour of Elisabeth Welch, who had co-starred in the film with Paul Robeson. When we met, Elisabeth told us that she hadn't seen the film since its London premiere at the Plaza Cinema in 1936. Over time it had become something of a 'lost' film, though it was fortunate that the BFI had kept a print in their archive. Elisabeth greeted each appearance of her co-stars with enthusiasm: Paul Robeson, Esme Percy, Robert Adams. She applauded Connie Smith, who appeared as Queen Zinga in the prologue, set in West Africa in 1700.

Afterwards, Elisabeth reminisced about the film and I asked her about Smith. Her face lit up with a broad smile when I mentioned Smith's name. Elisabeth explained that they worked together several times, though they hadn't become close friends, just friendly theatrical acquaintances. She believed that Connie had come to Britain from America in the late Victorian era, with a choir or a show, and never returned home. 'I think she lived in Brixton. A lot of theatrical people did,' she explained. Later on, I discovered that the two women had worked together on several BBC Radio shows, including a variety programme, *Molasses Club* (1936), and a musical play specially written for Elisabeth called *Broadway Slave* (1944), in which Smith played her mother. Elisabeth was very fond of Smith but had no idea what became of her. Five years later I found out.

In 1988 I made one of many visits to a community bookshop near my home known as the Peckham Bookplace. On arriving I found myself looking at the bookshelves, but not for anything in particular. Then I saw it. Edward Scobie's *Black Britannia*, published in 1972. I have no idea why a pristine first edition of Scobie's book was in a Peckham bookshop in 1988, but there it was, one of the first books ever published about the history of Britain's Black community. For me it became a wonderful resource, and there, on pages 176 and 177, was Smith's story. I later found out that Scobie had been based in Britain in the 1950s and 1960s and interviewed quite a few Black theatre people, including Smith.

He wrote with warmth about Smith, whom he believed had been born in Brooklyn, New York, and whom he described thus: 'A sort of Black Fanny Brice, with a soothing lisp in her Brooklynese voice, she left New York in 1894 to play the capitals of Europe in the show *The South Before the War*.'[1] Scobie also noted that Smith had died not long before the publication of his book.

It was easy to access a copy of her death certificate and in doing so I discovered that she had been living in Lambeth, not far from me. Smith had died in a Catholic nursing home on 11 May 1970. The following year, when I interviewed the former actress Pauline Henriques at her home in Brighton, she smiled when I mentioned Smith's name. She willingly shared with me the happy times they had spent together in the 1940s and 1950s:

> Now and again, we shared dressing rooms and became quite close. On stage Connie had a presence, even though she was

> very small and very quiet. She had discipline and a subtle way of playing. She had a very different presence from someone like Paul Robeson, who I had seen in *Othello*. His stature and beautiful speaking voice made everybody look at him. Connie had this quiet discipline and I would say she was the first Black professional in the theatre I ever met. Perhaps in the music halls you have to have more discipline than you do in straight legitimate theatre. She would be on time for rehearsals and she never missed a cue. However tiny the part, she studied it meticulously. I thought, 'this woman's got what I want', so I modelled myself on her. She was always very encouraging to younger actors, especially those of us who were Black. I recognised that she had something very few Black actors have had – enormous experience in the theatre.[2]

I found out more about Smith when I accessed a copy of the December 1956 issue of the African American magazine *Ebony*. Edward Scobie had published 'The Old-Timers', an affectionate, feature-length tribute to Connie and two of her friends. They had all been London residents since the turn of the century, and came together every week to reminisce about their lives in show business and sing a few songs at the piano. At the time of Scobie's interview, Connie Smith was 81, Norris Smith (no relation) 73, and Ed Wallace 85. Scobie described what happened when the trio reunited at 340 Kennington Lane, Lambeth, the south London home of Ed Wallace:

> At precisely 1pm every Thursday, spry 85-year-old Ed Wallace locked the doors of his busy London liquor store and joined two old friends in a sentimental journey. With old-time entertainers Connie Smith and Norris Smith, Ed takes a rousing excursion back to the time when the trio made hot musical news all over Europe and back, even further, to their youth in the American homeland they have not seen for over 45 years.

In 1926 Norris Smith had organised The Southern Serenaders, which Connie and Ed joined, and together the trio entertained the British public in music halls, concerts and on BBC Radio:

> The weekly trip into the past begins when Ed mounts the stairs to his flat above the store. There, his wife Marion already has a friendly fire crackling in the Victorian-style hearth and is preparing a modest feast of cold cuts, salad and canapes on the old-fashioned dining table. While he waits for the others to appear, the retired musician takes his 60-year-old saxophone out of its age-worn case and blows a few bars from some long-remembered tune.

Ed Wallace, born in Knoxville, Tennessee in 1871, had arrived in Britain in 1899 and made his debut at London's Middlesex Theatre as a member of the Old Plantation Trio. They billed themselves as 'Novelty Instrumentalists'. Wallace played alto saxophone, doubling on banjo and cornet. When work became scarce, Wallace and his wife Marion, whom he married in 1940, ran an off-licence. Though he entered his profession as 'vocalist and travelling instrumentalist' in the 1939 Register of England and Wales, Wallace made occasional stage appearances as an actor. In 1939, in London's West End, he played the supporting role of Crooks – the lively, sharp-witted Black stable hand who takes his name from his crooked back – in the adaptation of John Steinbeck's novel *Of Mice and Men*. Said Scobie:

> As they have done every Thursday afternoon for the past 15 years, the other old-timers arrive in a flurry of excitement. First to breeze into the Wallace's flat is Connie, a lively former music hall singer-dancer who likes to boast that she is still 'a working girl.' She is followed by Norris, the chief merry-maker who is the 'youngster' of the group.

Norris Smith travelled to Ed's home from Islington in north London. He was born in Columbia, Missouri, in 1883, and arrived in London with the cast of *In Dahomey* in 1903. In 1905 he became a member of the vocal quartet The Four Black Diamonds and toured with them all over Europe. He was also the London correspondent for the *Chicago Defender*, an African American newspaper. For years the paper published his reports about Black artistes in Britain and Europe. In 1928, as a baritone, he understudied Paul Robeson in *Show Boat* at the Theatre Royal, Drury Lane. He also played a small role in the musical and recorded 'Ol' Man River' when Robeson was prevented from doing so due to a contractual agreement in America. Until he retired in 1954, Norris Smith alternated work as a 'straight' actor in West End plays, such as Lillian Hellman's *Watch on the Rhine* (1942) at the Aldwych Theatre, and touring the country in all-Black revues like *Harlem to Kentucky* (1944), based on *Uncle Tom's Cabin*, in which he sang spirituals. In 1947 he was in the supporting cast of *The Coral Snake* with Connie Smith at London's Q Theatre:

> After helping themselves at the table and cautiously partaking of Ed's stock of fine liquors, the old-timers gather around the piano and lustily sing the old songs that brought them fame and fortune as The Southern Serenaders back in the 1920s.

Connie Smith did not have far to travel far to Ed's home. She was also a resident of Lambeth, having lived in Brook Drive, behind the Imperial War Museum, since the 1930s. Smith was born Cornelia Johnson in South Carolina in 1875 but raised in Brooklyn, New York.[3] Pauline Henriques recalled, 'She told me that she worked in a factory in New York and was desperate to get out of it because Black people were being terribly exploited and poorly paid. She had a lovely singing voice and decided to become a music-hall entertainer.'[4]

In 1894, Smith left New York to tour Germany and Denmark in a production called *The South Before the War*. During the tour she met Augustus 'Gus' Smith, a variety artist from Philadelphia. In 1895 they quit the tour and travelled to Hull, England, where they were booked to appear as a double act in the Alhambra

Theatre. They billed themselves as Smith and Johnson and, for over thirty years, found plenty of work in music halls. They married while on tour in Liverpool in 1902. In 1914, with the outbreak of the First World War, they could have returned to America, but they decided to stay because the British public had been good to them. Smith later recalled, 'We never had any sort of insult or suffered any indignity from the English.'[5]

When Gus died in 1927, Smith was heartbroken, but she kept on working, having already joined Norris and Ed in the Southern Serenaders. On 29 January 1928 they took part in a charity concert at the London Pavilion in Piccadilly Circus. This was in aid of the Mayor of Westminster's Flood Relief Fund. It was described as 'the greatest all-star coloured show ever staged' and it had been organised to raise money for the victims of flooding caused by the swollen River Thames. Other artists on the bill included Josephine Baker, who flew in from Paris specially for the occasion to dance the Charleston (it was also her British stage debut), the cabaret entertainer Leslie 'Hutch' Hutchinson and the American blues singer Alberta Hunter. A few months later, on 3 May, when *Show Boat* opened at the Theatre Royal, Drury Lane, Hunter was cast as Paul Robeson's wife, Queenie, and Smith was her understudy.

In London, Smith became well known among agents, producers and playwrights, and in the 1930s she made a successful transition from variety artiste to character actress. When a part for an older Black actress became available, Smith was considered. Her many West End plays included Lillian Hellman's *The Little Foxes* (1942), *Stage Door* (1946) and *Hattie Stowe* (1947). When she joined the cast of Eugene O'Neill's *SS Glencairn* (1947) at the Mercury Theatre, Smith was reunited with Pauline Henriques.

As she grew older Connie found herself in growing demand. She appeared in several repertory productions including revivals of *The Little Foxes* and *Deep Are the Roots*. In 1956, at the age of 80, she joined the distinguished English Stage Company at the Royal Court Theatre. Her first role for the company was the slave Tituba in Arthur Miller's *The Crucible* (1956), directed by Tony Richardson. The cast also included several future stage stars. Mary Ure, Joan Plowright, Kenneth Haigh, Alan Bates and Robert Stephens were among them. In 1958 came Barry Reckord's *Flesh to a Tiger* starring Cleo Laine. One of Smith's last radio plays was Andrew Salkey's *The Dry Time* (1959) with Pauline Henriques. Said Scobie:

> During the weekly reunions of The Southern Serenaders, conversation invariably turns to 'back home'. For the one longing which the old-timers have in common is to pay a final visit to America. While they seem unaware of it, the America they would find would have little similarity to the land they left behind.

The 'old-timers' did not see America again. Norris died at the age of 76 on 31 October 1959 in Islington. Ed died at the age of 94 on 26 December 1965 in Lambeth. Smith made her final stage appearances in *Mister Johnson* (1960) and a German production of *The Emperor Jones* (1961), learning to cope with a foreign language at the age of 86. She was approaching her 90th birthday when ill health forced her to retire.

When Smith died at the age of 95, a mass was read for her at St George's Cathedral in Lambeth Road before her funeral service. She was laid to rest in the variety artistes' section of Streatham Park Cemetery. Pauline Henriques said, 'It doesn't surprise me that Connie is buried in an unmarked grave because she underplayed everything. She would be perfectly happy with that.'[6]

On a visit to the cemetery, I was given Smith's plot number but the gravesite was impossible to find. However, I felt her presence on that warm, sunny day. I had also made the acquaintance of friends who spoke with such warmth and happiness about the trailblazing actress once described by Edward Scobie as 'a little old lady with a big heart'.

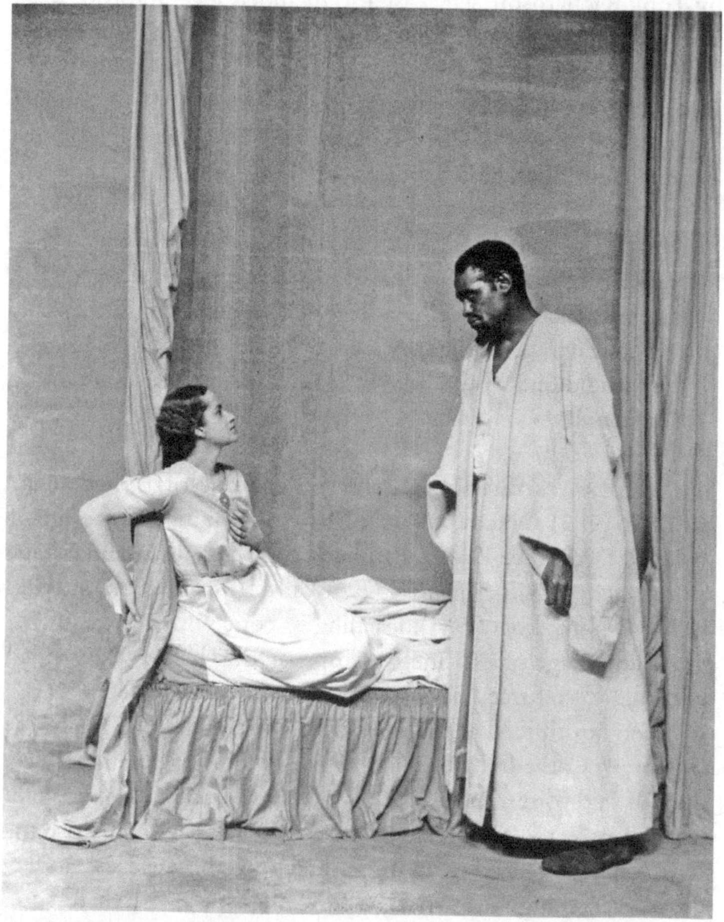

Peggy Ashcroft and Paul Robeson in *Othello* at the Savoy Theatre, 1930. (Author's collection, courtesy of Peggy Ashcroft)

8

Paul Robeson: Magical Fires

In 1984 I befriended Junior 'J.D.' Douglas. He had curated an exhibition about Paul Robeson for Battersea Library, and when he successfully applied to the GLC for funding to expand the exhibition, he asked me to come on board as a consultant. My primary interest was in Robeson's acting career, so I focused on that section. J.D. and the GLC agreed to present the new version of the exhibition at the Royal Festival Hall in London's South Bank. During this time, my involvement brought me into contact with some of the people who had known Robeson personally or had some connection to him.

At a private viewing of the first exhibition at Battersea Library, I met Dame Peggy Ashcroft, who had played Desdemona to Robeson's Othello at the Savoy Theatre in 1930. Graceful and charming, she was theatre royalty to me and reminded me a little of the Queen Mother. She had the utmost respect for Robeson as an actor and political activist, and talked to J.D. and myself about her working relationship with him.

On that day J.D. also introduced me to Marie Seton, who, in 1928, had seen Robeson in *Show Boat* at the Theatre Royal,

Drury Lane, and befriended him when he had played Othello with Ashcroft. In 1934, Seton accompanied Robeson and his wife Eslanda to Moscow to meet the renowned film director Sergei Eisenstein. They remained friends and she later wrote one of the best biographies of Robeson. It was superior to many others because Seton had personal knowledge of him. In her biography she drew upon many fascinating anecdotes about his life and career. Seton's *Paul Robeson* was published in 1958, the same year as Robeson's autobiography *Here I Stand*, but Robeson found time to consult with Seton and make corrections to her final draft. In her biography, Seton acknowledged that Robeson exposed the 'white world' to facets of the Black man they had never seen before, 'one strikingly different from those who expressed themselves in jazz, dancing, humour … Robeson had an almost monumental quietness; he lacked the "dynamic" qualities popularly and too tritely ascribed to Negroes by those who admired Negro music and dancing.'[1] Regrettably, Marie Seton did not see the new version of the exhibition at the Royal Festival Hall. She died on 17 February 1985.

The Trinidadian historian, journalist and socialist C.L.R. James also attended the private viewing at Battersea Library. Aged 84, he looked physically frail in his wheelchair, but mentally he was as sharp as a tack. He expressed his appreciation for the long-overdue recognition of Robeson, for whom he had a great deal of admiration and respect. In 1936 it was James's friend Seton who made it possible for his play *Toussaint L'Ouverture* to be staged with Robeson in the lead. Seton took the playscript to the Stage Society and they agreed to produce it if Robeson became involved. To coincide with the Royal Festival Hall exhibition, C.L.R. James reflected on Robeson in the 1930s in the radical journal *Race Today*:

> People of all kinds, particularly those advocating equality, were able to point to him and say: 'Look, here is a Black man. See the kind of person he is. You can't look upon him and

> think he is inferior.' And that is why Robeson represented so much. His performances and the force of his personality represented and symbolised the great change that was taking place in the new conceptions that were flooding human consciousness in the thirties.[2]

One day, when J.D. and I were setting up the exhibition at the Royal Festival Hall, Paul Boateng from the GLC, who had been instrumental in approving the funding for the exhibition, insisted that we join him for lunch. The other guests were Ken Livingstone, then leader of the GLC, and Robeson's son, Paul Robeson Jr, who had travelled from America to open the exhibition. Boateng informed us that he had been named in honour of

Poster for the GLC's Paul Robeson exhibition at the Royal Festival Hall, 1985. (Author's collection)

Paul Robeson, but for me the lunch was a challenge. I felt overwhelmed in this gathering, and let J.D. speak for us. I was out of my depth in the company of Robeson's son, though I needn't have worried because he was a gracious and friendly gentleman.

The opening of the *Paul Robeson* exhibition on 24 April 1985 attracted a huge crowd of honorary guests and attendees. These included the Labour leader Neil Kinnock; C.L.R. James; actor Sam Wanamaker, who had played Iago to Robeson's Othello at Stratford in 1959; a number of well-known Labour Party politicians who had known Robeson or just admired him, including Jennie Lee, Illtyd Harrington, who at that time was Deputy Leader of the GLC, Bernie Grant, Tony Benn, Andrew Faulds and Lord David Pitt; the folk singer and actress Nadia Cattouse, whom I befriended a few years later; Elisabeth Welch, Robeson's leading lady in two films; and Rachel Thomas, the Welsh actress who had co-starred with Robeson in the 1940 film *The Proud Valley*.

When I look back, I realise these brief encounters helped to give me insights into Robeson. He was a man who was loved and cherished by the British public but, at the height of his fame, was demonised and ostracised for his political beliefs in his homeland during the McCarthy era of the 1950s. I also discovered that he meant different things to different people: singers, actors, writers, socialists, communists, Labour Party politicians and Marxists all had their own Paul Robeson. His fans, especially those who had no strong political beliefs, just wanted to hear his glorious singing.

Said Tom Hutchinson in the *Highbury and Islington Express* (27 March 1998):

> He was magnificent, called by some an 'artistic and social genius' and by enemies 'a Marxist traitor to the United States'. Current stars such as Harry Belafonte revere him. Without him there would have been no Malcolm X or Spike Lee … Paul Robeson survives as an icon to his own people – and all

> people ... He was a man of Biblical stature and, after a lifetime of struggle, glory is still all around his presence.

In the 1930s, Paul Robeson reigned supreme in the world of British entertainment. He was one of the country's most popular singers, but he also had a successful career as an actor in films and on the stage. However, he probably suffered more disappointments than any other actor of his generation. For Robeson, who was a highly educated and forward-thinking artist, there were hardly any opportunities to play challenging or realistic roles; as he refused to play one-dimensional stereotypes, there was little that appealed to him. Nonetheless he persisted in seeking out plays that would help him to make progress as an actor and as an ambassador for his race. Against the odds, and despite this scarcity of roles, Robeson somehow managed to gain prominence in the world of theatre.

In spite of his illustrious stage career, he never saw himself as a technically great actor. His son, Paul Robeson Jr, explained, 'He didn't try to be. Didn't care about that. He was interested in the impact on an audience. He felt he had to project a Black male image of power and dignity and cultural integrity.'[3]

Paul Robeson was born in Princeton, New Jersey, in 1898. He was a law student in 1920 when he made his acting debut in *Simon the Cyrenian*, the story of the Black man who carried Jesus's cross. This one-act play was staged at the Harlem branch of the Young Women's Christian Association by an amateur group called the Coloured Players' Guild. Robeson had no interest in acting professionally; however, two years later he was persuaded to return to the stage. In 1922 he made his professional debut in Mary Hoyt Wiborg's *Taboo* in New York. He played a wandering minstrel who dreams about his former life in Africa. A British version, renamed *Voodoo*, soon followed, with the famous actress Mrs Patrick Campbell as the star. It opened on 17 July 1922 at Blackpool's Opera House, but it was not a success. It didn't even reach the London theatre world for which it was destined. In a BBC Radio interview Robeson later spoke about discovering his magnificent singing voice during the opening performance. The end of the first act required him to whistle, but Robeson couldn't whistle, so he substituted a well-known spiritual called 'Go Down Moses':

> I was startled to hear Mrs Pat whispering off-stage, for all the theatre to hear, 'Sing another song!' So, I sang another spiritual. In all my supposedly heavy dramatic scenes, Mrs Pat would nudge me, and off I'd go – singing! – the audience seemed to love it! I got very nice reviews from it and found out that I was a singer, the first time *I* knew.[4]

During his trip to England in 1922, John Payne invited Robeson to his London home. Payne, an African American ex-patriate, was a singer and choirmaster who made his home, 17 Regent's Park Road, a haven for African American visitors, most of whom came from the world of music. When Robeson stayed with Payne during his 1922 visit, he befriended another African American guest, Lawrence Brown, a gentle, charming composer, arranger and pianist who was an expert on American Negro spirituals. According to one of Robeson's biographers, Martin Bauml Duberman, 'One night at Payne's, Robeson sang a few songs "just for fun", and thus began the highly successful musical collaboration between Robeson and Brown.'[5] Brown recalled, 'He had the most magnificent natural voice. I knew at once that it was possible for him to become a great singer.'[6] Brown introduced Robeson to his arrangements of Negro spirituals and Robeson later said:

> It was this musician who clarified my instinctive feeling that the simple, beautiful songs of my childhood, heard every Sunday in church … should become important concert material. Lawrence Brown … was firm in his conviction that our

> music ... Negro music of African and American derivation – was in the tradition of the world's great folk music.[7]

In 1925, Robeson and Brown began their long and successful professional association as singer and accompanist, which would last into the 1960s.[8] Robeson told Marie Seton he thought he was more articulate through the songs he sang than anything he ever said, 'that his singing was the truest expression of himself as a man as well as an artist; that song had always been a form of speech for him.'[9]

It was in 1925 that Robeson made his London stage debut at the Ambassadors Theatre in Eugene O'Neill's *The Emperor Jones* (1925). It seemed that British audiences had forgotten Ira Aldridge from the Victorian era. Robeson's name was unknown to theatregoers. However, according to the *Sunday Times* (13 September 1925), on opening night he received 'a great ovation at the close. It was a wonderful performance.'

In 1930, Robeson's wife Eslanda, affectionately known as 'Essie', described the impact London had on her young husband in the previous decade:

> There were few inconveniences for him ... he did not have to live in a segregated district; he leased a charming flat in Chelsea near his friends; he dined at the Ivy, a delightful restaurant with marvellous food, directly across from the theatre; he ate at many other restaurants in town with white or coloured friends without fear of the discrimination which all Negroes encounter in America. He was a welcome guest in hotels at the seaside places where he spent many week-ends. This was important for his general well-being ... So here in England, where everyone was kind and cordial and reasonable, Paul was happy. 'I think I'd like to live here,' he said; 'someday I will.'[10]

The Robesons did make London their home, and, in 1928, Paul enjoyed great success with his appearance as Joe, the Mississippi riverman, in the musical *Show Boat* at the Theatre Royal, Drury Lane. Seton later described what happened after he sang 'Ol' Man River':

> The pathos of Robeson's voice called up images of slaves and overseers with whips. How had a man with such a history risen? … A most startling quality appeared in Robeson as he accepted the applause. He stood as if it were his naked spirit which was receiving the response of the audience. He was visibly touched and yet remote. He seemed to have no greed for applause and he appeared to be a man stripped bare of mannerisms.[11]

The following year, Seton attended one of Robeson and Brown's Sunday concerts at the Albert Hall. She was struck by the startling contrast between his appearance as the Mississippi riverman in *Show Boat*, and the formal attire he wore for the concert. Then he sang:

> Every word was distinct … The first Spiritual which came wholly alive to me was 'Sometimes I Feel Like a Motherless Child' … The wistfulness of the words and the melody seemed to rise to an expression of the universal. There was something almost painful about this massive man with strong, forceful features speaking in song with such infinitely tender and sorrowful yearning.[12]

In 1925, Amanda Ira Aldridge, the London-born daughter of Ira Aldridge, befriended the Robesons. Essie kept a diary, and in her entry for 19 October 1925 she described Aldridge as 'the most charming, interesting and lovable woman. She gave us her father's stage earrings that he wore as Othello, and said she hoped Paul would wear them when he played the role.'[13] Robeson never wore the earrings but Ira Aldridge remained an inspiration to him as an actor throughout his career. Amanda helped to prepare Robeson for his first appearance as Othello, opposite Peggy Ashcroft as Desdemona, which was staged at the Savoy Theatre in 1930. To prepare for the role he studied thoroughly, as he explained to *The New York Times* (18 May 1930):

> I have read virtually everything of Shakespeare … Now that I know the English people and really understand what their country means to them, now that I am in touch with the English spirit, I feel I can play *Othello* … I have played various parts in America, but I always cared more for my singing. Now I want to act. Shakespeare amazes me.

Regrettably, the production was hampered by an inadequate director, Maurice Browne, who also insisted on playing Iago. For some, Robeson's performance was disappointing. The Jamaican-born actress Pauline Henriques has testified to this. She had come to Britain with her middle-class family in 1919, and regularly attended the theatre. She was just 16 when she saw Robeson as Othello and, when I interviewed her in 1991, she recalled:

> I always had tremendous admiration for him because he had such a wonderful voice – there was not another like it. He also had tremendous presence, charisma. But I was disappointed with his performance as Othello, because, although he had tremendous size and presence augmented by his gorgeous voice, he was, in my opinion, quite wooden. He carried the part with presence, but that wasn't really enough. When you are as deeply immersed in the theatre as I was, you want something different and I found lacks in Robeson's portrayal of a man torn apart by jealousy.[14]

In spite of any shortcomings in his performance, theatre audiences adored him. Seton remembered how they showed their approval on the opening night of *Othello*:

> Notwithstanding flaws in the Savoy production, at the end of the first performance there were twenty curtain calls. Paul Robeson had swept away all doubts of his ability to act Shakespeare's noble Moor. There were cries of 'Robeson! Robeson! Speech! Speech!' At last he stepped forward. 'I took the part of Othello with much fear. Now I am so happy,' he said.[15]

One of Robeson's most successful London stage appearances took place in 1933 at the Embassy Theatre (later moving to the Piccadilly Theatre) in Eugene O'Neill's *All God's Chillun Got Wings*, a powerful, emotionally charged study of an interracial marriage in America, where such unions were then outlawed in the majority of states. Robeson played Jim Harris, a young law student who falls in love with and marries Ella Downey, a white woman who had been his childhood friend. Resistance to their relationship from all sides, including Jim's family, leads to Ella's mental breakdown. The critics raved about Robeson and his leading lady, Flora Robson.

The first night was an intoxicating experience. The stars were named as a major new team. 'Mr Robeson [has] the simplicity that gives pathos its depth and the dignity that saves it from historical declamation,' claimed *The Times*.[16]

All God's Chillun was directed by André van Gyseghem, who later described his experience of working with the two stars as unforgettable:

> I had the feeling of being on the edge of a violent explosion; I had touched it off but the resulting conflagration was terrifying in its blazing intensity. I have seldom known two performances fuse so perfectly; Miss Robson's emotional power and the uncanny skill with which she stripped bare the meagre soul of the wretched Ella was almost more than one could bear at such close range. Such a technically superb performance found a perfect foil in Robeson's utter sincerity

> – he *was* Jim, he had the facility for making imagination visible; his magnificent voice seemed to vibrate with truth and to take command of his body until one was blinded by naked suffering made solid and tangible. His giant frame, his awkward, ungainly movements seemed to make his tenderness and humility more moving, more truthful. He was, instinctively, a great artist.[17]

During his film and stage career in Britain, Robeson met and befriended many Africans who worked on his productions as extras or had small roles. Some of them were dock workers who had been recruited from the seaports of Cardiff, Liverpool and London; others were students from various universities. They included Jomo Kenyatta, who later became the first President of Kenya. Culturally, Robeson found himself drawn to the Africans he encountered. He discovered his African identity and became radicalised by the African anti-colonial fighters of the 1930s. In 1936 his wife, Eslanda, took their young son Paul to Africa. Eslanda was an anthropologist who had also befriended Africans in Britain, but she was keen to learn about African people in their own land. In 1946 she wrote about this visit in *African Journey*:

> These Africans, these 'primitives,' make me feel humble and respectful. I blush with shame for the mental picture my fellow Negroes in America have for our African brothers: wild Black savages in leopard skins, waving spears and eating raw meat. And we, with films like *Sanders of the River*, unwittingly helping to perpetuate this misconception.[18]

In Britain, Robeson faced criticism in the Black community from those who resented the roles he accepted. They said that some of his film and stage roles promoted colonialism and showed the British Empire in a positive light. *Sanders of the River*, a film he made in 1935 and then disowned, was often the target of such criticism. One of the most outspoken Black critics was Marcus Garvey, the Jamaican nationalist leader who is credited with inspiring Black consciousness on an international scale. In the late 1930s, while residing in London, Garvey denounced Robeson's choice of film and stage roles. In the American journal *Black Man*, Garvey said:

> Paul Robeson is a good actor. There is no doubt that he is one of the front liners of the profession, but featured as he is as a Negro he is doing his race a great deal of harm. The Producers have been using Paul Robeson … to put over a vile and vicious propaganda against the Negro. It is true that in some of the plays Robeson is used as a hero, but even in that the propaganda is more pronounced … The promoters are skilful in putting over their propaganda. The wonder is that Paul Robeson cannot see that he is being used to the dishonour and discredit of his race … Robeson is pleasing England by the gross slander and libel of the Negro.[19]

In 1987, Rupert Lewis observed in *Marcus Garvey: Anti-Colonial Champion*:

> Garvey felt that Black creative artists should not only identify with the struggle of their own people but that their work should be a direct contribution to this struggle. Overall, Paul Robeson did not fail that test for he was a political fighter who used his 'art' to combat racism.[20]

In 1935, Robeson took the lead in *Stevedore* at the Embassy Theatre. He played Lonnie Thompson, a dock worker who becomes involved in trade union conflict. It was an American play, written by Paul Peters and George Sklar, and had been produced in New York in 1934. In London, André van Gyseghem was the director. Seton described it as an important play because for the first time in the theatre, Black characters were shown fighting for their rights and their lives, with white workers joining them in their resistance to a racist mob. Said Marie Seton:

> Lonnie Thompson was the first class-conscious Negro character to be the hero of a play and die an heroic death in defence of his union and his people ... Robeson gave expression to feelings and thoughts taking shape within him. He was consciously using his ability to act in a play which accorded with his newly developing ideas. His views and his role had fused as never before.[21]

In New York it hadn't been difficult to find the high number of Black actors and actresses needed for the supporting cast, but in Britain it was not such an easy task. Apart from Robeson the only African Americans in the cast were his friends John Payne and Lawrence Brown, who were not professional actors. The handful of British professionals in the cast included Robert Adams from Guyana and Orlando Martins from Nigeria. Robeson's leading lady was Kathleen Davis, who was born in Trinidad. She had already appeared in the role of an African dancer in *Basilik*, a play that starred Paul Robeson at the Arts Theatre (1935), and she would later appear with Robeson again in *Toussaint L'Ouverture* (1936). Davis was also in the dancing chorus of *The Sun Never Sets* (1938) at the Theatre Royal, Drury Lane, before the Second World War interrupted her career and she returned to Trinidad. Other roles had to be filled by non-professional Africans and West Indians who were then residing in London.

Some of them were recruited from Aggrey House, the hostel and social club in Doughty Street where African and West Indian students gathered and socialised. Amy Ashwood Garvey and George Padmore, two prominent Pan-Africanists, were consulted and they were helpful in recommending people who might be interested. Others were found in London's East End docks through an intermediary called Miss Maukaus, an African who had come to London and opened a restaurant for Africans.

Kathleen Davis and Paul Robeson in *Stevedore* at the Embassy Theatre, 1935. (Courtesy of Christian Holder)

She was described by Seton as the sworn enemy of imperialism in her native Africa: 'She sat in the printed calico dress commonly worn by African women, her head bound tight with a crimson kerchief ... She was determined to help, but she wanted to be absolutely certain that no one was going to be exploited.'[22]

In 1935 there was talk of Robeson making a film in Russia for Sergei Eisenstein called *Black Majesty*. It was going to be based on the life of the Haitian revolutionary Toussaint L'Ouverture. Regrettably, it came to nothing, but Robeson did portray the heroic role on the London stage in 1936 in C.L.R. James's *Toussaint L'Ouverture*, presented by the Stage Society at the Westminster Theatre. James's 'dramatised biography' told the story of the famous general, who rose from slavery to become the independent ruler of San Domingo before he was captured by the French to die of starvation in prison. James came to Britain from Trinidad in 1932. A writer and historian, he was passionate about the Caribbean gaining independence from the

British. James's masterwork was *The Black Jacobins*, a study of L'Ouverture published two years after the stage play.

James later described Robeson as 'the most marvellous human being I have ever known or seen':

> He was as gentle a man as one could meet. He never gave the slightest impression of being aware of all that he was. He spoke a lot. But Paul was always listening to what you had to say, listening and giving it great consideration … if I had to sum up his personality … I would say it was the combination of immense power and great gentleness … He was not satisfied that he as a Black man was confined to playing Othello among Shakespeare's plays. Often enough he said: 'I believe that the Negro actor should be able to play Hamlet, Macbeth, King Lear, and that he should not be confined to Othello because Othello is a Black man. I am quite certain that if he played them as well as I know he will be able to play them, people will ignore the fact that this actor is Black. The play's the thing.'[23]

In 1936, André van Gyseghem, who had directed Robeson in *All God's Chillun* and *Stevedore*, co-founded the Unity Theatre in London. Unity aimed to provide a showcase for left-wing dramatists. When it opened at new premises on 25 November 1937, Robeson took part in the opening ceremony, singing spirituals and 'Ol' Man River'. In the latter he altered Oscar Hammerstein II's lyrics from 'I'm tired o' living but scared o' dying' to 'I must keep struggling until I'm dying'. Sean Creighton has observed: 'Explaining his involvement in Unity, he said that as an artist he needed a working-class audience. Most scripts sent to him went into the wastepaper basket because they did not deal with ideas of social progress.'[24]

One of the scripts he rejected at this time was *The Sun Never Sets*, a 'melodrama based on the West African stories of Edgar Wallace'. Robeson had already publicly condemned his film *Sanders of the River*, and he flatly refused to resurrect the character of Bosambo from that film and portray him in a lavish West End play with songs. Instead, Robeson agreed to act in a Unity production for far less money: Ben Bengal's American strike drama, *Plant in the Sun* (1938). In his autobiography, *Reflected Glory* (1958), Peter Noble remembered going to see the play after it had become an enormous success at Unity due to Robeson's participation:

> After a long and honourable career as an actor and singer all over the world, Robeson had announced his strong affiliation to socialism, had also visited the Soviet Union and had sent his small son to school there for a time. One of the most revered and most popular figures in the left-wing movement, Paul had given up a great deal of money to work at Unity Theatre … Robeson's name and personality attracted people who had never been to Unity Theatre before … Unity was well and truly on the theatrical map.[25]

Plant in the Sun would be Robeson's final stage appearance as an actor in Britain until he returned just over twenty years later for *Othello* in 1959. In *The Young Paul Robeson* (1997), his friend Lloyd L. Brown summarised what happened:

> For forty years the man was a headline personality, first gaining fame as a football star and then going on to win international acclaim both as a concert bass-baritone and a starring actor of stage and screen. After World War II he emerged as a controversial Black militant whose intransigence made him a target of mob attacks, blacklisting and governmental repression during the McCarthy era. Asserting that 'Paul Robeson's travel abroad would be contrary to the best interests of the United States,' the State Department denied him a passport for eight years, until the Supreme Court reversed that decision.[26]

When his passport was finally returned, Robeson came back to Britain, where he was welcomed as a hero. He made his final stage appearance as an actor when he played Othello at the Shakespeare Memorial Theatre in Stratford-upon-Avon. Now aged 60, he decided to play Othello as an ageing warrior in his declining years. In the view of his son Paul Robeson Jr, this *Othello* had an unorthodox director who shaped a non-traditional production: 'Tony Richardson's production included a fireworks display, drums beating out rock and roll, three Great Danes running across the stage, a scene acted behind a smoke screen, a ferocious combat scene with thrown swords, and the death scene on a high platform.'[27]

In spite of the pressures of making his first acting appearance since 1945, and facing the demands of a 'non-traditional production', Robeson survived the opening night on 7 April. He received fifteen curtain calls and his performance was hailed as a triumph. Afterwards, at the cast party, Robeson said this was one of the greatest nights of his life. 'The reviews reflected a near-total validation of Paul's strategy and execution,' said his

Paul Robeson with Sam Wanamaker and Mary Ure at a press conference for *Othello* at the Shakespeare Memorial Theatre in 1959. (Author's collection, courtesy of Sam Wanamaker)

son.[28] Among them was W.A. Darlington's piece for the *Daily Telegraph* (8 April 1959):

> Paul Robeson is now the second best Othello I have ever seen, the best being Godfrey Tearle. In my estimation this represents a great advance by Mr. Robeson since he played the part in London 29 years ago, for I did not then find that I could praise him wholeheartedly. He had many fine moments, but there were times when he lacked that air of confident authority that a Negro general would have to make a successful commander of European troops. He has that authority now ... He is able therefore to use his impressive stature and magnificent voice to full advantage. Also he can be savage without barbarity and tender without mawkishness. Where he falls short of Tearle is in the actual delivery of the verse ... Mr. Robeson has a moving sincerity but leaves one's heartstrings untorn.

Micheal MacLiammoir commented in the *Observer* (12 April 1959), 'Paul Robeson has a majesty of voice and of presence that illumines everything he does with magical fires.'

Othello ran from April to November. Thirteen consecutive performances were scheduled before the run was reduced to two or three performances a week until the end of November, with two ten-day breaks in July and August. 'Having triumphed on opening night, Paul remained in command of the performance throughout the initial run,' Robeson Jr recalled. 'My father seemed fulfilled and at peace in the Stratford environment.'[29]

If critics were kind to Robeson, they were vitriolic towards the excesses of his director, Tony Richardson, who later reflected, 'The production, though a success with audiences, was mauled savagely by the critics ... What we thought of as traditional ... was called revolutionary and vulgar.'[30]

The success of *Othello* wiped away Robeson's concerns about taking on the demanding role in his 60s. As Lindsey R. Swindall observed in *The Politics of Paul Robeson's Othello*:

> The Stratford appearance functioned as a vital symbol of resurgence in Robeson's artistic career following the passport victory. Yet, his triumph at Stratford was also a public acknowledgment of Robeson's posture as a political performer during the cold war. One insightful critic writing about the Stratford opening, Mervyn Jones, asserted that the line between cheering for Robeson as Othello and Robeson's personal character was increasingly blurry: 'Robeson could do it [play Othello] I feel, because of the man he is – brave, simple, loyal, supremely fitted to become, for a space, Othello. So we applauded him through I don't know how many curtain calls. We were not, I saw later, cheering a great piece of acting. We were welcoming Paul Robeson for what he is, and for that I will clap my hands sore any time.'[31]

While Britain, Russia, Australia and other countries welcomed and embraced Robeson, he continued to be overlooked in the United States. In 1956, when the House Committee on Un-American Activities asked him why he did not make his home in Russia, Robeson replied, 'Because my father was a slave, and my people died to build this country, and I am going to stay right here and have a part of it, just like you. And no fascist-minded people will drive me from it. Is that clear?'[32]

Ostracised for his radical views, Robeson was immediately airbrushed from American history. Lloyd L. Brown observed that by the 1960s the airbrushing was so successful that, though he was still alive, 'Robeson was an unknown figure to the ghetto militants and campus rebels who echoed his earlier preachments. And because of his poor health … he could not be active in the civil rights movement that gave rise to such spokesmen as Martin Luther King Jr., Malcolm X, and others.'[33]

There was one final reunion with his friend and former co-star Elisabeth Welch in January 1963, when she was appearing with Cleo Laine and Cy Grant in the stage musical *Cindy-Ella*. Paul and Essie attended a matinee and afterwards they came backstage to greet Elisabeth. She recalled the reunion during her appearance in the 1985 Paul Robeson memorial concert at London's Queen Elizabeth Hall:

> There was Paul and Essie and I hadn't seen them for years. He told me he was leaving to go back to America. He took me in his arms and gave me one of his warm, bear-like hugs but something came over me and I thought 'this is goodbye' and it was. I never saw him again. He had this intense love of humanity. We all know he fought for years. He gave all his strength, everything he had, until illness hit him and knocked all the force and strength out of him. He was a wonderful person. His humour was so great. I can stand anybody saying anything to me as long as there are smiles and laughter and, my god, when he smiled, the whole world lit up.

Robeson returned to the United States in ill-health and retired. After Essie's death in 1965, he lived in seclusion at his sister's home in Philadelphia, where he died at the age of 77 in 1976.

After the *Paul Robeson* exhibition in 1985, I continued to participate in projects about Robeson. Among the highlights was the 1998 centenary conference at the School for Oriental and African Studies organised with the Black and Asian Studies Association, of which I was a founder member. I gave an illustrated talk about his British films and met Robeson's friend, Lloyd L. Brown, who had collaborated with him on *Here I Stand* (1958). Also in 1998, I curated *Paul Robeson: Songs of Freedom*, for the National Film Theatre. This centenary retrospective included some of his films as well as television documentaries. I was interviewed in two documentaries about him: BBC Television's *Speak of Me As I Am* (1998) and *Paul Robeson: Here I Stand* (1999), made for the *American Masters* series. In 2001 I consulted on the Theatre Museum's *Let Paul Robeson Sing!* exhibition, during which I was reunited with Paul Robeson Jr. I was thrilled when he complimented me on my contribution to the *American Masters* documentary. Robeson Jr then signed my copy of his recently published first volume of a biography of his father, *The Undiscovered Paul Robeson: An Artist's Journey, 1898–1939*. The second volume, subtitled *Quest for Freedom, 1939–1976*, was published in 2010.

I was aware that Paul Robeson had an emotional effect on people, whatever their background or political beliefs. The script of his final British film, *The Proud Valley*, had enabled Robeson to express his socialist beliefs and portray his strong affinity with the people of South Wales. He played an American coal miner who is 'adopted' by the close-knit community of a Welsh mining village. During the making of the film, in 1939, just before he returned to the United States at the outbreak of war, the Welsh people took Robeson to their hearts. Said Marie Seton, 'Music was as deep a part of their heritage as it was of his: but it seemed they found something else in him; the decency and simplicity of their own folk.'[34]

After appearing in *The Proud Valley*, Robeson was never forgotten in South Wales. In the years the American government denied him a passport, the Welsh people were among the most vocal and active groups who came to his support. In 1958 he explained in *Here I Stand*:

> It was in Britain – among the English, Scottish, Welsh and Irish people of that land – that I learned that the essential character of a nation is determined not by the upper classes, but by the common people, and that the common people of all nations are truly brothers in the great family of mankind. If in Britain there were those who lived by plundering the colonial peoples, there were also the many millions who earned their bread by honest toil. And even as I grew to feel more Negro in spirit, or African as I put it then, I also came to feel a sense of oneness with the white working people whom I came to know and love.[35]

Left to Right: Amy Barbour James, Una Marson, Desmond Buckle, Stephen Thomas, Dennis Degazon and Stella Thomas at a rehearsal for *At What a Price* from *The Keys*, April–June 1934.

9

Una Marson: London Calling

On 1 February 2024 I had the honour of being one of the guest speakers at the opening of the new Una Marson Library, a public library in Thurlow Street, Southwark. This is in the London borough where I live. Two days later, within walking distance of the library, I attended the launch of the Camberwell Black History Walk on Camberwell Green. I had created this with the encouragement of a local group called the SE5 Forum. In addition to Una Marson, it had been my idea to celebrate the lives of eight Black historical figures with connections to the local area.[1] Una had lived in Brunswick Square, Camberwell, in the mid-1930s, several years after arriving here from Jamaica and continuing her career as a trailblazing poet, playwright and activist. Before the end of the decade, she embarked on a career as broadcaster for BBC Radio.

However, none of this recognition for Una would have been possible without the publication, in 1998, of Delia Jarrett-Macauley's comprehensive biography *The Life of Una Marson 1905–65*. Said Hakim Adi in the newsletter of the Black and Asian Studies Association: 'what emerges from this finely crafted biography is the story of a woman whose story had to be told: Marson was a pioneer in many fields, unconventional and individualistic, yet a personality with a deep social conscience and concern for others.'[2]

In 2009 I nominated Una for a Southwark Heritage Blue Plaque and I was thrilled when she was shortlisted and awarded the plaque by a public vote. Delia Jarrett-Macauley agreed to unveil the plaque outside Una's former home in Brunswick Square. I took part in the unveiling ceremony and met Delia, who had done so much to raise the profile of this remarkable Jamaican pioneer. Until we had Delia's biography, Una had remained a forgotten figure in British history, in spite of her achievements.

Una was born in 1905 but, as a young woman, she found that there were few openings for her to expand her creative work as a poet and playwright in Jamaica. She wanted to spread her wings and believed that Britain, in those days referred to as the 'Mother Country', would provide her with the opportunities she desired. Before leaving for Britain, Una worked as the assistant editor of a Jamaican political journal before, in 1928, launching her own magazine, *The Cosmopolitan*, which dealt with local, feminist and workers' rights issues. In 1930 she self-published her first collection of poems, *Tropic Reveries*. This was followed by *Heights and Depths* (1931).

In Jamaica, Una also wrote a play in the summer of 1931 in collaboration with her friend Horace Vaz. They called it *At What a Price*. It was mainly her work and Vaz later praised her as 'a pioneer who had stressed the importance of Jamaican themes, characters and settings'.[3] The main character is Ruth Maitland, a young middle-class Black woman who relocates from the countryside to Kingston, Jamaica, to work as a stenographer. After she is seduced by Gerald Fitzroy, her attractive white boss, Ruth discovers she is expecting his baby. As far as women are concerned, Fitzroy is a rogue, which Ruth discovers when he betrays her. Consequently, she is forced to return home. Said

Jarrett-Macauley: 'While the ending was nothing but safe and conservative, the play itself presented emancipated women in a world still hostile to their independence.'[4]

At What a Price was first staged at Kingston's Ward Theatre on 11 June 1932 and the popular newspaper the *Daily Gleaner*, while highlighting that the drama had a few 'weak spots', called for 'more such productions' and greater public support for local writers.[5]

In less than a month, with the money she had earned from *At What a Price*, Una was on her way to Britain. She arrived in Plymouth on 9 July 1932 on board SS *Jamaica Settler*. She soon found a place in Black social and political groupings. On her arrival, Una was assisted by Dr Harold Moody, also from Jamaica, and his wife Olive. They offered her lodgings in their home at 164 Queen's Road, Peckham, and Dr Moody gave her a job as the unpaid assistant secretary to the League of Coloured Peoples (LCP). This was the first significant Black-led civil rights organisation. It had been founded by Dr Moody in 1931. However, paid work was hard to find. She was qualified to work as a secretary but, she later said, 'I tried to register for work as a stenographer. One agent told me that she didn't register Black women because they would have to work in offices with white women. Another agent tried to find me a position and he told me that though my references were excellent, firms did not want to employ a Black stenographer.'[6] Meanwhile, Una's creative and literary talents were channelled into writing plays, short stories and poetry.

Also lodging at the Moodys' home was Sylvia Lowe, a Jamaican student who became a prominent Christian activist in Jamaica, where she had a distinguished medical career. It wasn't long before Una met other Black women, all of them from middle-class backgrounds and associated in some way with the LCP. These included Stella Thomas, a Nigerian barrister, who lived in Bloomsbury, an affluent part of London, and Viola Thompson, who was an LCP executive member. Una also made friends with Amy Barbour-James, who lived in Acton. British-born of Guyanese parents, Amy was a civil rights activist and a mezzo soprano, often giving recitals at concerts of spirituals.

When Una staged a performance of *At What a Price* on 23 November 1933, she played Ruth, the main role, and recruited LCP members for the cast, which also included three of Dr Moody's children: Christine, Harold and Joan. According to the theatre historian Colin Chambers, the LCP cast members included several who went on to illustrious careers:

> the future British Communist and noted Ghanaian anti-colonial fighter Desmond Buckle; Eric Campbell, who became a member of the Jamaican House of Representatives for the People's National Party; Fred Degazon, Dominica's first president after independence; Keith Gordon, a barrister who became a senior judge in the Caribbean and was knighted; founding LCP executive member and LCP librarian barrister Stella Thomas, a Nigerian of Sierra Leonean descent, Pan African activist, the first African woman to qualify as a barrister, and the first woman to be appointed a magistrate in Nigeria (in 1943); and her brother Stephen Thomas, LCP secretary who became a judge in Nigeria.[7]

The performance took place at the Young Women's Christian Association (YWCA) Central Club Hall on Great Russell Street in Bloomsbury. The January 1934 edition of the LCP's journal *The Keys* explained that they had 'tackled the gigantic task of putting on a Jamaican play with a cast of twenty, all coloured. As our readers are doubtless aware, the majority of our members are students in London and therefore cannot afford much time for rehearsing, and getting twenty together for rehearsals was a gigantic task.' However, before the play could be seen again, a copy of the script had to be sent to the Lord Chamberlain's Office for censorship. This had been in place since 1737 and would continue until 1968. Plays were examined and then decided to be allowed on the stage or banned.

In 2023, when Alexander Lock, the British Library's Curator of Modern Archives and Manuscripts, and Kate Dossett, Professor of American History at the University of Leeds, looked at the Reader's Report on Una's play dated 29 December 1933, they believed that the people who read the script in the Lord Chamberlain's Office didn't appear to recognise that Ruth, the main character, was Black. Said Professor Dossett:

> The examiner of plays says 'We understand that this was produced by the League of Coloured Peoples, but it seems to have no particular relation to the objects of that institution except that the scene is in Jamaica and some of the minor characters are of colour and speak a more or less diverting dialogue.' What we see here, then, is that the reader of this play doesn't understand that this is about interracial relationship. He assumes that Ruth, the heroine, is white … certainly doesn't understand that she's a Black, educated Jamaican … no educated young woman could be Black, so he assumes she is white but also only understands characters to be Black if they speak in what a white person imagines to be a Black Jamaican dialect. I suspect they didn't know who Una Marson was and certainly didn't make any inquiry as to her racial identity though they know that she is associated with the League of Coloured Peoples. The reader's report we have here says 'nothing to censor.' It describes the play as 'an artless, old-fashioned kind of affair.'

Professor Dossett concluded: 'We might speculate that if they had a better grasp of what this play was about they might have censored some of the scenes around the interracial relationship because it's not a good look, senior white man harasses young Black woman in the workplace.'[8]

Following its London debut at the YMCA and, after securing permission to stage it at a professional venue, *At What a Price* played for three nights, beginning on 15 January 1934, at the 1,130-seat Scala Theatre in Charlotte Street in central London. The cast remained the same. Said Dr Harold Moody in his 'President's Message' in *The Keys* (January 1934):

> This play is being put on to accomplish many purposes. I believe that it will in the first place bring home to the British public the fact that we can manage our own affairs effectively and therefore need not to be forever under tutelage. It will also bring our own people together and help us to have more confidence in ourselves, dissipate from among us any inferiority complex which still exists, and assist us to find a basis of fuller co-operation among ourselves. Its effect must also spread overseas to be a source of inspiration to our race.

Una was delighted with the positive reaction of the audiences, and their enthusiastic applause. Reviews were good too. *West Africa* (20 January 1934) described it as a 'delightful Jamaican comedy'. The critic for the *Manchester Guardian*, cited in *West Africa*, singled out Stella Thomas who played Ruth's friend Myrtle. They described her as 'memorable': 'When she came in on one scene in a magnificent orange dress ... the whole audience broke into applause.' Spike Hughes in the *Daily Herald* (16 January 1934) commented that the accents of the cast varied and included 'the rich language of the African coast, the staccato sing-song of Jamaica and a few natives of London with a genuine Cockney accent'. In 1934 it just wasn't possible for Una to find a cast with convincing Jamaican accents. *The Keys* (April 1934) noted that Una's play was staged with great success at the Scala and the press notices received were most gratifying: 'As our President said we did not make money but we made history as it was the first time that a play written and performed by coloured colonials had been staged in London.'

It is a little known fact that Una made another acting appearance on the London stage. John Wexley, a white American dramatist, had staged his play *They Shall Not Die* in New York in February 1934. Wexley documented the notorious and widely publicised case in which nine Black teenagers from Alabama – some as young as thirteen – were falsely convicted of raping two white women in America's racially segregated South. They were sentenced to death, and held in prison while their fate was debated through the courts. It was known as the Scottsboro Boys case, and in the 1930s it became a rallying point for the international Left. In Britain, colonial students, especially the West African Students' Union, were very active in the London-based Scottsboro Defence Committee. Said Hakim Adi: 'In the London School of Economics alone over 800 students and teachers signed a petition condemning the judgement of the American courts.'[9]

A group called Left Theatre, which was founded in 1934 by progressive-thinking theatre professionals, including André van Gyseghem who had worked with Paul Robeson, were responsible for staging Wexley's play at London's Holborn Empire on 1 July 1934. Situated in High Holborn, this was a large and very popular variety theatre with almost 2,000 seats. As far as I am aware, Chambers is the only theatre historian who has identified Una as a member of the cast.[10] He has kindly shared his copy of the programme which confirms that there were two further performances of the play at the Greenwich Borough Hall (8 July) and East Ham Town Hall (15 July). Two other cast members from *At What a Price* were also in the production: Amy Barbour-James and Viola Thompson. Una, Amy and Viola played the mothers of three of the boys. Viola, born in Sierra Leone in the 1880s, had a semi-professional acting career in Britain in the 1930s and 1940s. In the 1940s she is credited as the costume designer for Berto Pasuka's Les Ballet Negres company. In 1948 she played the mother in a stage adaptation of Richard Wright's *Native Son* at the Boltons Theatre in London. This was another rare occurrence of the staging of work by a Black playwright at that time.

Another cast member of *They Shall Not Die* was the Nigerian Orlando Martins who played one of the Scottsboro Boys, the main defendant Heywood Parsons. From the 1920s to the 1960s he had a long and productive acting career in British cinema and theatre.

An article that appeared in the *Dominica Tribune* (1 September 1934) said:

> Londoners who saw the play when it was presented before a packed house at the Holborn Empire were so moved by the incidents in the trial of the nine Negro boys, that, at the conclusion of the last act, a resolution was passed voicing the objections of the English people. The audience pledged themselves to support all movements for the unconditional release of the boys and a sum of £32 was collected to contribute towards the defence committee in the case.

After *At What a Price*, Una didn't have any other plays produced in Britain but, after her return to Jamaica in 1936, she founded the Kingston Drama Club. The following year she staged *London Calling*, a comedy of student life in London. In 1938 she presented *Pocomania*, which revealed the influence of an African religious cult on a young middle-class woman. In 2001, Susan Croft commented in *She Also Wrote Plays*: 'While her significance as a ground-breaking poet has begun to be recognised, her theatre work has remained a footnote until Delia Jarrett-Macauley's rescue work.'[11] Further 'rescue work' has been undertaken by Alison Donnell who has written widely about Una and, in 2016, contributed the introduction to a published edition of *Pocomania* and *London Calling*.[12]

In the early years of British theatre, hardly any Black women dramatists had their work produced. Una was the first but there followed a twenty-five-year gap before America's Lorraine Hansberry had her acclaimed play *A Raisin in the Sun* produced in London at the Adelphi Theatre in 1959.

In 1938 Una returned to Britain and it wasn't long before she was employed by BBC Radio. In 1941 she became an assistant producer in the BBC's Empire Programmes department. Her series *Calling the West Indies* helped to bridge the gap between the Caribbean and its people who had left home to serve overseas in the armed forces. Una would invite groups of them into the studio to read messages to their loved ones. Una also created a weekly feature in *Calling the West Indies* which included poems and short stories by Caribbean authors. The segment, known as *Caribbean Voices*, ran until 1958. It is now recognised as the single most important literary catalyst for both creative and critical writings in the Caribbean. After the war ended, Una returned to Jamaica and continued her work in politics, broadcasting and literature. She died in Kingston, Jamaica, in 1965.[13]

Florence Mills in *Dover Street to Dixie* at the London Pavilion, 1923. (Author's collection/Mary Evans Picture Library)

10

Florence Mills: Beautiful Eyes and a Joyful Smile

In 1981, Florence Mills was briefly portrayed in an episode of the critically acclaimed television series *Brideshead Revisited*, starring Jeremy Irons and Anthony Andrews. She is seen at a noisy party attended by a large crowd of white upper-class Bright Young Things and Black musicians of the 1920s Jazz Age. This remains true to the source material, Evelyn Waugh's novel of the same name, in which Mills is mentioned. She did attend such parties, but the portrayal of her couldn't have been further from the truth. She is shown as an intoxicated, sleazily dressed blues 'shouter', belting out a song about a 'red-hot mama from Savannah' in the manner of Bessie Smith, the Empress of the Blues. Lena Horne's description of Mills as 'a little like Judy Garland' was closer to the truth. She was 'a waif they would cry over and pity sometimes ... tiny, with small bones, enormous eyes and skinny legs. Her voice was high and sweet and pure.'[1]

When *Brideshead Revisited* was published in 1945, the Jazz Age was well and truly over and Mills, who had died young, was largely forgotten by the public. Waugh had been around in the 1920s when she reigned supreme over London's West End in her famous *Blackbirds* revue which, at the London Pavilion in 1926, attracted huge audiences, including members of the royal family. Following her meteoric rise to fame as a star of musical revues in the 1920s, Florence captivated audiences at home in America and on the London stage. Regrettably, when she died in 1927, she left no films or recordings for future generations to see and hear. All we have left of her are a collection of photographs that capture her playfulness and vivacity, and the first-hand testimonies of those who were fortunate to see her on stage. These include Britain's famous showman Charles B. Cochran, who described her as one of the greatest artists that ever walked onto a stage. The African American writer and civil rights activist James Weldon Johnson commented:

> She was indefinable. One might best string out a list of words such as: pixy, elf, radiant, exotic, Peter Pan, wood-nymph, wistful, piquant, magnetism, witchery, madness, flame; and then despairingly exclaim: 'Oh, you know what I mean.' She could be whimsical, she could be almost grotesque; but she had the good taste that never allowed her to be coarse. She could be *risqué*, she could be seductive; but it was impossible for her to be vulgar, for she possessed a naivete that was alchemic. As a pantomimist and a singing and dancing comedienne she had no superior in any place or race.[2]

In 1993, I interviewed Elisabeth Welch about Mills for a BBC Radio 2 music documentary called *Black in the West End*. In her beautiful London home in Knightsbridge, at the age of 89, Lis remembered seeing Mills at Daly's 63rd Street Theatre over seventy years earlier:

> We used to rush up there to see *Shuffle Along*. I was a kid then. It was a lovely, intimate theatre and Florence was a gentle child who had beautiful eyes and a joyful smile. We adored her. It wasn't a big voice but it came over. The joyousness.

> She sang her songs very quietly. Very hushed. Even if she was playing with a big chorus. That was cute. And Lew Leslie chose songs to suit her personality which was clean, happy, young and without any evil at all. She didn't belong in show business really [*laughs*]. She was married to U. S. Thompson. We called him United States Thompson because we didn't know his name was Ulysses! He was a very nice man and a wonderful acrobatic tap dancer.[3]

Florence Mills was born in Washington, DC, in 1896. She began her career as a young child and theatre audiences knew her as 'Baby Florence'. A few years later she joined her two sisters, Olivia and Maude, in a singing and dancing act called The Mills Trio. By the 1920s Florence was working in vaudeville with her husband, the comedian and dancer U.S. (Slow Kid) Thompson. Her big break came in 1921 when Noble Sissle, composer of the smash hit Broadway musical revue *Shuffle Along*, heard her singing and invited her to replace the star of the show. The African American poet Langston Hughes recalled in his autobiography *The Big Sea*, '*Shuffle Along* was a honey of a show. Swift, bright, funny, rollicking, and gay, with a dozen danceable, singable tunes … Florence Mills skyrocketed to fame in the second act.'[4]

Claude McKay, a Jamaican writer and poet who was a central figure in the Harlem Renaissance, recalled in his autobiography, 'She ran away with the show, mimicking and kicking her marvellous way right over the heads of all the cast and sheer up to the dizzying heights until she was transformed into a glorious star.'[5]

Mills's career progressed rapidly from her initial success in *Shuffle Along*. In 1922 she starred in Lew Leslie's *Plantation Revue* at New York's Plantation Club, situated on the roof of the Winter Garden Theatre. Leslie was a white impresario, primarily associated with revues of the 1920s that featured all-Black casts. In 1939, when he employed the young Lena Horne for a

Broadway show called *Blackbirds of 1939*, he attempted to transform her into another Florence Mills, but failed to repeat the success of the shows he had produced in the 1920s:

> Lew would sit backstage and tell me stories about his travels with Florence Mills, and tears would come to his eyes as he talked. Working with her had been the greatest thing in his life, and I believe he was always trying to find someone like her and in that way, to recapture the best part of his past … Her most famous number was one in which she appeared dressed like a little boy in a checked shirt and little, cut-up denim overalls with straps over the shoulders. She carried a bandanna-wrapped bundle suspended at the end of a stick and sang 'I'm a little blackbird, looking for a bluebird.'[6]

In 1923 the English impresario Charles B. Cochran brought Mills and the *Plantation Revue*, which was renamed *Dover Street to Dixie*, to the London Pavilion. Two years later, in his autobiography, Cochran recalled:

> She controlled the emotions of the audience as only a true artist can. There was not a false note in any part of her performance. Every night she appeared at the London Pavilion, Florence Mills received an ovation each time she came on the stage – *before* every song she sang. That is a tribute which in my experience I have never known to be offered to any other artist.[7]

Not everyone loved Black artistes, however, and there had been rumours of a demonstration against the cast. The journalist Hannen Swaffer was considered left-wing but contributed mostly to right-wing publications, and he had been attacking Black artistes in one of the newspapers he wrote for. On Cochran's instructions, Swaffer and other theatre critics were excluded from the first night of *Dover Street to Dixie*, but Swaffer managed to gain entry to the theatre. On discovering this, Cochran manhandled him and threw him out 'with one hand on Swaffer's neck and the other on the seat of his trousers, bundling him out, shouting furiously, "Get out of my theatre."'[8] It was the only time that Cochran was known to lose his temper in public.

In his autobiography he told of the spell Mills cast with her performance: 'after the opening verse of her first song, "The Sleepy Hills of Tennessee", I knew she had London in her hands.'[9]

On her return to New York in 1924, Mills triumphed yet again at the Plantation Club in the revue *Dixie to Broadway*. This was the first 'integrated' musical to appear in New York in years. George Gershwin contributed some songs, including 'Lady be Good', and there was dancing by the young Fred Astaire and his sister Adele in the first half. Mills starred in the second half.

Charles B. Cochran brought Mills back to London in 1926 to star at the London Pavilion again, this time in Lew Leslie's sensational revue *Blackbirds*. Opening on 11 September, it was Florence's biggest success. One of her big numbers was 'Silver Rose', which captivated audiences, and her version of the energetic Charleston dance stunned them. It was this famous dance which horrified a Bristol vicar named Reverend E.W. Rogers: 'Any lover of the beautiful will die rather than be associated with it. It is neurotic! It is rotten! It stinks!' The Bishop of Coventry disagreed, albeit more mildly: 'It is a very nice dance.'[10]

Theatre critics loved Florence and *Blackbirds*. The *Daily Mail* of 13 September 1926 described the show as first-rate entertainment:

> The dancing must be seen to be believed. There has been nothing like it in London for years. Florence Mills is unquestionably one of the outstanding personalities of this type of singing and dancing in the world. She has a song called 'I'm a Little Blackbird Looking for a Bluebird' that sent a section of the first-night audience wild with delight, and she is also a most accomplished dancer and a real comedian. It is impossible to compare her with anyone else. She is original.

One month later it was reported in the British press that the show had been seen by the Prince of Wales, the future King Edward VIII. The following year gossip columns in the newspapers claimed that the Prince had seen *Blackbirds* twenty-two times and hinted that he and Mills were having an affair. Nothing could have been further from the truth, asserted Elisabeth Welch:

> Florence wouldn't have had an affair with anybody but her husband Ulysses. There wasn't a sign of theatre about her, no sign at all. She wasn't flamboyant in dress or character. She didn't roar with laughter. We were noisy in those days but she was a gentle creature. I mean, if you met her at a party, you'd think 'Who's that over there?' She didn't go out of her way to impress, but she had this natural personality. When she went on the stage you just loved her.[11]

In 1927, Lew Leslie planned to star Mills on Broadway in a lavish revue called *Blackbirds of 1928*, but she underwent an operation for appendicitis and died on 1 November 1927. She was just 31 years old.

When Mills died there was a public outpouring of grief on a large scale. African Americans all over the world remembered where they were when they heard the news of her death, the way they recalled the moment in 1968 when they heard of the assassination of Dr Martin Luther King, Jr. Over 50,000 people filed past her coffin before a service at the Mother Zion African Methodist Episcopal Church on 136th Street in New York. The streets of Harlem were packed with a crowd estimated at 250,000. Mills was buried in a $10,000 coffin: 'It was a replica of the one that took Rudolph Valentino to heaven, and eternal glory.'[12]

Elisabeth Welch remembered:

They gave her a star's funeral. The cortege moved through Harlem with the drums beating at that slow funeral pace, and the sidewalks were jammed with people. Then an airplane appeared and released flocks of blackbirds overhead. A few years later, when I came to London, Charles B. Cochran asked me to record her theme song, 'Silver Rose'. I was very proud to do so. Florence should not be forgotten.[13]

Elisabeth Welch in 1946. (Author's collection, courtesy of Elisabeth Welch)

11

Elisabeth Welch: A Marvellous Party

For six decades Elisabeth Welch was one of the most popular singers working in Britain and a radiant, sparkling presence in London's West End musical theatre, from Cole Porter's *Nymph Errant* in 1933 to the all-star tribute concert *A Time to Start Living* in 1992. Elisabeth regarded herself as American by birth but English in thought and interest. When a curious journalist enquired about the singing technique she had sustained for over eighty years, her simple, direct reply was, 'I have no technique. No art, no training. Nothing! Just myself. I describe myself as a singer of popular songs.'

Born in New York of mixed parentage, Welch was a trailblazer for women of colour in Britain. The public were drawn to her beauty and elegance, her soft, lovely voice and her perfect diction.

I met Elisabeth for the first time in 1982. It was the closing night of her triumphant series of one-woman shows at the Riverside Studios in Hammersmith. I had attended the concert, which included songs by some of the great composers and lyricists of the twentieth century: Hoagy Carmichael, George Gershwin, Richard Rodgers, Lorenz Hart, Cole Porter and Ivor

Novello. After the concert I visited her crowded dressing room. Feeling shy, I stood in a corner. One by one, excited friends and fans greeted Elisabeth. Eventually, she saw me, hovering in the corner, too shy to approach her. Sensing my awkwardness, she called me to her. I introduced myself. She took my hand and I immediately felt at ease. 'Cold hand, warm heart,' she said. 'I bet you're a Scorpio!' She was right.

Some months later, in response to a letter I had written to her, she invited me to her beautiful home, a mews cottage hidden away in Capener's Close, off Kinnerton Street, in Knightsbridge. I was impressed that Elisabeth had kept most of her elegant art deco furnishings of the 1930s. In her drawing room, painted a dusky pink, I was invited to make myself comfortable on her large sofa and gazed in wonder at her baby grand piano (I had never seen one before), which had a large coffee-table biography of Cole Porter resting on the top.

Elisabeth was full of joy and she possessed a loud, impressive laugh. I immediately warmed to her – and her laugh. She told me she loved to be with people who had a sense of humour, and she was fun to be with and interesting to talk to, though guarded about her private life. I didn't ask about it. I also discovered that Elisabeth was more interested in the person she was talking to than in talking about herself. I gradually found myself telling her about my work, family and interests. This is what made Elisabeth so special. She may have rubbed shoulders with the likes of Cole Porter, Charles B. Cochran, Noël Coward and Paul Robeson, but she made me, a young lad who couldn't sing, read music, or play a musical instrument, feel at ease, and as important and interesting as her show business friends. In her cosy, comfortable home, Elisabeth was animated, down-to-earth, friendly and entertaining. Though I couldn't help feeling star-struck, I kept it to myself.

I did not expect to see Elisabeth again, but I was lucky. The following year I received a call from Andrew, a mutual friend of ours who worked for the BFI. Andrew explained that he had befriended Elisabeth at a party and had organised a private screening for her of *Song of Freedom*, the first film she had made with Paul Robeson. Would I like to join them? Just a few months after visiting her in Capener's Close, I found myself sitting next to Elisabeth in a viewing theatre at the BFI. Thereafter, Elisabeth and I were occasional guests of Andrew's for lunch at Kettner's in Soho, followed by an afternoon screening of a film from the National Film Archive, chosen by Elisabeth.

By the mid 1980s, a 'renaissance' in Elisabeth's career was well under way, and it was a joy for me to witness this revival in interest of one of the great ladies of British musical theatre. The turning point was her showstopping appearance at the Donmar Warehouse in *Kern Goes to Hollywood*, an intimate revue that celebrated the songs of Jerome Kern. Critics and audiences 'rediscovered' her beauty, magic and charisma. Critical acclaim, a nomination for a Laurence Olivier Award, and several guest appearances on radio and television all played their part in returning Elisabeth – in triumph – to her native New York in 1986. It was a 'comeback' that earned her a nomination for a Tony Award. Though Elisabeth's full diary sometimes prevented her from meeting up with Andrew and me for lunch and screenings, we kept in touch by phone and letter.

Elisabeth had settled in London in 1933. She came here because the composer and lyricist Cole Porter had written a song for her to sing in the musical *Nymph Errant*, produced by Charles B. Cochran. Elisabeth's rendition of Porter's 'Solomon' stopped the show and endeared her to British theatregoers. Her scrapbook includes letters of appreciation from Cochran and Porter. When asked about Porter, she always acknowledged the wit and elegance of his songs, which suited her, especially in cabaret and, later, her one-woman concerts: 'Irving Berlin wrote for the general public but Cole for a much more sophisticated audience.'

After seeing Elisabeth in *Nymph Errant*, Ivor Novello decided to feature her in his musical *Glamorous Night* as a stowaway called

Cleo Wellington. The show opened at the Theatre Royal, Drury Lane, on 2 May 1935:

> I had one number in each of the two acts: 'Far Away in Shanty Town' and 'The Girl I Knew'. They're not in the script. They're not in the score, either. Ivor just put me there as a stowaway dressed in rags on board a ship who is dragged on to sing 'Shanty Town' at the ship's concert. Later, during a difficult scene change in Act 2, I went on in front of the curtain, this time dressed in a chic Victor Stiebel costume, and sang 'The Girl I Knew'.

Elisabeth continued to work in London's West End in revues like *Let's Raise the Curtain* (1936) and *Sky High* (1942), but it was Ivor Novello who brought her back into a 'book' musical when he featured her in *Arc de Triomphe* (1943). She said, 'I played a French cabaret singer called Josie, who was based on Josephine Baker, all feathers, jewels and sequins. I sang "Dark Music" on a barge lit by fairy lamps on the River Seine in Paris.'

Next came one of Elisabeth's most popular stage successes, *Happy and Glorious*. Opening at the London Palladium on 3 October 1944, it ran for a record-breaking 938 performances until May 1946:

> I was so happy working with Tommy Trinder in *Happy and Glorious* at the Palladium. Two shows a day. We were in the theatre about half past eleven in the morning and we got out about seven at night. It was a big revue, very glamorous, with lovely dancing girls, and we were in the midst of another Blitz – this time Hitler was sending over the V-2 rockets – and we just had to cope.

After the war, Elisabeth reigned supreme in London's West End in three sophisticated revues devised and directed by Laurier Lister: *Tuppence Coloured* (1947), *Oranges and Lemons* (1948) and

Penny Plain (1951). There was also *Pay the Piper* (1954). Each of them gave her opportunities to shine as an artiste and, true to form, in each production, Elisabeth stopped the show. For example, in *Tuppence Coloured*, which opened at the Lyric Theatre in Hammersmith on 4 September 1947 and transferred to the Globe Theatre the following month, Elisabeth co-starred with Joyce Grenfell and Max Adrian, and introduced 'La Vie En Rose' to Britain. This was the signature song of Edith Piaf in France.

In *Tuppence Coloured*, Elisabeth introduced another song to Britain, Irving Berlin's 'Supper Time'. This was first performed by Ethel Waters in 1933 in Berlin's Broadway revue *As Thousands Cheer*. It told the story of an African American woman who is feeding her children, waiting for her husband to come home, not knowing he has been lynched. This song marked a dramatic change for Elisabeth, and her reviews for *Tuppence Coloured* were outstanding. In her scrapbook they stand as a testament to her artistry and onstage brilliance. For example, *Time and Tide* enthused: 'she is an enchantment, and turns the dear little Lyric into a real Parisian *boîte*. No microphone, no display – just witty words or telling sentiment, a good tune and the rest, all technique, personality and attack.'

In 1952, Elisabeth declined the supporting role of Butterfly, a bandanna-wearing mammy, in the West End musical *Love from Judy*. She was having too much fun playing glamorous and sophisticated women of the world in the revues.

In 1959 in *The Crooked Mile*, Elisabeth played her first leading role in a West End 'book' musical. She had been featured in several musicals, and had starred in revues, but there had never been a leading character created for her. She was cast as the romantic fantasist Sweet Ginger, the owner of an ironmonger's shop. Set in London's Soho, *The Crooked Mile* was a tale of gang warfare in the underworld, with outstanding music composed by Peter Greenwell. Peter Wildeblood contributed the amusing book and lyrics, drawing on his autobiographical novel *West End People* about running a club in Soho. Apart from the lead, Wildeblood's Damon Runyon-esque characters included Jug Ears (Jack MacGowran), a spineless gang leader loved by Sweet Ginger, and Cora (Millicent Martin), a tart with a heart of gold.

The Crooked Mile opened at the Cambridge Theatre on 10 September and Elisabeth had two showstoppers: 'Meet the Family', a lively duet with Millicent Martin, and a solo ballad, the haunting 'If I Ever Fall in Love Again', which she sang beautifully.

Elisabeth's next stage musical, *Cindy Ella (or I Gotta Shoe)*, opened at the Garrick Theatre on 17 December 1962. This was a reworking by Caryl Brahms and Ned Sherrin of the Cinderella story. Elisabeth and her co-stars, Cleo Laine, Cy Grant and George Browne, all played multiple roles. An enthusiastic review in the *Spectator* (28 December 1962) summed up its appeal: '*Cindy*'s progress is punctuated by a glowing crop of jazz songs and negro spirituals which the mercurial Miss Laine and her companions put over with dazzling artistry. The effect is of a sophisticated charade.'

London-born Laine had already established herself as one of Britain's top jazz singers before she branched out into straight acting and musical theatre. She had first worked with Elisabeth in a BBC Radio play (*Under the Sun*, 1958) and they became great friends. The impact Elisabeth has had on other singers is, perhaps, best expressed by Laine, who, as a child in the 1930s, first heard her singing on BBC Radio:

> I've always admired Elisabeth. Before I came into the business, I imitated the way she sang. I loved her voice. When I had the opportunity to work with her, that was a dream come true. She's great fun to be with. Elisabeth has been a mentor to a lot of singers. People in the business adore her.[1]

In 1970, when the Hampstead Theatre Club in London presented Noël Coward's *Tonight at Eight* starring Millicent Martin and Gary Bond, it was suggested that Elisabeth make an appearance in a one-woman show after the performances. Taking the title *A Marvellous Party* from one of Coward's songs, the show, devised and directed by Paul Ciani, became a musical history of the 1930s. It incorporated some of Coward's songs, and some associated with Elisabeth. Opening on 30 December, it marked a turning point in Elisabeth's career and became the template for her future one-woman shows. The reviews were enthusiastic, among them B.A. Young's in *the Financial Times* (4 January 1971):

> Any party with Elisabeth Welch as hostess is bound to be marvellous, and this late show at Hampstead certainly is. Miss Welch leans heavily on Cole Porter and Noël Coward for her repertoire and she does them proud. She puts over the lyrics with a sympathy and understanding never heard in the popular singers nowadays. Note especially such details as the *diminuendo* at 'every love but true love' in Cole Porter's 'Love for Sale', injecting at that climactic point the fundamental tragedy lurking behind the defiant words. This is artistry of a high order.

On 30 October 1973, at Her Majesty's Theatre, Elisabeth made a long-overdue return to West End musicals as Berthe in *Pippin*, with music and lyrics by Stephen Schwartz, the American composer best known for *Godspell*. The Broadway version had received several Tony awards. True to form, Elisabeth stopped the show cold with her rendition of the rousing 'No Time at All'.

The high point of Elisabeth's 'renaissance' in the 1980s was her appearance in the revue *Kern Goes to Hollywood* at the Donmar Warehouse. Critics raved and, without exception, they singled out Elisabeth. Said Mike Mills in *What's On in London* (6–12 June 1985):

> Elisabeth Welch is a phenomenon. In a world of illusion and fake sentiment, she is the real thing, a singer whose vitality and humour, humanity and dignity shine through everything

> she does. She sings sweet and true as ever and when she chooses she can make anyone else on stage disappear.

Elisabeth was nominated for a Laurence Olivier Award for her performance in *Kern Goes to Hollywood*. At the 1985 Royal Variety Performance, she sang 'Smoke Gets in Your Eyes' from the Kern revue, and single-handedly transformed the vast Theatre Royal into an intimate cabaret. The audience, including Queen Elizabeth II, rewarded her with rapturous applause, which clearly moved the 81-year-old singer.

More adulation followed for Elisabeth when the Donmar Warehouse revue, now called *Jerome Kern Goes to Hollywood*, transferred to Broadway. Opening at the Ritz Theatre in 1986, it was Elisabeth's first appearance in a Broadway show since 1931. The New York critics adored Elisabeth, and her performance prompted Frank Rich of *The New York Times* (24 January 1986) to make this famous comment: 'We must write letters to our Congressmen demanding that Miss Welch be detained in the

Elisabeth Welch with Stephen Bourne at the Museum of the Moving Image in London, December 1994. (Courtesy of Peter Everard Smith)

United States forthwith, as a national resource too rare and precious for export.'

Elisabeth retired in the mid 1990s and passed away on 15 July 2003 at the age of 99. In 2012, on what would have been her birthday, 27 February, the playwright and critic Bonnie Greer unveiled an English Heritage blue plaque at Ovington Court in Kensington, where Elisabeth had lived from 1933 to 1936. In her speech, Greer said:

> It was a very rare art form that she practiced, the supper clubs, cabaret, and that's about being an actor, as well as being a great singer. For her, it was about freedom, and she gives people like me, and many of us, permission to pursue our lives, she gives that to everybody.

Buddy Bradley. (Author's collection)

12

Buddy Bradley and Berto Pasuka: On With the Dance

Dance holds an important place in the history of Black British theatre, whether in the choreography of West End musicals, ballet or on the streets of Notting Hill during the annual carnival celebrations. Two trailblazers in this field are the African American choreographer Buddy Bradley and the Jamaican ballet dancer Berto Pasuka. In the 1930s Bradley worked on a number of West End shows and films and often collaborated with Jessie Matthews, Britain's number one star of musicals, while in the 1940s Pasuka founded Britain's first Black ballet company, Les Ballets Nègres, yet neither of them have been given the attention and recognition they deserve as dance innovators.

Bradley was born in Harrisburg, Pennsylvania, and learned how to tap dance after moving to Harlem, New York, in the 1920s. At the Billy Pierce Dance Studios, Bradley choreographed routines for gangsters' molls and many Broadway stars like Mae West, Eddie Foy, Clifton Webb, Ruby Keeler, Lucille Ball, Eleanor Powell and siblings Fred and Adele Astaire for \$250 a routine. Bradley worked behind the scenes on several Broadway musicals in the 1920s, but he was not allowed to officially choreograph an American show with a white cast. Interviewed in London by Marshall and Jean Stearns, he said, 'They called me in to patch them up when they realised how bad the dancing was. I never saw half the shows my stuff appeared in. I wasn't invited, and besides I was too busy teaching.'[1] This did not happen when he arrived in London in 1930 and began a long and successful career in British musicals. Bradley was always given credit.

It was Fred Astaire who persuaded impresario Charles B. Cochran to bring Bradley, and another Black dancer, Billy Pierce, over to London to stage the dances for the West End musical *Ever Green* at the Adelphi Theatre in 1930. The show starred Jessie Matthews, a fabulous and versatile young dancer, and she worked well with Bradley. In fact, they became a 'team'. Bradley said, 'In all modesty, no coloured person had ever been given so much responsibility.'[2] He was in charge of sixty-four dancers: sixteen regulars, sixteen Tiller girls, sixteen show girls, and sixteen chorus boys. It is likely that Bradley was the first Black choreographer of an entire 'white' show and, unlike on Broadway, he was fully credited for his contribution.

After *Ever Green*, Bradley remained in England and collaborated with Matthews on *Hold My Hand* at the Gaiety Theatre, by which time Bradley had made his first appearance on the British stage at the London Pavilion in *Cochran's 1931 Revue*. In 1932 he staged the dances for Jerome Kern's *The Cat and the Fiddle* at the Palace Theatre and Noël Coward's *Words and Music* at the Adelphi Theatre. At Jessie Matthews's request, Bradley moved with her into films, choreographing the film version of *Evergreen* (1934; the title became one word). For several years the Bradley–Matthews partnership was one of the most creative and successful in British cinema, and yet British film and theatre historians failed to mention his name in any of their books. However, he was interviewed by Marshall and Jean Stearns in their American book *Jazz Dance* (1968), and he was included in three editions of the British *Who's Who in the Theatre*.

In addition to his film and theatre work, Bradley opened a popular dance school, known as the Buddy Bradley School of Stage Dancing, at 25a Old Compton Street, Soho, in 1932. (It later moved to nearby 12 Denman Street.) In 1932 he collaborated with the ballet dancer and choreographer Frederick Ashton in creating Britain's first jazz ballet, *High Yellow*, in which the celebrated ballerina Alicia Markova starred for Sadler's Wells. This upset a few people. According to Ashton's biographer, Julie Kavanagh:

> Despite being conceived as a novel experiment, *High Yellow* caused more of a stir than Ashton intended, shocking [society hostess] Lady Cunard and upsetting [Russian ballerina] Olga Spessivtseva, who did not want it to appear on the same programme as her 'beloved *Swan Lake*'. The *Dancing Times* was unpleasantly patronising about what it dubbed as a 'darkey' ballet, saying it belonged in a revue … 'It was a matter of absolute impossibility to teach a company of ballet dancers the necessary n***** steps and movements' … But although its impact was short-lived (with only a few subsequent performances), *High Yellow* proved a valuable touchstone as far as Ashton was concerned, a practice run in a new dance vernacular that he would go on to 'balleticise' with much greater finesse.[3]

Bradley also created a cabaret act for the ballet dancers Vera Zorina and Anton Dolin, but he was most in demand for West End musicals and revues. In 1935 he choreographed the London production of Cole Porter's *Anything Goes*, followed by many other successful productions including Charles B. Cochran's *Follow the Sun* (1936); Lew Leslie's *Blackbirds of 1936*, with a cast that included the Nicholas Brothers; *I Can Take It* (1939) with Jessie Matthews; *Light's Up* (1940); *Full Swing* (1942); *Big Top* (1942); *Something in the Air* (1943); and *It's Time to Dance* (1943) with Jack Buchanan and Elsie Randolph, in which he also appeared as 'Buddy'.

In 1935, when he was interviewed for *Film Weekly*, he gave some insights into his thought processes:

> Let's begin at the beginning. All modern dance creations have African rhythm and movement as their rudimentary bases. People lose sight of the fact that all these modern dance creations, stretching over the past fifteen years, beginning with the Charleston and carrying on through the Black Bottom, Pickin' Cotton, Beguine, Rhumba and Carioca [danced by Fred Astaire and Ginger Rogers in the 1933 film *Flying Down to Rio*], all have African rhythm. The idea is to 'localise' that African basis. Take the Rhumba. In this you must introduce Spanish touches, as it has a Spanish background, hands on hips and bending back from the waist, for instance. With the Carioca you still have the Rhumba movement, but here the background is South American, so it's much more fiery and tempestuous, as against the languor of the Spanish … We must study the National Dance, and add to it newer movements, mostly African in origin, but now universal in practice.[4]

In 1949, Bradley was responsible for Jessie Matthews taking over from Zoe Gail in Cecil Landeau's revue *Sauce Tartare*, at the Cambridge Theatre, which was the last time they worked together. The young Audrey Hepburn, who was in the cast of that production, also studied dance at Bradley's academy. Bradley choreographed the sequel to this revue, *Sauce Piquante*, again at the Cambridge, in 1950. His widow, Dorothy Bradley, commented that throughout his career Bradley gave opportunities to younger Black dancers, such as the Guyanese Ken 'Snakehips' Johnson.[5]

In 1964, Bradley directed a revue called *Blackbirds of 1964* at the Palladium in Edinburgh. The all-Black cast included the Trinidadian comedian and compère Horace James, a 'Carnival in Trinidad', a 'Shebeen in Johannesburg' featuring the South African Manhattan Brothers, and a New York cabaret as a finale.

Bradley closed his studio in 1967 and relocated to New York with his wife Dorothy. He died five years later. When the American journal *Variety* published an obituary (26 July 1972), it stated:

> As often true of show business innovators, Bradley was famous among his contemporaries but little known to the general public. His dance ideas were well ahead of his time and the knowing performers of the musical comedy stage flocked to him. He was personally popular in the profession, together with respect given to his creative choreography. He pre-dated and may have influenced Busby Berkeley.

Early attempts to establish Black theatre companies may have been short-lived, but there was one that was successful and managed to survive: Les Ballet Nègres, a company founded in 1944 by the Jamaican Berto Pasuka. With his dancers, Pasuka successfully staged aspects of Jamaican and African history and culture, but the going could be tough. Lack of funding eventually led to the demise of Les Ballet Nègres in 1952, though Pasuka survived to become a successful artist in France.

Pasuka was born in Kingston, Jamaica, in 1917. After he left school, his father apprenticed him to a dentist. However, Pasuka's interests lay elsewhere. As a young man growing up in Jamaica he mixed freely with the inhabitants of Maroon Town. They were descended from runaway slaves and their energetic dances had originally evolved as a form of catharsis from the oppression of slavery. Pasuka was fascinated by their rhythmic dances and, influenced by the Maroons, he became an expert dancer himself. In 1931 he took part in the political activist Marcus Garvey's vast theatrical extravaganza, staged at Edelweiss Park in Kingston. At this event Pasuka befriended another dancer, Richie Riley. Abandoned by his family, Pasuka found a home and companionship with Riley, and together they toured the island, appearing in every theatrical event they could find.

Berto Pasuka. (Author's collection, courtesy of Tom Sargant)

With his knowledge of Maroon dances, Pasuka saw the potential for expanding their appeal to a wider, international audience. He was aware that London was accommodating new art forms and he moved there in 1939. However, several years passed before 'Bertie', using a new professional name, Berto Pasuka, realised his ambition to take Black dance to another level and to new audiences. Meanwhile, to survive as a young gay Black man in London, he danced in cabaret shows in West End nightclubs and worked as an artist's model. Other gay Black men, including a fellow Jamaican, Granville 'Chick' Alexander, led similar lives at this time. Pasuka, admired for his fine physique, also found himself in demand as a model for sculptors, photographers and painters. These included Angus McBean, whose exquisite photographic portraits of Pasuka have now found a home in the collection of the National Portrait Gallery.

To improve his skills as a choreographer, Pasuka enrolled at the Russian Dancing Academy in King's Road, Chelsea, which had been founded by Serafina Astafieva, formerly a dancer with Diaghilev's Ballets Russes. In *British Ballet*, Peter Noble confirmed that, from 1941 to 1946, Pasuka studied pure ballet technique at the Academy under Anna Severskaya and Mme Verushka.[6] However, the young student felt that classical ballet was 'unsuitable, too conventional for me and my people'.[7]

A breakthrough came in 1944 when Pasuka was employed as a dancer in the film *Men of Two Worlds*. Pasuka and the other Black dancers were not assigned a dance director. Eric Johns in *Theatre World* explained, 'They were just told to dance, to make up a dance "out of their heads" … the dancers acquitted themselves so well that Pasuka decided he would endeavour to establish a negro ballet company in London.'[8]

After preparing for two years, Pasuka launched Les Ballets Nègres, Britain's first Black ballet company, at the Twentieth Century Theatre in Westbourne Grove, London, on 30 April 1946. Two months prior to the company's debut, Pasuka gave the following insights into his work in an interview with Glyn Kelsall in *The Stage*:

> Negro dancing is the complete antithesis of Russian ballet … Negro dances are evolved from a blending of spontaneous and basic steps … the Negro dances quite naturally on the occasion of weddings and funerals. He dances as easily as he sings, when he is happy or when he is sad. Just as Dvorak used Negro melodies as the core of the New World Symphony, so I am using simple Negro dances as a basis for my ballets. There will be no pointwork and no entrechats. Instead, the audience will see rhythmic movements of the hips, head, and shoulders, and they will discover that a dancer's eyes can be a useful instrument of expression.[9]

In 1946, Pasuka's friend Richie Riley left Jamaica to join him in London. He is credited as one of the founders of Les Ballets Nègres. When Riley arrived, he discovered that Pasuka was friends with the Bloomsbury intellectual circle and in a relationship with Adam Meredith, an affluent professional bridge player. Meredith had a passion for ballet and backed Les Ballet Nègres with the hard-earned savings he had amassed at bridge.

Pasuka created four new ballets for their debut: *De Prophet*, based on the story of a religious maniac who tried to convert villagers; *They Came*, which depicted the clash of races when white Christians first landed in Africa; *Aggrey*, based on the teaching of the Ghanaian philosopher James Emman Kwegyir Aggrey who advocated racial co-operation; and *Market Day*, a light-hearted impression of tourists in a Caribbean marketplace.

In *British Dance: Black Routes* (2017), Thea Barnes described the eighteen members of the company as both amateurs and dancers who had been trained in ballet, jazz and Pasuka's own method technique. Despite their French name, the members of the company were mostly born in Britain and the Caribbean. The West African Rhythm Brothers, a group of drummers led by the Nigerian Ambrose Campbell, provided the music.

'Their dancing will be an entirely new experience,' wrote Eric Johns in *Theatre World* (April 1946). 'It is a blending of basic and spontaneous steps and rhythms. It is extempore dancing, reminiscent of Isadora Duncan, who never knew the precise pattern her dance would take until she found herself on the stage and heard the music.'[10]

Les Ballets Nègres were successful and gained the support of several famous people including George Bernard Shaw, Aneurin Bevan and Dame Sybil Thorndike, who declared Pasuka to be 'a genius'. Critically acclaimed and attracting large audiences, for several years Les Ballets Nègres toured throughout Britain and visited such countries as Holland, Belgium, Sweden and Switzerland. In 1947 the Jamaican Noel Vaz described the company as:

> The first indication of a theatrical medium African in origin and motif, often West Indian in flavour … which promises to

> become a serious and permanent contribution to the Theatre, not only as a vital contribution to Ballet, but also to the propagation of Negro ideals, ideas and problems.[11]

A major setback occurred in 1951, when the organisers of the Festival of Britain turned down Pasuka's application to take part. They rejected Les Ballets Nègres on the grounds that this was going to be an event that was exclusively a celebration of 'traditional' British culture.

One of their final appearances was a three-week engagement in September 1952 at the Twentieth Century Theatre, where they had made their debut in 1946. Soon afterwards, the company disbanded. Pasuka had invested his life's savings in the company but at the end he struggled to pay the dancers' wages.

Pasuka died in London on 23 April 1963 and his final resting place is an unmarked grave in Streatham Park Cemetery.

Part 3

A New Era

Pauline Henriques (Emilia) and Valerie White (Desdemona) in the Arts Council tour of *Othello*, 1950. (Author's collection, courtesy of Pauline Henriques)

13

Enter, Stage Left: The First Black Drama Students

When drama schools first opened their doors, there was very little or no opportunity for aspiring Black actors to secure a place. There is hardly any documentation that tells us what it was like for the few who did manage to gain access. I met and befriended one of the few, Pauline Henriques, in 1989.

She had arrived in Britain from Jamaica as a child and settled with her middle-class family in the leafy London suburb of St John's Wood. She told me that she had always been passionately interested in theatre. Pauline's father, Cyril, was a successful import and export merchant who wanted his six children to have an English education. While growing up in London, Pauline went to the theatre regularly with her siblings and acted out plays with them at home. In spite of the lack of opportunities for a young Black British actress at that time, Pauline dreamed of becoming a professional actress.

In 1932, with her parents' support, she joined a drama course at the London Academy of Music and Dramatic Art. Situated in Talgarth Road, Hammersmith, it was founded in 1861 as the

London Academy of Music (drama courses were added later) and it has a reputation for being one of the best of its kind:

> I started going to the theatre when I was seven. I lost my Jamaican accent rather quickly, so when I went to drama school, I had an English accent which was perfect for 'classic' roles. The course lasted for one year, and I appeared in many school productions, but I had to play my parts in white face, including Lady Bracknell and Lady Macbeth! I went along with it because I was very anxious to learn my craft, and to be taken seriously as a dramatic actress ... However, after leaving drama school, I finished up playing comic Black maids in American plays and one line – 'Yessum. I'sa coming!' – which I learned to express about eighteen different ways.[1]

In 1945, the charismatic Jamaican folklorist and poet Louise Bennett, popularly known as 'Miss Lou', was awarded a British Council scholarship to the Royal Academy of Dramatic Art (RADA), situated in Bloomsbury in central London.

In 1945, RADA was short of money. Wartime London had been a very dangerous place to be and student numbers had dropped. After the war, it was a truly vibrant place. RADA students returning from the war included ex-servicemen and women who had a different outlook on life. They had different attitudes to authority.[2] The Trinidadian Pearl Connor-Mogotsi has also explained that, immediately after the war, the British government and other organisations, including the British Council, wanted to show some appreciation for all the people from the colonies who had contributed to the war effort.[3]

It was in this climate that Bennett successfully applied for a place at RADA. However, there was a misunderstanding. She had been accepted as a student, and had a letter from the British Council to prove it, but no one had informed RADA. Though the war was nearly over, she risked her life by travelling across the Atlantic on a ship protected by wartime convoys. On her arrival at RADA, Bennett was asked to audition. She agreed and, for diction, Bennett presented an excerpt from George Bernard Shaw's *Caesar and Cleopatra*. She then dazzled the assessors by performing all the characters in a courthouse scene, as she had enjoyed seeing in Jamaica. Speaking in Jamaican dialect, Bennett played the judge, policemen and a character called Matilda Slackness. The assessors at RADA were about to award Bennett a scholarship when she explained that she had already been given one in Jamaica. The audition had been unnecessary, but the assessors had been entertained and impressed by her remarkable talent.

At RADA, Bennett attended classes in theatre history, dramatic structure, acting, voice and speech, movement, mime, but she refused to lose her Jamaican accent and identity: 'I just let them know that I didn't come to lose any of the cultural things that I had acquired,' she later told an interviewer.[4]

Bennett acted in plays by several European dramatists, including Shakespeare. In a RADA production of *Romeo and Juliet* she was highly commended for playing the Nurse in Jamaican Creole. Bennett was considered an outstanding student in mime. When another Jamaican, Leonie Forbes, joined RADA about a decade later, she found instructors in mime who still remembered Louise Bennett.[5]

After completing her RADA course, Bennett decided not to pursue a career as an actress in Britain. There were few opportunities anyway. Instead, she returned home to Jamaica and successfully applied for another British Council scholarship that enabled her to continue her passion for collecting folklore from Jamaica and other Caribbean islands. Almost single-handedly, Bennett saved Jamaican folklore from extinction. Leonie Forbes remembered an inspirational visit by 'Miss Lou' to her school in Jamaica:

> That was the first time I heard someone doing the alphabet with things that we could recognise. She said: 'A is for Ackee,

> saltfish best friend,' and so on. I was completely taken with it and I just thought this lady was out of this world. I couldn't believe that somebody could take our foods, our things, and put it into a song that was going to help Jamaican children learn their ABCs.[6]

'Miss Lou' gave Jamaicans a pride in their language and culture, as well as their future. The Jamaican dub poet and activist Linton Kwesi Johnson said:

> She gave my generation of writers the confidence to use our ordinary everyday Jamaican speech as a legitimate vehicle for poetic discourse. What Miss Lou's poetry does is to offer a mirror to Jamaican people in which Jamaicans can see themselves in all their various manifestations, with all their strengths and their weaknesses.[7]

It is highly likely that Bennett was the first Black student at RADA, but very few openings followed in the 1950s and 1960s. Two exceptions were also Jamaican women: Leonie Forbes, who graduated in 1963, and Mona Hammond, who graduated in 1964. There was also Horace James from Trinidad, who graduated in 1961, and Ramsay Blackwood in 1962.

In 1961, when Forbes arrived in London, she discovered a vast new world. She said, 'The city was cold, lonely and alien – different from anywhere I'd ever been or known.'[8] She wasted no time in making contact with friends from back home, including the actors Charles Hyatt, Frank Cousins and Trevor Rhone. She found RADA 'somewhat intimidating at first, yet truly exciting, and I was making great strides by the end of my first term'.[9] At first, she was afraid of speaking:

> I sounded so different from the other students. Some tutors seem to think that if you're Black and from the Caribbean or any Black country, you won't be able to communicate in

> English. Also, their theatrical history was so vast and so well set that one easily felt like an outsider. There were things I wasn't sure I could handle, because I didn't understand them, I hadn't been exposed to them … And although I was diligently studying all this wonderful standard English, these English customs and social graces and so on, nearly every time I got a role they wanted me to be from Trinidad, Jamaica or Nassau or South America.[10]

Before her graduation from RADA, Forbes took part in a Shakespeare Commemoration Service at Southwark Cathedral on 27 April 1962, and later that year, at RADA's Vanbrugh Theatre in Bloomsbury, she played the title role in a student production of *Cinderella*. In March 1963, also at RADA's Vanbrugh Theatre, she played Cleopatra in a student production of Shakespeare's *Antony and Cleopatra*. In the *Birmingham Daily Post* (4 March 1963), the theatre critic J.C. Trewin noted that Forbes has 'presence and impulse: she can take the stage'.

The Trinidadian folk singer Edric Connor arrived in Britain in 1944 and desperately wanted to go to RADA. In his autobiography he explained that, as far as he was concerned, it was blatant racism that prevented him from becoming a student there in 1945. The principal of RADA preferred him to take private lessons from one of the teachers, the distinguished Irish baritone Frederick Ranalow. 'We worked mainly on *Othello*,' Connor recalled. 'They were very good lessons and Mr. Ranalow a very great teacher, but as I couldn't go to the Academy, I felt I was getting second-best and merely being tolerated.'[11]

Earl Cameron said that it was impossible for a young Black actor to gain access to a drama school in the 1940s. When he understudied Gordon Heath in *Deep Are the Roots* in 1947, Earl instead took advice from his friend Ida Shepley and approached Amanda Ira Aldridge for lessons in elocution and voice projection. Amanda was the daughter of Ira Aldridge and had given voice lessons to Paul Robeson to prepare him for his appearance in *Othello* in 1930. Even in her 80s she kept her studio open in Hanover Square in London's West End.

Cameron said, 'She was a courteous, beautiful human being … I had the highest regard for her, and we got on extremely well. She helped me tremendously and I continued having lessons with her for at least two years. She told me about her father, and showed me pictures of him.'[12]

The lessons Earl had with Amanda Ira Aldridge worked, for he eventually took over the leading role from Gordon Heath in *Deep Are the Roots* and acted in the play to critical acclaim in repertory productions into the 1950s. He continued acting until he was in his 90s.

Before he became a highly respected dramatist, theatre historian and author of the classics *Shakespeare in Sable: A History of Black Shakespearean Actors* (1984) and *The Cambridge Guide to African and Caribbean Theatre* (1994), Errol Hill, from Trinidad, is credited with being partly responsible for forming the modern era in Caribbean theatre. As early as 1946 he founded, with another Trinidadian, Errol John, the Whitehall Players, one of the first theatre companies in the Caribbean. With British Council support and their headquarters at Whitehall, Port of Spain, the Players adopted the policy of taking their productions to the people, performing at hospitals and other public institutions and in the open air in small towns and villages. When the need for accessible plays with Caribbean themes and language became apparent, Hill not only wrote his own, but also assisted in advancing Caribbean drama with his innovations.[13]

In 1949, Hill received a British Council scholarship to study at RADA. He appeared in a succession of plays, including Shakespeare's works, as part of his training. He said:

> Being the only Black student, I made up white for my roles … The only significant Black role I ever had in an academy production was assigned to me when one of the directors

> sympathised with my situation and decided to produce *Deep Are the Roots*. Now one of the white students had to make up in blackface to be my mammy! The production was so successful that the director took the play on tour to workers' union halls around London. This was most unusual for a Tory school.[14]

When the time came for Hill to graduate, he selected Othello. Judging his performance were Vivien Leigh and Sir Lewis Casson:

> They awarded me distinction in acting, probably influenced by the school's principal, Sir Kenneth Barnes, who could never get it straight that I came from the West Indies where I had spoken English all my life. He believed I was from darkest Africa and thought my cultivated English accent was a remarkable achievement.[15]

By the time Hill gained his diploma in 1951, he had acted with the left-wing Unity Theatre in *Longitude 49*. He was also awarded a diploma in dramatic art from London University. At the Colonial Students' Residence in Hans Crescent House, Knightsbridge (behind Harrods), Hill directed members of the West Indian Student Association in two productions: Sophocles' *Oedipus Rex* (1951) and Derek Walcott's *Henri Christophe* (1952). The casts included several names that would soon become well-known in Caribbean literature, culture and politics.

Like Bennett before him, Hill did not wish to pursue an acting career in Britain, and accepted an offer to work in the extra-mural drama programme of the University of the West Indies in Jamaica. He also travelled to other parts of the Caribbean, encouraging the writing and production of indigenous plays to lay the groundwork for a West Indian national theatre. Hill's calypso verse-play *Man Better Man* represented Trinidad and Tobago at the Commonwealth Arts Festival in Britain in 1965.

In 1956, aged just 17, Yvonne Brewster travelled from her middle-class home in Jamaica to Britain to train at the Rose Bruford School of Drama in Kent. In 2005, when Brewster was Sue Lawley's guest on BBC Radio 4's *Desert Island Discs*, Lawley erroneously described her as the first Black female drama student in Britain. There had, of course, been Pauline Henriques and Louise Bennett before her, but Brewster was probably the first at the Rose Bruford School of Drama. Brewster recalled:

> They viewed me as a curiosity, and indeed I was, and Miss Bruford took one look at me and, very kindly I think, said 'Well, you do know you will never work' and I looked at her and I said, 'Watch this space.' When you're 17 I just thought she was funny. She was saying she would take the money, because my father had paid my tuition three years in advance. He had anticipated they might want to get rid of me and I wouldn't work because I was Black.[16]

Brewster described Britain in the late 1950s as having 'many bleak moments'. This was a turbulent time for Black Britons, most of them recent settlers from Africa and the Caribbean. Against a backdrop that included the Notting Hill Riots of 1958, and the racist murder of student Kelso Cochrane in 1959, Brewster said she survived by forcing herself to think that people were not *deliberately* racist: 'I had to think that or else I couldn't go through. I couldn't go back to Jamaica without a piece of paper because my father would have cut my head off! So, I had to get through those moments and say I will overcome.'[17]

Brewster did get through the drama course and she went on to have a brilliant career in British theatre. Among her many achievements was the founding of the Talawa Theatre Company in 1985 with Mona Hammond, Carmen Munroe and Inigo Espejel. Brewster was Talawa's Artistic Director until 2003. She later explained the meaning of the word Talawa and why she chose it as the name of the company:

> Talawa means small, female and powerful and not be threatened. I know it as a Jamaican saying because my mother was a small but powerful woman. And when I was little people would say, 'Bwoy, she little but she talawa.' When I looked it up, I discovered it comes from Ghana but it defines what the company set out to be. We don't set out to be grand or grandiose but to be strong and substantial even though we are not big.[18]

While writing this book in 2021, I spoke to my friend Anni Domingo about her experiences of being a drama student. In 1967, Anni auditioned in Sierra Leone for Rose Bruford's School of Drama. They never saw her in person because Anni auditioned on an audio tape and sent it to England. The teaching staff at Rose Bruford were impressed and, based on what they heard, offered her a place. Anni joined Rose Bruford in September 1968 for a three-year course. She recalls: 'I was in the same year as some fantastic actors and they included Anton Phillips, Stephen Boxer, Ron Cook and Michael Hebden, who is now best known for playing Norris in *Coronation Street*.' There was no student accommodation, so Anni found digs within walking distance of the college in what she described as an 'international house' because the landlady housed female students from across the globe.

During the three-year drama course, Anni worked for the BBC World Service:

> I acted in radio plays that were broadcast in Africa with some wonderful actors like Louis Mahoney and Yemi Ajibade, but I kept it a secret from the teaching staff at Rose Bruford. I got my full Equity card by doing this, but I kept quiet about it. I knew I wanted to act, but at the school I was only offered boys' parts and maids in student productions. The BBC World Service provided me with opportunities to play a lot of different parts, and I also acted in some television plays for broadcast to the Commonwealth.

At Rose Bruford, Anni's voice teacher encouraged her to lose her 'natural' Sierra Leonean speaking voice and to speak standard English only, but Anni refused. 'I spoke up for myself,' she says, 'and I have been this way ever since. I will not compromise.'

Anni found an agent before she graduated and, just before the end of the final term, in 1971, she left Rose Bruford to begin her professional acting career. She says:

> Rose Bruford herself advised me to accept what work was offered to get my full Equity card. I replied, 'But I already have it.' She was taken aback, so I explained what I had been doing with the BBC World Service for the last three years and how it had led to me being given my full Equity card. She wasn't too happy about my 'secret'.

In addition to studying at Rose Bruford, Anni regularly went to see plays and opera, to help learn her craft. She also went to the ballet and made friends with Margot Fonteyn. In addition to being a governor, she now teaches at Rose Bruford, but advises her students 'not to rely on everything the college tells you'.

Ida Shepley. (Author's collection)

14

Ida Shepley: A Gentle, Friendly Star

Ida Shepley was a singer who had an ambition to become a dramatic actress but, for a British woman of colour, this was almost impossible in the 1940s. However, though she has been described as 'gentle', Ida must have had a strong personality and a will of iron to achieve her goals. She succeeded too, even when the odds were against her and acting roles were rare. It is sad that, in spite of her fascinating career in music and drama, all memory of Ida has slipped away.

Ida Humphrey was born in 1908 in Monks Coppenhall, Crewe. Although her birth certificate states that her parents were Clement and Gladys Humphrey, it is doubtful that they were married. There is no trace of a marriage certificate. Clement appears to have been an absent father (though Ida's younger brother Cyril was born in 1912) and, when Gladys married John Shepley in 1919, she entered 'spinster' on their marriage certificate. Ida then took her step-father's surname. Meanwhile, Clement, a Trinidadian, claimed he was a 'herbalist' or 'music hall player', which is probably true, but what has also come to light is that he spent several periods in prison for various crimes (including fraud) and died in HM Prison Parkhurst on the Isle of Wight on 30 January 1928.

Apart from snippets in various newspaper reports of the 1940s and 1950s, little is known about Ida's early years. One source says that she was educated at the Ursuline Convent School in Crewe; another adds that she attended a finishing school in Paris. In 1937 she won a singing competition and a newspaper gives her address at the time as 21 Arundel Gardens. This was also the home of the voice coach Amanda Ira Aldridge, daughter of Ira Aldridge (see Chapter 4). Ida took lessons from Amanda and they remained friends until Amanda died in 1956. Meanwhile, Ida came to the attention of the theatrical agent Keith Prowse who recommended her to the BBC: 'We have heard a vocalist whom I would like to introduce – a contralto – she has a voice of rare and sweet quality, and very pleasing indeed.'[1]

Soon afterwards Ida commenced a long association with the BBC, appearing in such popular radio shows as *Band Waggon* (1938), *Mississippi Nights* (1938), *Brief Interlude* (1939) with Elisabeth Welch and many other music and variety programmes during the Second World War. She also broadcast for the BBC to the forces and on their Empire Service to West Africa and the Caribbean. In *The Stage* newspaper she advertised herself for variety stage tours as 'Radio's Charming Contralto' and 'The Bronze Girl With the Golden Voice'.

In 1943, on one of her many wartime variety tours, Ida was featured in a concert called *Brighter Black-Out* at the Palace Theatre in Tamworth, Staffordshire. This was organised to raise funds for merchant seamen and their families. Ida was mentioned in a local newspaper, the *Tamworth Herald* (20 February 1943), and the information given about her is intriguing. It claimed that Ida was the daughter of a West African chief who was killed during a tribal feud and that she came to England at the age of 5. This was more than likely the creation of a journalist with an over-active imagination, but the rest of it sounds as if it could be accurate, such as claiming she entered a convent where her musical gifts were observed: 'She began her musical studies in Paris as a pianist, and there it was discovered by Miss Aldridge that her vocal possibilities were outstanding. Consequently she has been under her guidance ever since … She sings in five different languages – English, German, French, Italian and Spanish – and has appeared in the best-known opera houses of Europe, including Berlin, Vienna, Budapest and Paris.'

It is correct to say that Amanda Ira Aldridge encouraged Ida's 'vocal possibilities' and she certainly helped her to make the transition from singer to dramatic actress. In reality, very little information comes to light about Ida until 1937 when she married a motor engineer, Charles Skilbeck Smith (1893–1957), and was mentioned in several newspapers when she won the singing competition. As for the *Tamworth Herald*, when they reviewed the concert, they had nothing but praise for Ida 'who charmed by her artistic use of a beautiful voice. She sang a group of Negro spirituals with a depth of feeling and simple sincerity which was intensely moving, and in her second group of popular songs showed that her exceptional talent ranges over a wide repertoire.'

In 1944 Ida made her 'straight' acting debut in a production of Eugene O'Neill's *All God's Chillun' Got Wings*. It was presented by the Colchester Repertory Company and starred Robert Adams. Ida was cast as his sister, Hattie Harris, who objects to her brother's marriage to an emotionally unstable white woman. The supporting cast included three other Black actors who were making their way in the profession: Orlando Martins, Earl Cameron and George Browne. In 1946, when Ida and Robert Adams were cast in the Left-wing Unity Theatre's production of the same play, *The Stage* (21 February 1946) praised Ida for playing Hattie with a 'confident touch, obviously with complete psychological grasp of the part which she successfully projects'.

Further dramatic roles in London's West End came her way in plays like *Caviar to the General* (1947) at the Whitehall Theatre and *The Vigil* (1948) at the Prince of Wales Theatre. She also replaced the African American actress Evelyn Ellis as

Gordon Heath's mother Bella in the American play *Deep Are the Roots* at the Wyndham's Theatre. It was a role she would return to in various repertory productions such as the Londonderry Guildhall and with the Colchester Repertory Company, both in 1949.

In between dramatic stage roles, Ida continued to work as a vocalist for BBC Radio and in variety tours. For these appearances she advertised herself as having been born in Trinidad, which would have sounded more 'exotic' to post-war British audiences. Then, in 1952, she made her debut in pantomime in *Dick Whittington* at the Alexandra Theatre in Birmingham. For its casting of Ida, the *Birmingham Daily Gazette* (28 November 1952) praised the theatre: 'it can always be looked to for some touch of originality in a largely traditional field of pantomime.' It also explained that Ida's casting as the 'Queen of Cantata' replaced the customary Emperor of Morocco.

There followed a busy period touring variety theatres in musicals: *Music for the Millions* (1952–54) with Max Wall and Beryl Reid; *New York to New Orleans* (1954) with the trumpet player Leslie 'Jiver' Hutchinson and Cy Grant, advertised as 'the greatest of all-coloured musicals'; and as Butterfly in *Love from Judy* (1955–56), replacing Adelaide Hall who had created the role in London's West End.

During the tour of *Love from Judy*, the *Manchester Evening News* (24 September 1955) claimed that 'Ida is planning a holiday in her native West Indies when the tour ends. Ida came to England when she was eighteen months old. She has never been back. But her name is well known in the West Indies. She has broadcast regularly in the BBC Overseas Service.'

There was another West End play, *The Best Damn Lie* (1957) at the Winter Garden Theatre, and on BBC television, in addition to music and variety programmes, she acted in George Bernard Shaw's *Back to Methuselah* (1952), *Halcyon Days* (1954) and *The Green Pastures* (1958). On ITV she was seen as Mrs Kumalo in *Cry, the Beloved Country* (1958) and *All God's*

Chillun' Got Wings (1959) in the same role she had played on stage in the 1940s.

Ida never stopped working. The 1960s began with the London production of *Flower Drum Song*, the penultimate Rodgers and Hammerstein musical. Opening at the Palace Theatre on 24 March 1960, Ida played Madame Liang, a Chinese character. In the original Broadway production this role had been taken by an African American, Juanita Hall. One of the highlights of the show was Ida's show stopping number 'Chop Suey'. In 1961 she replaced Pearl Connor in Barry Reckord's play *You in Your Small Corner* at the Royal Court and repeated the role in the television version in 1962.

In 1964 Ida returned to London's West End as the Narrator in Langston Hughes's *Black Nativity* at the Vaudeville Theatre. Peter Hepple observed in *The Stage* (8 October 1964) that Ida narrated the tale 'with simple charm'. She then joined the Negro Theatre Workshop, appearing in their productions of *The Dark Disciples* (1965) and *Mr Hubert* (1966). She even found time to visit Ireland to play Lady Thiang in a production of Rodgers and Hammerstein's *The King and I*.

In 1968 Ida made her final appearance in the West End at the London Palladium when she replaced Hilda Haynes as Ma Wellington in the musical *Golden Boy* starring Sammy Davis Jr. In 1969 she appeared in W.J. Weatherby's *Breaking the Silence* at the Liverpool Playhouse.

Though Ida never achieved the fame of her British-based African American contemporaries Elisabeth Welch and Adelaide Hall, she remained a familiar face in theatres up and down the country from the 1940s to the 1960s. She enjoyed success in a variety of productions and made it possible for a British-born woman of colour to make a breakthrough in the challenging world of theatre, even if she did occasionally pass herself off as a 'Trinidadian' or 'West Indian'. This suggests that Ida believed a Caribbean identity would make her more 'acceptable' to producers and casting directors than if she said she was British-born.

Ida clearly loved to sing and act, and she did so with remarkable determination and success. Sadly, her point of view cannot be heard. Interviews with her are almost impossible to find. However, positive reviews by theatre critics of her performances are a testament to her many gifts.

Ida died at St Christopher's Hospice in Sydenham on 12 March 1975. One year later a notice was published in *The Times'* 'In Memoriam' section, describing her as 'A gentle, friendly star'.

Robert Adams and Louie Bradley in *All God's Chillun Got Wings* at the Unity Theatre in 1946. (Author's collection, courtesy of Terry Bolas)

15

A New Feeling: Britain's First Black Theatre Companies

Before the 1970s there were several attempts to establish Black theatre companies in Britain, but they were all too often unsuccessful in gaining financial support and a base. Consequently, Black theatre companies surfaced from the 1940s to the 1960s, only to vanish before they could become fully established.

One of the earliest was Robert Adams's Negro Arts Theatre in 1944, but it barely got off the ground. During the long and successful 1947–48 run of the American import *Anna Lucasta*, the Black British understudies of the African American cast formed their own group. They called themselves the Negro Theatre Company.

In 1983, when I was contributing to *Staunch* magazine, I wrote an article about the trailblazer of early black theatre, Robert Adams. In the 1930s and 1940s, Adams had some success and celebrity status as the first non-American Black actor to secure leading roles in British theatre, films, television and radio. In 1946 he attracted attention for two major roles: the first was Jim Harris in Unity Theatre's production of Eugene O'Neill's *All God's Chillun Got Wings*, which he then repeated on BBC Television; the second was Kisenga, the African pianist and composer, in the film *Men of Two Worlds*. And yet, in spite of these breakthroughs, by the 1980s he was completely forgotten. There was no mention of him in British film history books, including early editions of the popular *The Filmgoers Companion*, until I wrote to Leslie Halliwell, the author. Halliwell agreed to include Adams in the next edition and accepted my entry for him and several other Black British film actors. Adams wasn't acknowledged in any British theatre books, either, except two editions of *Who's Who in the Theatre* (1947 and 1952).

These oversights meant that Adams became an 'invisible man' and it was an erasure that was so complete that I haven't been able to find out what happened to him after 1960. That year he made his final acting appearances in Britain on television in Errol John's *Moon on a Rainbow Shawl* and in Joseph Losey's film *The Criminal*. Then he completely vanished.

I wrote to his friend Peter Noble, then editor of the weekly magazine *Screen International*. Unfortunately, Noble couldn't help me. 'I have completely lost touch with him,' he said. 'Disheartened with his acting career, he went home to Guyana and took a job as a headmaster, also working in the Information Department of the Guyana Government.'[1] I had a similar response from the Guyana High Commission in London: 'Further to your enquiry regarding Mr. Robert Adams the Ministry of Home Affairs, Guyana, has not been able to trace him and his family further than June 1960 when he returned to Guyana from London.'[2] The outgoing passenger list for the *Amakura* from Liverpool to Georgetown, Guyana, on 14 June 1960 confirms that Adams travelled home with his wife and daughter, but there the trail ends. What became of Adams after June 1960 remains a mystery.

Adams was born in Georgetown, 'British Guiana' (now Guyana), and while teaching there in the 1920s he produced and acted in amateur stage productions. After his arrival in Britain in 1931, he was forced to earn a living in low-paid jobs such as labouring before a sports promoter persuaded him to become a professional wrestler. Film and stage work followed, including *Stevedore* (1935) at the Embassy Theatre and *Toussaint L'Ouverture* (1936) at the Westminster Theatre, both starring Paul Robeson. But Adams didn't have to wait long for his first leading role in a stage production: in 1938, he was cast as Brutus Jones, the role made famous by Robeson, in Eugene O'Neill's *The Emperor Jones*. The production was staged at the Cambridge Arts Theatre.

His association with the left-wing Unity Theatre began in 1939 with an appearance as a Caribbean strike leader in a play called *Colony*. Then London's West End beckoned and during the war he played supporting roles in Lillian Hellman's *The Little Foxes* (1942), *The House of Jeffreys* (1943), *The Judgement of Dr Johnson* (1943) and *He Signed His Name* (1943). However, Adams was ambitious. He was approached to play Othello for the Old Vic in 1942, but the opportunity did not materialise. He explained:

> Everything was apparently satisfactory, then suddenly a continental was given the chance to do it. While he brought a much needed virility to the part, his lack of knowledge of English was obviously a drawback. His power was alright but his inflections were ludicrous. Yet what was the explanation for rejecting me? I was told that I had not sufficient Shakespearian technique.[3]

Adams dreamed of having his own Black theatre company. In 1944, when he played Jim Harris in Eugene O'Neill's *All God's Chillun Got Wings* for the Colchester Repertory Theatre, it was promoted as the inaugural production of Adams's Negro Arts Theatre. One critic, in the January 1945 newsletter of the League of Coloured Peoples, declared, 'I have seldom seen a better performance than that of Robert Adams. This was power on the stage, a power which caught all the light and shade and poetry of the play and made it quiver and burn with life.'

In interviews, an ambitious Adams spoke of his plans to stage work by Black writers as well as ballet and dance. He planned to extend the work of the Negro Arts Theatre by touring America and the British Empire under the auspices of the British Council. But Adams was unsuccessful. What became clear to Adams in the 1940s was that Britain was not going to accept – or fund – a Black theatre company.

In 1948, before he withdrew from acting and focused on a career in law, Adams played Bigger Thomas in *Native Son*, a repertory production staged at Boltons Theatre in Kensington. It was based on the celebrated novel of the African American Richard Wright. Reviews were good and *The Stage* (26 February 1948) praised Adams: 'It is chiefly a one-man play. Robert Adams dominates everything as the native son, not merely physically – he is a giant of a man – but as a towering personality capable of expressing instantly every changing emotion from tenderness to barbaric wildness, from diffidence to terror.'

Why wasn't Adams given an opportunity to play Othello? Perhaps the following letter he sent to a friend explains the reason. It was written in November 1948 at the same time he had qualified as a barrister:

> I had read for the Bar for several reasons. The Stage as it exists for the Negro is a most precarious type of existence. If one manages to succeed on the Music Halls like HUTCH [cabaret star Leslie 'Hutch' Hutchinson] then one may if one lives carefully look forward to a somewhat secure old age. But the position is different for the Dramatic Artiste, and that is my Field. The parts are few and far between and when one reaches Stardom the position becomes more difficult still. Apart from this the main objection is the Negro stereotype which seems to be the standard for the Coloured Artiste. When one raises objections one immediately hears that one's head is getting too big … When I was in the League of Coloured Peoples and working with Dr Moody it was I who passed on to him the idea of the Cultural centre, but

> after his death [in 1947], and my dissociation from the League I have to continue alone to get the idea over ... Perhaps one day when I shall have succeeded the Government may then realise how useful the idea is both as a contribution to the stabilising and continuance of Empire relationships, and to improved human relationships and understanding.[4]

After a long break from acting, Adams returned to the London stage in a supporting role in Eugene O'Neill's *The Iceman Cometh* (1958). By then a new, younger generation of African and Caribbean actors had replaced him: Edric Connor, Earl Cameron, Cy Grant, Frank Singuineau, Harry Quashie and the African American Gordon Heath. The casting of the latter as Othello by the BBC in 1955 angered Adams, who then protested to the corporation.

In 1946, when Robert Adams played the lead in BBC Television's *All God's Chillun Got Wings*, his sister was played by Pauline Henriques, who had trained to be an actress at the London Academy of Music and Dramatic Art in the 1930s. In 1947, Pauline was thrilled to be an understudy for one of the cast members of an American Negro Theatre production called *Anna Lucasta* when it transferred from Broadway to London:

> There was an enormous build-up for this American theatre company, and everybody was quite feverish because rumour had it that they were going to have British Black understudies. I was thrilled when I got the part understudying Georgia Burke. She was the oldest and frailest member of the cast, but she never missed a single performance! I was one of the understudies who never went on stage. *Anna Lucasta* had a tremendous impact on the British public and we knew almost immediately that the play was going to run.[5]

Pauline had always wanted to act, and in the late 1940s opportunities began to come her way, even though roles for Black actresses were rare. Pauline couldn't sing or dance, so she knew there would not be much work on offer. However, 1947 was a good year for her. Before understudying in *Anna Lucasta*, she was seen in *Caviar to the General* at the Lindsey Theatre and Noël Coward's *Point Valaine* at the Embassy Theatre. Pauline's understudy work in *Anna Lucasta* gave her the opportunity to put together a showcase for Black British actors and they called themselves the Negro Theatre Company.

Pauline recalled that, after the British understudies had rehearsed their parts for a few weeks, they realised that they were going to have a lot of evenings with nothing to do. She thought that it would be a good idea if they got together and did their own play readings:

> We chose one-act plays such as Thornton Wilder's *The Happy Journey*, a rather unusual play about some people going on a

Negro Theatre Company rehearsal in 1948, with Pauline Henriques directing Harry Quashie and Ida Shepley. (Author's collection, courtesy of Pauline Henriques)

journey in a car. We had to do quite a lot of miming, so it was an imaginative production. That was the nucleus of what we were beginning to think of as the British Black theatre movement. We didn't actually give ourselves a grand title. Many of us had so little experience in the theatre that we couldn't really compare ourselves to the American actors. But we had good strong voices, and decided to get experience by seeing if we could do this play and put it on as a serious production.[6]

Pauline then booked a little theatre in Hampstead in north London, and tried out *The Happy Journey* on a Sunday evening:

> We were very lucky because we had good support from the *Anna Lucasta* company. They were really wonderful. They gave us some publicity, came to the show, and got some of their friends to come as well. I think we did something really important with that production. It helped to launch people by giving them the confidence to get on and take parts when they came along.[7]

Next came the idea of staging a more ambitious production. Another *Anna Lucasta* understudy, Neville Crabbe, contributed an article called 'Negro Theatre Company' to the magazine *Checkers* in October 1948 about this venture. Music, dancing and slapstick comedy had been the parts allocated to Black artistes; Pauline, Neville and their colleagues aimed to change that situation. Support came from Frederick O'Neal from the American Negro Theatre and others who were in the cast of *Anna Lucasta*. There was also interest from the well-known Trinidadian folk singer Edric Connor, and from Dame Sybil Thorndike, who agreed to be the Company's patroness. Neville told *Checkers*:

> It was decided that while the training of artistes was of primary importance – it would also be good policy to put on a show to publicise the group and raise funds for the purpose

> of establishing classes in stage technique. It was agreed that Miss Pauline Henriques, who already had some years' experience as a producer and actress, should produce the dramatic items on this first programme.

The production, a mix of musical and dramatic items, was called *Something Different*. It was staged at Maccabi House in Compayne Gardens, West Hampstead, on Sunday, 4 July 1948. Among the women in the cast were Ida Shepley, who acted in an excerpt from *Golden Boy* and sang spirituals, and Mabel Lee, who sang several numbers. Crabbe told *Checkers*, 'There were many mistakes made, but many lessons learned. Perhaps the most important of these was the fact that the group learnt to appreciate the value of team-work, and it was this co-operative spirit that they are going to work for in the future.'

Negro Theatre Company rehearsal in 1948, with Harry Quashie, George Browne, Neville Crabbe and Ida Shepley. (Author's collection, courtesy of Pauline Henriques)

Checkers reported on a farewell party organised by the Negro Theatre Company on 31 October 1948, just before several of its members left to go on tour with *Anna Lucasta*. The evening's entertainment, produced by Pauline, included a mix of songs and dramatic interludes. Songs were provided by Ida Shepley. Rita Stevens, who had been understudying the role of Stella in *Anna Lucasta*, acted in Eugene O'Neill's 'miniature play' *Before Breakfast*.

In 1950, Pauline realised her ambition to act in a Shakespeare stage production. Kenneth Tynan cast her as Emilia in a touring version of *Othello* with the African American actor Gordon Heath in the lead. She said:

> I loved the excitement of working in the theatre, but I felt I could do better. I had a voice, but it wasn't until Kenneth Tynan cast me as Emilia in *Othello* that I realised what a wonderful thing it was to act in a Shakespeare play on the stage, and to speak those marvellous lines.[8]

The *Burnley Express* (14 October 1950) commented, 'The audience expressed their appreciation of Pauline Henriques' entrancing Emilia. For once one sympathised with Iago's fears. Miss Henriques completely captivated and culled the last ounce from her scenes with Desdemona.'

After the tour ended, Pauline found herself struggling to find fulfilling stage work: 'I eventually gave up acting because I realised it was useless to depend on it for a living, and I needed to have a full-time career.'[9]

Gordon Heath on the cover of *New Theatre* in 1947, the year he opened at the Wyndham's Theatre in *Deep Are the Roots*. (Author's collection/Mary Evans Picture Library)

16

Gordon Heath: A Very Unusual Othello

In 1950, Gordon Heath became the first Black actor since Paul Robeson to play Othello in Britain. It was an innovative production, staged for the Arts Council by the theatre critic and producer Kenneth Tynan, and it toured all over the British Isles. At first, Heath was reluctant to take on the role, as he feared being compared with Robeson. According to another cast member, Pauline Henriques, Heath was a 'slim, sensitive American actor who was really a folk singer, but he had a lot to give the theatre. We were all amazed that he had the range to play the part but he was a very good and a very unusual Othello.'[1]

Regrettably no film was ever made of Robeson's performance as Othello, although in the 1940s, when he played the role to critical acclaim on Broadway, a sound recording was produced. It was released on disc and has since been reissued on a CD. Thank goodness something has survived, and it serves as a testament to Robeson's artistry. His speaking of Shakespeare's lines is beautiful and very moving.

We do, however, have film of Heath playing Othello. Five years after the Arts Council tour, Gordon Heath played Othello again, this time for BBC Television. His director was the up-and-coming Tony Richardson. This was in the days of live television, when drama output on the BBC heavily relied on stage productions. Very few recordings of BBC programmes from this early period have survived; but the 1955 *Othello* is one of them. It was telerecorded (filmed on 35mm from a television monitor), and this rare footage gives us an opportunity to see Heath in action.

Heath's Othello is a revelation, and it is exciting to have an example of a Black actor playing the role on screen in an early production. Heath gives an extraordinary, gentle, softly spoken, bejewelled interpretation, so different from Laurence Olivier's over-the-top, fire-and-brimstone Othello covered in boot polish. And what a face Gordon has! It is an expressive face, and he made full use of the opportunities to register the turbulent emotions of Othello when the camera came in for close-ups.

'I admired Heath's interpretation of the difficult role, so quiet, so imposing in the early stages, so rapidly revealing a latent barbarism once jealousy has been kindled,' wrote John Minty in the *Birmingham Daily Gazette* (16 December 1955).

Philip Hope-Wallace, in the BBC journal *The Listener* (22 December 1955), described Heath's Othello as 'noble as an emperor of Abyssinia … vulnerable, and delicate in the finest manner of his race. That he should be duped was wonderfully believable – whereas so many white Othellos smeared with soot and porridge look so guileful, we never understand how they can be so naïve.'

There should have been more possibilities for Heath as an actor, especially on camera. Anything was possible. He could have been a delicious villain in a James Bond movie; I can imagine him sizing up Sean Connery. But, alas, it was not to be. In spite of his talent, his career did not flourish in the way that it should have done except, perhaps, in France, his adopted home. It was in France, from the 1950s onwards, that his friend Leslie Schenk saw some of Heath's best theatre work, both as an actor and director:

> Like Olivier, Garbo, Dietrich and Brando, Gordon had such presence that others vanished beside him. All the more interesting to note the great care with which he created his roles ... The actors Gordon directed were not Oliviers or Brandos for the most part, yet Gordon's analytical faculties permitted them to get inside their roles as they never would have been able to on their own. As great an actor as he was – on the level of Olivier, I would say – he was an even greater director.[2]

Gordon Heath was born in New York City in 1918, and his early stage roles included Shakespeare's Hamlet for the Hampton Institute in 1945. Later that year he made his Broadway debut in *Deep Are the Roots*, the critically acclaimed drama by Arnaud d'Usseau and James Gow about racism in America's South. Heath played Brett Charles, an American army officer who returns home to the plantation on which was raised by his mother, Bella. She is the devoted servant of the white family who own the plantation. While serving in Europe during the war Brett has been treated as an equal, but at home he is forced to confront the virulent racism of America.

Deep Are the Roots opened in London on 8 July 1947 at the Wyndham's Theatre, but not before Heath had embraced London's theatreland. The first production he saw was *Richard II* at the Old Vic, starring Alec Guinness. 'I continued to devour London theatre in great gulps,' he recalled in his memoir, which was also called *Deep Are the Roots*:

> The freemasonry of the profession and the publicity surrounding *Roots* gave me easy entrée to 'back stage' and, stage-struck and star-struck as I was, I walked into dressing rooms without presenting credentials. Noël (as far as England was concerned there was only one Noël – dieresis included – in the United Kingdom) invited me to see him, in his own bitchy comedy *Present Laughter*. He was mischievous and

> witty – wittier than the play – and adored by the public. I went around to the stage door. His valet stood outside his dressing room and as I approached said, 'Mr Heath?' which was typical of Noël's thoughtfulness and friendliness.[3]

Deep Are the Roots was a success in London, and Heath recalled how the setting of the drama and the interracial love story:

> Were strong enough to hold and effect an audience even if it was as the reviews put it, 'a problem with which Britain has little or no concern.' Our first night was triumphant and, as we held hands and bowed, the orchestra played 'God save …' and we looked forward to the future.[4]

Heath received enthusiastic reviews and was featured on the cover of *Theatre World* (September 1947). In the same issue, Eric Johns praised his acting, saying he had a 'fine voice and commanding stage presence – obviously an artist capable of getting completely under the skin of any real character, and therefore not limited to the playing of Othello and the Emperor Jones'. In the same article, 'On Being a Negro Actor', Heath explained how he chose his roles:

> I try not to think of myself as a Negro actor. When considering a part, I ask myself – Am I temperamentally suited to play it? And if I think I am, that is all that matters. I played Death in *Death Takes a Holiday* and Professor Higgins in *Pygmalion*. I felt that I understood them and could project them effectively on the stage. So, I played them. It is possible to cast Negroes for parts without calling any particular attention to their colour. The audience accepts them, as they accepted Canada Lee playing a 'white' part [Bosola] in Elisabeth Bergner's Broadway production of John Webster's Jacobean tragedy *The Duchess of Malfi*.

Gordon Heath and Betsy Drake in *Deep Are the Roots* on the cover of *Theatre World*, 1947. (Author's collection/Mary Evans Picture Library)

A positive outcome of the West End run of *Deep Are the Roots* was that it generated a lot of interest in the play from repertory theatres all over Britain. For several years, the role of Brett Charles provided work for Black British actors such as Earl Cameron (who had understudied Heath in the West End production) and Frank Singuineau.

In 1949 Heath relocated to Paris, where he lived with his partner, Lee Payant. They had been having a relationship in America for seven years. Together they ran a popular Left Bank café where they entertained customers with their folk singing. In 1995 I met one of their friends, Leslie Schenk, who explained:

> Heath discovered that the French were colour blind. He loved it. Lee was a wonderful guy. A sweetheart. He gave up his life

> for Gordon. They had a great deal of love for each other and they both liked Paris. It was such an exciting place in those days and, when it came to race and your private life, you were left completely alone.[5]

In the 1950s, Paul Breman, the writer, antiquarian bookseller and publisher, became friends with Heath and Payant, and wrote about their life in Paris in *The Independent*:

> The proud, haughty, temperamental, extrovert New Yorker found in Lee Payant, a gentle leprechaun from Seattle, a partner to make all of life possible and most of it enjoyable. For nearly 30 years they appeared every evening, seven days a week, in their crowded little folksong 'club', l'Abbaye, behind the abbey church of St Germain, entertaining starry-eyed youngsters and habitues of growing years who knew they would meet or hear news of every friend they had ever had in Paris.[6]

In 1950, Heath undertook the exhausting but exhilarating Arts Council tour of *Othello*. In towns where there were no theatres, the cast performed in working men's clubs, town halls or libraries. The tour opened at the Library Theatre, Manchester, on 28 August 1950. The reviews were favourable. The *Burnley Express* (14 October 1950) praised Heath for his range:

> From the confident, magnificent figure of the Commander of the Venetian army, ardent yet guileless in love, to the shaken, jealousy-ridden murderer, terrible in his hate. Heath's was a performance most convincing in his virility, its depths, and, above all, in its plausibility. There was a time when a man of colour was denied the part, yet who but such a man could plumb the depths of the wonderful agony of Othello?

Thereafter, Heath occasionally returned to Britain for acting work, and these appearances included BBC Television versions

Julian Somers (Iago), Valerie White (Desdemona), Gordon Heath (Othello) and two unidentified actors with Pauline Henriques (Emilia) in the Arts Council tour of *Othello*, 1950. (Author's collection/Mary Evans Picture Library, courtesy of Pauline Henriques)

of *Deep Are the Roots* (1950), *The Emperor Jones* (1953) and *Othello* (1955). There were also occasional stage appearances: the revue *Cranks* (1955), *The Expatriate* (1961), *The Man on the Stairs* (1964) and *In White America* (1964) with Earl Cameron. In the 1960s, Heath directed several American plays for the Studio Theatre of Paris, among them Arthur Miller's *After the Fall*, Thornton Wilder's *The Skin of Our Teeth* and Tennessee Williams's *The Glass Menagerie*. He acted in French as well as English in Paris.

Towards the end of 1990, I hoped to interview Heath. When I contacted his agent, she warned me that he was unwell but said that he might agree to a short telephone interview. Thankfully, he did agree, and so I made the call to him in Paris. Though he spoke in a whisper, which sometimes made it difficult to understand what he was saying, he told me how much he had enjoyed the opportunity to play Othello not once, but twice, in Britain. He described Kenneth Tynan's 1950 Arts Council tour as a breakthrough. He also recalled the demands of the live 1955 BBC Television transmission, directed by Tony Richardson. He was aware of the BBC telerecording that had survived in the archive of the British Film Institute. When I asked him if he had seen it, he replied that he had, during a visit to London with his mother in 1973. He was disappointed with the *technical* quality of some of the picture and sound. However, he agreed with me that it was a miracle a recording had somehow survived from a period when few television programmes were recorded and saved for posterity. He chuckled when I mentioned Robert Adams. He said, 'I played the role practically over his dead body.'

Gordon Heath and Lee Payant were together for a very long time, and when Lee died in 1976 it was a terrible blow to Gordon. He decided not to continue with l'Abbaye. Gordon died in Paris on 28 August 1991 from an AIDS-related illness. When I asked Leslie Schenk whether, had Gordon stayed in America, he would have had the fame that Sidney Poitier had in Hollywood films of the 1950s and 1960s, he replied:

> Gordon would not have enjoyed that kind of international fame and popularity. He preferred to remain a free agent … He loved the theatre, and a great cross he had to bear was that there were not enough roles for him to play, but he didn't make this a crutch, as some people do, not at all. He just got on with his life and made the best of things. He didn't let it destroy him.[7]

Edric and Pearl Connor at the Shakespeare Memorial Theatre in Stratford-upon-Avon in 1958. Autographed by Pearl at the National Film Theatre in 1998. (Author's collection/Mary Evans Picture Library, courtesy of Pearl Connor-Mogotsi)

17

Edric Connor and Pearl Connor-Mogotsi: Against the Odds

During my career as a historian of Black Britain, I have met and become close friends with many extraordinary and inspiring people, but there was one I couldn't meet: the Trinidadian folk singer, actor and storyteller Edric Connor, who had passed away in 1968 at the age of 55.

By the 1990s, I had learned a few things about his life and career, but sadly not a great deal was available and he was missing from the many film and theatre books I read. He was never included in any volumes of *Who's Who in the Theatre*, even though he was the first Black actor to appear in a Shakespearean role at the Stratford Memorial Theatre in Stratford-Upon-Avon. He was never mentioned in any books about the BBC, even though he was an important figure in radio and television broadcasting from the 1940s to the 1960s. Almost single-handedly he introduced Caribbean folk songs to the British public, and yet I discovered that it was impossible to find his recordings. Even today, only a fraction of his recording output is available on CD.

It was not until I met his widow, Pearl Connor-Mogotsi, at her home in Wembley in 1989, that Connor's story began to unfold. Pearl explained that her late husband's archive, including his private papers and material relating to his acting and singing career, was no longer in this country. She told me that when no British archive or university showed an interest in taking it she packed everything into boxes and sent them to Trinidad, but the boxes went missing in transit. Some years later Pearl was informed by a friend that they had mysteriously surfaced in New York's Schomburg Center for Research in Black Culture. Pearl told me she was confused about this, and was unable to find out the truth about what had happened, but she was thankful the archive had survived.

Then, in 1993, I researched his music in the BBC Music Library for the Radio 2 series *Salutations*. The series was my idea and there were nine programmes in total, all of them about Black British, Caribbean and African singers and musicians in Britain from the 1930s to the 1960s. Among those I profiled were Leslie 'Hutch' Hutchinson, Evelyn Dove, Reginald Foresythe, Ken 'Snakehips' Johnson, Winifred Atwell, Ray Ellington, Cy Grant and Shirley Bassey.

I devoted one of the programmes to Connor, so I was given some of his recordings to listen to. All of them were on vinyl: 78 discs or LPs. I shall never forget the time I spent in a small room in the BBC Music Library, with a record player, headphones on, listening to these old recordings from the 1940s and 1950s. Connor's strong, powerful, emotionally charged baritone moved me to tears. He was a great singer in the tradition of his idol, Paul Robeson. The recordings included his 1944 version of the Lord's Prayer, spirituals and calypsos. During this session, it all fell into place. It made sense to me what I was doing. I was making a radio documentary about Connor for BBC Radio 2. I had found his music. I had interviewed Pearl for the programme. Against the odds, I was making it possible for Connor's remarkable but forgotten life and many achievements to be recognised again. I felt that it was Connor who was making this happen. I don't know how or why, it is a mystery to me how such things *can* happen, but I did feel his presence around me, willing me to introduce him to the British public again.

In the BBC Music Library I was confronted by a member of staff who criticised me for taking the idea for the series to the BBC. Not only was he surprised that Radio 2 had commissioned it, he was dismissive of the idea and questioned why I was making a special case for *Black* British artistes. As far as he was concerned, most of the names I had selected for the programmes, including Connor, were long forgotten, and were no longer important. However, I knew what I was doing and, though I was deeply offended by the staff member and thereafter kept my distance from him, I carried on with the research and writing the scripts. *Salutations* was broadcast in 1993, and the series was a success. They were all excellent programmes, and were given high production values by Ladbroke Radio, the independent company that made them, but Connor's was the one I was most proud of. I played it again while writing this chapter and it still moves me to tears. The following year the series was recognised with a Race in the Media Award from the Commission for Racial Equality for Best Radio Documentary. It was presented to me by Rudolph Walker, who had begun his acting career in Edric and Pearl's Negro Theatre Workshop.

Since that time I have presented an illustrated talk about Connor for the National Film Theatre and written about him in journals, books (including *The Oxford Companion to Black British History* and *Under Fire: Black Britain in Wartime 1939–45*) and the *Oxford Dictionary of National Biography*. I wish I could have done more. I wish I could have persuaded someone to reissue his songs on a CD, but I have done as much as I can, against the odds.

In 2020 it pleased me that Connor was included in Patrick Vernon and Angelina Osborne's *100 Great Black Britons*, because Connor deserves to be there alongside Olaudah Equiano, Bernie Grant, Stuart Hall, Darcus Howe, Claudia Jones, John La Rose, Andrea Levy, Dr Harold Moody, Olive Morris, David Olusoga,

George Padmore, Mary Seacole, Benjamin Zephaniah and many others. Before this, he had been overlooked or marginalised by historians, including those who wrote about Black Britain.

Pearl told me that she met Connor in Trinidad in 1948 during his 'welcome home, hero' tour. Trinidadians were aware that he had made a name for himself as a folk singer and actor in Britain, and that he was a popular broadcaster on BBC Radio and Television. They welcomed him back with open arms and as a national hero. That same year, Pearl accepted Connor's proposal of marriage and soon joined him in London. Together they became instrumental in promoting the life and culture of the Caribbean in post-war Britain. In 1956 they started the first agency for Black and minority ethnic actors. There had never been anything like that in Britain. While Connor spent most of his time working as an actor and singer, Pearl worked hard to increase employment opportunities for Black artistes.

During that first encounter in 1989, Pearl was a rich source of information about many of the people I was interested in. She even put me in touch with several actors I wanted to interview, including Pauline Henriques, Isabelle Lucas and Frank Singuineau. In fact, she telephoned Frank when I was at her home. He was also a Trinidadian, and they had known each other for years. She told Frank that he should talk to me.

Pearl may have been a driving force in the promotion of Black actors in post-war Britain, but she told me that in the 1970s she 'burned out' and, after closing the agency in 1976, she withdrew from the business of show business. Pearl was a feisty, determined trailblazer, but it eventually became too much for her and affected her wellbeing. When I interviewed the actress Carmen Munroe, she told me that Pearl had been 'the mother of us all':

> She was a pioneer. She was wonderful. She was such a dynamic personality that she made things happen for us. She took chances. She took risks. She pushed and opened doors.

> And we learnt a lot from her life and the way she handled situations. We are all very grateful to her.[1]

Connor left Trinidad in February 1944 to come to Britain to study structural engineering. He carried in his luggage notes on Caribbean folk songs, which he had been studying and collecting for many years. Within two weeks of his arrival, Connor made his debut as a singer on BBC Radio in *A Musical Anthology*. Many more radio appearances followed, including an edition of *Travellers' Tales* in November 1944, which focused on songs and stories from Trinidad. Pearl told me that after the war ended in 1945, an effort was made to show some appreciation for all the people from across the British Empire who had contributed to the war effort:

> All our young men had gone and some of them had died. The people of those little Caribbean islands had all stuck their necks on the block. I think the British government and the BBC wanted to show some appreciation. They weren't locking us out yet. And this helped Edric get started in the business. He had a lot of talent, a lot of ideas. He was ahead of his time. Edric came to Britain at a good time. Doors were open to him. He didn't have to kick too hard.[2]

Pearl didn't tell me that one of the young men who didn't return to Trinidad was her brother, George Nunez, who had joined the RAF and flew in a Lancaster bomber, but was killed in action in 1943.

Pearl married Connor in London on 26 June 1948 and she described him as a relaxed, very handsome man:

> A very quiet man. He was a contained, disciplined person. Charming and soft-spoken. He was rarely agitated. He always gave the impression of being at ease. He was an independent man who believed in pulling his weight. He was always

> well dressed, he looked after himself, he believed he was an ambassador for Trinidad. He was an avid student. A self-made person. He read widely. He had a great collection of books on all sorts of subjects. He embraced literature, music and so on. He was self-taught. He was always learning. Always practising and developing his art. He was a perfectionist and believed in what he was doing. He wanted to be the best.[3]

In post-war Britain, Connor became a much-loved and respected ambassador for the arts and culture of the Caribbean. For example, in 1951 he proudly organised concerts for the Trinidad All Steel Percussion Orchestra during their ten-week stay. They made their debut at the Festival of Britain on London's South Bank. He released recordings of Caribbean folk songs: *Songs from Trinidad* and *Songs from Jamaica*, and, where he could, he would try to bring such music into a film or stage production.

In 1956, when he was cast as Daggoo, the harpooneer in John Huston's acclaimed film version of Herman Melville's novel *Moby Dick*, Connor made an important but easily overlooked additional contribution to the film, with Huston's consent. Daggoo is required to sing a sea shanty to inspire the men in their boats during the whale hunt. Connor chose 'Hill an' Gully Rider', a 150-year-old Jamaican folk song. Pearl remembered how Connor was fully aware that it would be recognised and appreciated by Caribbean audiences:

> 'Hill an' Gully Rider' is about the undulating land in Jamaica, but it was the undulating sea of *Moby Dick*, the ocean where they were looking for the whale, where Edric introduced the song. And it is a lyrical, lilting song, a beautiful thing that John Huston loved. And Edric was always trying to do that, introduce Caribbean music into the films he worked on, and letting people know about our songs. So Huston allowed him to have an input, which was very good for Edric, and good for the film.[4]

With her husband, Pearl met and befriended some of the great names in the worlds of theatre and music in post-war Britain. One of them was Paul Robeson, during his 1949 visit. He came to their home at 47 Lancaster Gate in Paddington:

> Edric had his heroes and he was a great admirer of Paul Robeson. We all admired him, and thought that he was one of the greatest artists, and a great man. We knew about his history. Edric hero-worshipped him. Paul was Edric's role model and Edric wanted to be like him. Not long after we were married, Edric brought him to our house for tea. I remember thinking my teaset wasn't up to scratch, so I had to rush out and buy a new china teaset! For me that was important, but I don't think Paul Robeson even noticed, he was so busy talking to Edric![5]

Robeson dominated Edric and Pearl's sitting room. He was a very big man. Huge and towering. Connor was big too, about 6ft 2in, but Pearl said even he looked small against Paul:

> We all looked up to Paul, ideologically and physically. Like Edric, he had great charm with a soft and gentle nature. The feeling between the two men was mutual. Paul liked this young man. Edric was fifteen years younger and he knew what was happening in our world, the Black world, in America and throughout the world. Edric wanted to hear about the civil rights struggle in America, and what Paul was doing. Paul admired him for that and, when he came to our home, it was a great honour he paid to Edric, and Edric never forgot it.[6]

Keen to develop his acting skills, in 1947 Connor accepted an invitation from Sir Stanley Marchant, Principal of the Royal Academy of Music, to play the Lord in a drama student's production of Marc Connelly's *The Green Pastures*. This led to

Left to right: James Clarke, Paul Robeson, Ulric Cross, Ida Shepley and Edric Connor, watching three singers perform in London, 1949. (Author's collection, courtesy of Pearl Connor-Mogotsi)

the start of his professional stage career. There were other plays, and musicals, including *Calypso* (1948), *The Shrike* (1953), *The Jazz Train* (1955) and *August for the People* (1961). In *Summer Song* (1956) a young Thomas Baptiste also appeared, and understudied Connor. He said:

> I remember Edric with great affection, admiration and a certain amount of sadness because, in the time he lived, he was a very important artist in this country, but he wasn't really appreciated. He was a great performer. He had a wonderful presence. He looked somewhat like a magisterial Jomo Kenyatta: tall, bearded, with square shoulders. And he sang magnificently. His voice was unique. It had a timbre like nobody else's except, perhaps, Paul Robeson. When I worked with him, I learned a great deal.[7]

Thomas said that he learned something that became important in his life. Connor always wanted to succeed, to prove that he was as good as anybody else. Thomas suspected he felt that he had to be twice as good as his contemporary British artists:

> But where he failed was not to realise he had the right to fail, and I think that's a pity. In that area I benefitted from him because, for myself, I know I have the right to fail. I must have failed hundreds of times! But not Edric. He felt if he did anything which did not work out positively, it was a reflection on his people. Black people. And I don't think anybody should carry that burden or responsibility on their shoulders. You can only do what you can as well as you can. But he was a great artist and should be remembered.[8]

In 1958, the innovative director Tony Richardson wanted to present a Black actor for the first time at the Stratford Memorial Theatre. He invited Paul Robeson to play Gower in *Pericles*. Richardson had Gower's lines set to music and sung but, when Robeson was unable to accept, he recommended Connor. Pearl described Gower as 'a beautiful role' and it was a high point of Connor's career in the theatre. The theatre critic for *The Stage* (10 July 1958) commented:

> Gower is played as a definite narrator of events, outside the development of the story, as with a small band of companions he links scene to scene, comments, or offers needful details which are not embodied in the principal story. He is a chorus who sings – this is a worthwhile innovation – a mirror and a guide, and is played with moving sincerity and simplicity by Edric Connor.

In 1956, Edric and Pearl founded the Edric Connor Agency which later became known as the Afro-Asian Caribbean Agency. For the next twenty years the agency represented artists, writers and performers from the Caribbean, Malaysia, India and Africa. Said Pearl:

> Edric was looked upon as a father figure in Britain's Black community, so when performing artists came from the Caribbean they came straight to our London home. In those days there were very few places where they could meet. When we moved to a new home in Crediton Hill in Hampstead, we had a very large living room with a fire, and this would be used as a meeting place. I would say that 90 per cent of African, Asian and Caribbean people who wanted to join the acting profession came to us for help and advice. We'd let them sleep on the floor until they could find a place to live. Calypsonians, dancers, Lord Kitchener himself. All those people came to us.

Edric Connor as Gower in *Pericles*, 1958. (Author's collection, courtesy of Pearl Connor-Mogotsi)

> Edric was a generous man, and he felt committed to helping these people. He was a giver.[9]

Edric and Pearl decided to do something for them, and they became the first agency to represent them. Pearl said she was 'full of beans' and would push them like mad, but producers kept inviting Black stars and actors over from America:

> At the Royal Court [in 1958] they brought over Vinnette Carroll and Earle Hyman for Errol John's *Moon on a Rainbow Shawl*. It was set in Trinidad, but they brought over Americans! And then Earle came back the following year for *A Raisin in the Sun*. This happened because they had a certain celebrity status which gave them the edge on Britain's Black performers. Americans were appreciated more. They were also considered better actors, which was unfair. We had no media attention. No press coverage. No general promotion. In Britain our Black actors had to make it on pure merit and friends. We even fought with Equity to give more chances to Black actors, because they kept bringing over Americans. We had a very difficult time convincing casting directors that our Black actors could act. We were always second-rate citizens, so it was very difficult to break through.[10]

In 1958, Pearl represented the agency at a meeting of British Actors' Equity to discuss whether ethnic artists were getting a fair deal. Pearl raised the problem of too many parts being given to Americans: 'British coloured artists are barred from rising above a certain level. American coloured artists are imported, which is unfair because the roles could be played equally well or better by resident British artists and there are no reciprocal arrangements whereby British subjects are given similar facilities in America.'

Pearl gave the example of Errol John's play *Moon on a Rainbow Shawl*, set in Trinidad, for which three African Americans, Earle

Hyman, Vinnette Carroll and John Bouie, had been imported to play leading roles, 'without West Indian artists in this country being considered'. Equity's representative, Hugh Jenkins, suggested that British 'coloured' artists should apply for the formation of a special committee to deal with the problems, rather than form their own group of British artists within Equity itself.[11] It would take another ten years of campaigning before Black British actors succeeded in forming their own pressure group within Equity.

In an attempt to create new acting opportunities for those they represented, and to support newcomers, in 1961 Edric and Pearl founded the Negro Theatre Workshop (NTW). It was launched at London's Lyric Theatre with a play called *A Wreath for Udomo*. Connor led a cast that also included Earl Cameron, Lloyd Reckord and Evelyn Dove. The NTW's most active period was 1964–67. It is perhaps best known for its productions of Wole Soyinka's *The Road* at the Theatre Royal, Stratford, which was part of the 1965 Commonwealth Arts Festival, and *The Dark Disciples*, described as 'a blues version of the St Luke Passion'.

With Pearl as its driving force, the NTW was an ensemble of professional and amateur actors, directors and writers performing original works in community centres, town halls, churches and cathedrals up and down the country. It also represented Britain at the First World Festival of Negro Arts in Dakar, Senegal. It was an ambitious project that hoped to maintain continuous productions of dramas, revues and musicals, and in doing so give Black actors experience and Black writers a chance to see their work performed. It was the NTW's ambition to develop and improve standards among Black actors and technicians in every branch of the theatre. The founding members also included Lloyd Reckord, Bari Johnson, Horace James, George Browne, Bobby Naidoo, Nina Baden-Semper, Tony Cyrus and Ena Cabayo.

With the support of Michael Slattery, who arranged for the NTW to have free use of the Africa Centre in London for

Lloyd Reckord, Earl Cameron and Evelyn Dove in *A Wreath for Udomo* at the Lyric Hammersmith, 1961. (Author's collection, courtesy of Pearl Connor-Mogotsi)

rehearsals, a number of productions – many touring – were organised between December 1964 and December 1965. These included *Bethlehem Blues*, *The Dark Disciples* and *The Prodigal Son*. Most of these productions were performed in churches throughout London because they offered their facilities free of charge. A BBC Television production of *The Dark Disciples* was broadcast at Easter 1966 in the *Meeting Point* series. George Browne (Jesus) and Bari Johnson (Judas) headed a largely unknown cast.

Throughout its life, the NTW's development was restricted by lack of funds or a permanent home. Negotiations were undertaken for an annual grant from the Arts Council, as well as trusts and charities, but these were handicapped by the company's lack of a permanent home and performance space. For some time negotiations with the Greater London Council for a lease to occupy Wilton's Music Hall looked promising, but in the end this came to nothing.

Although the NTW was comparatively short-lived, it was a seminal organisation. Its productions helped to train a number of actors, dancers, writers and directors and it built the reputations and raised the profiles of many in the profession. In this way it enabled them to obtain their equity cards.[12]

Rudolph Walker was a young Trinidadian actor who was starting his career when he became one of the 'newcomers' who benefited from the NTW. In 1991 he reflected:

> We went up and down the country doing plays in church halls and town halls. It was great. It's important to emphasise that this earlier generation of actors made an important contribution, just as we made and are continuing to make our contribution. I think one of the sad things is that there's a tendency now to criticise the older actors and to accuse them of playing certain kinds of roles, be they so-called Uncle Tom roles or whatever. What people don't understand is what that generation was going through professionally was just a stage. We must acknowledge that they made their contribution. The youngsters are where they are today because of what actors before me, and actors like me, have been doing.[13]

Edric Connor suffered a stroke and passed away on 16 October 1968 at the age of 55. He had written an autobiography in 1964, but the manuscript remained unpublished until 2007, when it finally saw the light of day as *Horizons: The Life and Times of Edric Connor*.

In 1971, Pearl married the South African singer and actor Joseph Mogotsi. When she passed away in 2005, she was described by Margaret Busby in *The Guardian* (2 March 2005) as 'a peerless historical resource ... she retained an energy that belied her age and was a much loved and iconic figure at cultural events in Britain, Trinidad and South Africa.'

Pearl was survived by the two children she had with Edric. Their daughter, Geraldine Connor, who passed away in 2011, is best known for having written, composed and directed *Carnival Messiah*.

In 1991, when I interviewed the Jamaican actor and director Lloyd Reckord, I asked him about Edric and Pearl and what they had achieved. His face immediately lit up:

> Edric and Pearl were constantly campaigning on behalf of us Black artistes. They were the salt of the earth, especially Pearl who worked solidly, like all small agents, for the people she represented. But, of course, with all small agents who represent young artistes she brought them up from nothing, only to find that after getting their first or second big break they left her and took on a bigger or more powerful agent to represent them. It's very sad. It has nothing to do with colour. It's a cruel business. We all know it's a cruel business.[14]

Lloyd described Pearl as a 'guardian angel' to all young Black actors. She never represented him as an agent but he knew Pearl as a friend:

> I would go to her place and she always had something for me to eat. She knew that young actors were always hungry, and she was wonderful. Her house was always a home for people like us. And she just worked continually, pushing Black actors, quarrelling with the powers-that-be, arguing 'Why can't Black actors get this sort of part?', and generally working for us. Edric, meanwhile, was working on his acting and singing career, but Edric had a rough time and has to be admired for what he achieved despite the many obstacles.[15]

When I interviewed Pearl in 1993, she reflected on Edric and the collective memory loss of what they and other Black artistes had achieved in Britain:

> I would think coming this country right after the war, as Edric did, and getting into BBC Radio, and moving among the people, he did a great deal of good for our own community. Setting standards. He saw himself as a self-appointed ambassador for his country, Trinidad. We believed we had a country worthy of recognition. Those were the things that attracted me to him … We Black people were being judged all the time, so we felt we had to show our best. But also we are human. We're made of the same stuff. If you cut us, do we not bleed?[16]

Pearl believed that Edric had a sense of his destiny, but he died much too young. He hadn't achieved everything he wanted to do:

> He moved into this country and took every opportunity he had here to make a lasting mark so that those who came after him would know that it was possible. Possibilities was what he was about, that if you had the chance, you could take it and make good … In Britain there is no record of the contribution we have made to the performing arts. Edric did good work, but it is lost in time and space. There is no memory in Britain for us. There is a hole in the ground, and we fall into it.[17]

Author, director and actor Clifton Jones, who founded the New Negro Theatre Company at Stratford East's Theatre Royal in 1960. (Author's collection, courtesy of Terry Bolas)

18

Surviving and Thriving: Later Black Theatre Companies

In the 1950s there was the West Indian Drama Group, and in the 1960s the New Day Theatre Company, New Negro Theatre Company, Ira Aldridge Players and Pan-African Players. The 1960s also saw the establishment of Edric and Pearl Connor's Negro Theatre Workshop, which managed to survive a little longer than its predecessors. In 1969, Frank Cousins founded the Dark and Light Theatre, and this was followed by the Keskidee Centre in 1971, founded by Oscar Abrams.

The Temba Theatre Company followed in 1972, launched by the actors Oscar James (originally from Trinidad) and Alton Kumalo of South Africa. They had worked for several years with the Royal Shakespeare Company, playing small roles from 1967 to 1971. Kumalo named Temba after the Zulu word for 'hope' and 'trust', and in its early years the company staged the first British productions of Athol Fugard's *Sizwe Bansi is Dead* and Mustapha Matura's *Black Slaves, White Chains*.

Two years later, in 1974, the actor Cy Grant was the co-founder, with John Mapandero, of Drum, a London-based

Black arts centre which provided training workshops for aspiring Black actors.

In 1956, the Unity Theatre activist Joan Clarke founded a drama group at the West Indian Students' Union in Kensington. The following year the West Indian Drama Group welcomed a new member, an aspiring actress called Carmen Munroe. She had arrived in Britain from Guyana in 1951. It was to be the beginning of a long and successful acting career. Munroe made an early stage appearance as Marthy Owen in the group's production of *Anna Christie* by Eugene O'Neill. This was produced by Joan Clarke and may have been the first time *Anna Christie*, first produced in New York in 1921, had been performed by an all-Black cast. It opened for a five-week run at the Unity Theatre on 13 November 1959. When Carmen was interviewed by Brenda Emmanus at the Museum of the Moving Image in 1996, she recalled:

> It was a great time. I joined the West Indian Students' Union. We met in this huge, wonderful building on the corner of Collingham Gardens, and students met other students. There were people from all walks of life. Mostly artists, and writers like Andrew Salkey and C.L.R. James. There was a lot of activity. It was marvellous. And if you couldn't get home, you put two chairs together and slept on them until morning. Also, we felt we were related to a bigger picture. When we came to England we quickly realised the Mother Country didn't know us, what we were, or what we were capable of. We had this low expectation until we became part of the West Indian Students' Union, and began to raise our level of expectation. We had this drive. We had to replace all the old attitudes with a new feeling. The feeling was that we were all away from home, so this meeting place helped us form relationships which were strong, very rich, supportive, caring and, above all, honest. I say that now because honesty is missing, and I do regret it. And I'm talking about the acting profession.[1]

Some of the actors Munroe befriended included Leonie Forbes and Charles Hyatt from Jamaica, and Horace James from Trinidad. She said:

> Horace would translate and transform Chekhov, and other classics, and take us all over Britain, performing wherever we could, in town halls, at universities. I remember travelling up to Leicester University, staying overnight, sleeping rough, and all the time being helped and pushed by Horace and Pearl Connor, who also came from Trinidad. We didn't work for any money. We just knew we had to do it, because we felt there was a gap in the understanding of our culture, where we came from and who we were.[2]

In 1960, Munroe joined the New Negro Theatre Company, launched by the Jamaican actor Clifton Jones at the Theatre Royal in Stratford East. Jones had established himself as an actor as the sailor in the Theatre Royal's 1959 production of *A Taste of Honey*, but he believed that Black British actors had more to offer. He directed a double bill: William Saroyan's *Hello, Out There* and Paul Green's *No 'Count Boy*. The company members included Johnny Sekka, Gloria Higdon, Mark Heath, Neville Munro and Tamba Allen. *The Stage* (28 April 1960) described it as 'a promising start ... Very wisely, the group were under rather than overambitious in their first production. Both plays were on the short side but they were sufficient to give us an exciting taste of the potentialities of the company.'

In November 1960, Clifton Jones and the company then presented a double bill of two of his own plays, *La Mere* and *The S Bend*, at the same theatre. Both were set in Jamaica. The two plays offered insights into the hopes and dilemmas of West Indian youths. *La Mere* explored the relationship between a mother and her son as they wait in vain for her husband and his father to come home. *The S Bend* focused on a boy's support for his imprisoned uncle, a Rastafari leader.

In 1966, the Pan-African Players, based in London, in association with the Negro Theatre Workshop, presented *Wind Versus Polygamy* at the Dakar Festival in Senegal. The cast included Earl Cameron and Horace James alongside a number of West African actors who had established themselves in Britain. These included Willie Jonah and Willie Payne. The Nigerian playwright Yemi Ajibade directed the production. When it was produced for BBC Radio in July 1966, the Jamaican actor Frank Cousins, a graduate of the Guildhall School of Music and Drama, narrated it.

In 1971, the Guyanese architect and cultural activist Oscar Abrams launched the Keskidee Centre. This was Britain's first arts centre for the local Black community and it was located in Gifford Street in Islington, near King's Cross. The Keskidee Centre became a popular meeting place for youths and those wishing to discuss and promote African and Caribbean politics and arts. It also developed its own exciting drama company, the Keskidee Theatre Workshop, which attracted multicultural audiences.

The workshop dedicated itself to Black theatre under the artistic direction of the African American Rufus Collins. Keskidee aimed to produce plays by new and established Black dramatists. An early production, opening on 22 June 1973, called *Voices from the Frontline*, included three dramatic pieces by Jamaican writers: *Babylon Ghetto* by Dam-X (Steve Hall), *Voices of the Living and the Dead* by Linton Kwesi Johnson (who was the first paid Library and Resources Officer at the Keskidee Centre) and *The Bus Rebel* by Eseoghene. In 1973, Jamal Ali directed his musical drama *Black Feet in the Snow*, which he then adapted for BBC Television's *Open Door* series in 1974. T-Bone Wilson had two plays produced: *Body and Soul* (1974), directed by Yemi Ajibade, and *The Jumble Street March* (1975). Howard Johnson directed Wole Soyinka's *The Swamp Dwellers* (1975) with a cast that included Imruh Caesar and Willie Payne.

In 1975, the actor Louis Mahoney contributed an article to *The Stage* in which he acknowledged a new publication called

White Media and Black Britain, edited by Charles Husband. Mahoney quoted one of the contributors, the Sierra Leonean playwright Yulisa Amadu Maddy, known to his friends and colleagues as Pat Maddy. Maddy told how his experiences as Head of Drama at the Keskidee Centre showed 'the horrible loss of cultural identity common among Black youths born in Britain'. He is scathing about the Arts Council, local authorities and commercial financiers, 'who readily plunge thousands of pounds into the coffers of the National Theatre, the Royal Shakespeare Company and other white cultural ventures but are loath to even part with £300 for an all-Black production except under white guidance'.[3]

The Keskidee Centre closed in 1992 but, in 2011, to celebrate the fortieth anniversary of its opening, Islington Council honoured its memory with a Green Plaque on the building. It was unveiled by David Lammy MP and former resident artist Emmanuel Jegede.

In 1974, the actor Cy Grant and the Zimbabwean John Mapandero joined forces to launch Drum, a Black arts centre based in London's Covent Garden. In addition to showcasing Black arts, Grant explained that workshops were introduced to assist in the training of young Black actors. He believed that Drum was a place where this could be achieved. A director was brought over from New York to run the workshops. In 1991, Grant said:

> It's essential for a Black person to see him/herself as Black. Identity is absolutely important. If you don't define yourself, someone else is going to do define you. So, we have to start by defining ourselves and finding pride in ourselves, and looking at our own history and at our own culture, and seeing the things that are worthwhile.[4]

South of the River Thames, from 1969 to 1975, the Dark and Light Theatre staged many productions under the artistic direction of Frank Cousins. Though some sources have erroneously claimed it was Britain's first Black theatre company, it was more than likely the first to have a home base, which was Longfield Hall in Knatchbull Road, Brixton. This was made possible with support from the Arts Council, Lambeth Council and several charitable foundations.

To commemorate fifty years since the Dark and Light Theatre was founded, in October 2019 it was formally recognised by Dr Jak Beula of the Nubian Jak Community Trust. A Nubian Jak Community Trust blue plaque was unveiled by Cousins at Longfield Hall. The ceremony was attended by many other important Black theatricals, including Yvonne Brewster, who directed Dark and Light's first Jamaican pantomime, and several actors, including Carmen Munroe and Rudolph Walker.

In his speech, Dr Beula described Cousins as a true visionary: 'He was an actor who talked the talk, then put his money and considerable talents where his mouth was, and walked the walk. I am so pleased he will witness his pioneering contribution to British theatre immortalised with a blue plaque in his lifetime.'

Nubian Jak Community Trust plaque at Longfield Hall, Brixton. (© Stephen Bourne, 2021)

At the ceremony, Cousins said: 'The Dark and Light was bound to happen. But how? Finding Longfield Hall was the beginning. Without premises you have nothing.'

In addition to the plaque, in 2019 the Longfield Hall Trust received funding from the National Lottery Heritage Fund for a project exploring the history of Cousins's Dark and Light Theatre.

With the Dark and Light Theatre, Cousins staged a number of Black plays from America, Africa, the Caribbean and Britain. He also created a touring circuit for the company, taking some of the productions to Black communities across Britain. These included Athol Fugard's *The Blood Knot* (1971), Amiri Baraka's *The Slave* (1972), Robert Lamb's *Raas* (1972), Eugene O'Neill's *The Emperor Jones* (1973) and Wole Soyinka's *The Trials of Brother Jero* (1973).

The Stage newspaper singled out some outstanding performances, including Anton Phillips in *Raas*: 'very good at suggesting the intelligence that is groomed into boredom and violence by lack of job opportunity and unthinking authority' (12 October 1972); and Thomas Baptiste in *The Emperor Jones*: 'plays the gradual disintegration of swagger into abject fear with remarkable control' (3 May 1973).

Emphasising that his aim for the company was truly multiracial, Cousins found the time to stage a fundraising all-star variety show on 4 July 1971 at the Fairfield Hall, Croydon. The American singing legend Eartha Kitt topped the bill while the BBC Radio DJ Tony Blackburn compered the show. Others who took part were Tony Hatch and his wife Jackie Trent, Cy Grant, Ram John Holder, Charles Hyatt and Derek Griffiths.

For Christmas and New Year 1972–73, Cousins presented *Anansi and Brer Englishman* at Longfield Hall, directed by Yvonne Brewster. It was advertised as the first ever West Indian/English pantomime. Anansi, part spider and part man, is a national folk hero in Jamaica. His character is taken from the folk tales of the Ashanti in West Africa. Anansi stories are often humorous and teach children lessons about the consequences of bad decisions, and that it is better to be clever than to be strong. *The Stage* (11 January 1973) noted that the audience, mostly Black children from Brixton, 'was loud in its approval'.

Cousins's pioneering work also included forming a youth theatre for the local Brixton community.

At the unveiling of the blue plaque at Longfield Hall, Carmen Munroe summarised the importance of the achievements of Cousins and his wife: 'Born of the greatest struggles and obstacles facing Black performers, the Dark and Light Theatre came into being thanks to the courage and the compassion of Frank and Gaie Cousins.'[5]

Errol John. (Author's collection, courtesy of Terry Bolas)

19

Barry Reckord, Errol John and the Royal Court

> We were very fortunate in having the Royal Court, and Oscar Lewenstein and George Devine who were the greatest friends Black artistes ever had. They gave us Sunday nights and the Theatre Upstairs, and put a lot of effort into getting Black artistes off the ground.
>
> *Pearl Connor-Mogotsi*[1]

In her introduction to *The Royal Court Theatre: Inside Out*, Ruth Little described the Royal Court in London as a theatre that has presented 'some of the most influential plays in modern theatre history … in fifty years of the English Stage Company at the Royal Court (1956–2006), the theatre has generated heated debate over its identity, mission and output.'[2]

The present Royal Court Theatre was built on the east side of Sloane Square and opened in 1888. Among its productions was *Back to Methuselah* (1928) by George Bernard Shaw. The cast featured some of the great names of British theatre including Gwen Ffrangcon-Davies, Laurence Olivier, Cedric Hardwick, Edith Evans and Ralph Richardson.

This impressive cast also included Emma Williams in a supporting role as the 'Negress' or Minister of Health in *Part 3: The Thing Happens*. It is set in 2170 and the action takes place in the official parlour of the President of the British Islands. Williams was not a white actress in blackface, but a West African who had joined Will Garland's Negro Operetta Company in 1913 at the age of 29. Williams then vanished from the records until 1926 when she resurfaced as Doll, the seventeenth-century London housekeeper of Samuel Pepys, in the West End play *And So to Bed*. After the Shaw play, Williams returned to the Royal Court for Eugene O'Neill's *All God's Chillun Got Wings* (1929) playing the mother of Jim Harris (Frank Wilson). Following a 1931 revival of *And So to Bed*, Williams vanished again. There is no further information about her. Such was the fate of many Black British stage actors and actresses from the early years.

The Royal Court ceased to be used as a theatre in 1932, but it reopened three years later as a cinema until bomb damage during the 1940 Blitz closed it. The theatre was reconstructed, refurbished and reopened in 1952 and George Devine was appointed its artistic director at the recommendation of the left-wing Oscar Lewenstein, a founder member of the English Stage Company (ESC).

The ESC opened at the Royal Court in 1956 as a subsidised theatre producing new British and foreign plays, together with some revivals of the classics. Devine wanted to discover and encourage new writers who shared his passion for radical new theatre and in doing so produce serious contemporary plays. Consequently, Devine and the Royal Court introduced theatregoers to the work of such dramatists as Eugene Ionesco, John Osborne, Arnold Wesker, N.F. Simpson, Samuel Beckett and Jean Genet. It was Devine who produced the ESC's third production, staged in 1956 at the Royal Court: John Osborne's controversial *Look Back in Anger*. The director was Tony Richardson, who had recently worked with Gordon Heath at the BBC in *Othello*.

In 1956, Richardson began to open doors for Black artistes at the Royal Court. The first was the former music-hall star Connie Smith, who was cast as Tituba in Arthur Miller's *The Crucible*. Smith then had a small role in Carson McCullers's *The Member of the Wedding* (1957), also directed by Richardson. For the complex leading role of Berenice Sadie Brown, a housekeeper and 'mother earth' figure in a white Southern home, he cast the African American jazz singer Bertice Reading, who had made her London debut in the revue *The Jazz Train* (1955). Reading was directed by Richardson again at the Court in *Requiem for a Nun* (1957).

Barry Reckord

Barry Reckord became Britain's first post-war Black dramatist to have a production staged in a major London theatre, in 1958 with *Flesh to a Tiger*. Reckord went on to write five plays for the Royal Court between 1958 and 1974 'on wildly different topics, but each one resonated in some way with the theatre's penchant for the radical, the political, and the subversive'.[3]

Having been awarded Jamaica's prestigious Issa scholarship (founded by the philanthropist Elias Issa), Reckord had travelled to Britain in 1950 to read English at Emmanuel College, Cambridge. After graduating, his teaching work – in Jamaica, Britain and Canada – complemented his playwriting. Reckord's first play, *Della*, was set in the working-class community of Trench Town in Kingston. It was first presented, as *Adella*, as a small, fringe production at the Theatre Centre in St John's Wood, London in 1954. It was directed by his brother Lloyd Reckord.

A reviewer in *The Stage* (22 July 1954) praised the writing: 'Scenes are well written and the author often draws poetry from the very expressive dialect in a way that is reminiscent of Irish drama. The principal characters are completely convincing.'

In spite of this, Reckord did not believe that he would continue writing for the theatre:

> God knows what inspired me to write in the first place. I had no background in theatre; the only theatre that I knew in Jamaica I was fairly contemptuous of. It was either English pantomime where I dressed up and played the lion and was ashamed of myself, or it was Bim and Bam, which was broad slapstick, not very funny except when it was very rude Jamaican comedy. I knew a little bit of both of those worlds; but neither of them impressed me, so I can't understand why I got wrapped up in theatre.[4]

In 1958, *Della* was produced at the Royal Court with the new title of *Flesh to a Tiger*. Tony Richardson took on the role of director, fresh from the success of *Look Back in Anger*, and cast the British-born jazz singer Cleo Laine in her first acting job. Richardson recalled in his autobiography that Reckord's play was 'clumsy in its construction' but 'had at moments a passion of language which was extraordinary'.[5]

Reckord viewed Richardson as a very flamboyant director, and recalled, 'he liked the poetry of the play':

> It was poetic, it didn't have enough drama, it was good in pieces, it didn't have that sort of crude dramatic thrust of, say, Arthur Miller's *The Crucible*. It was a similar kind of play, it was about religious superstition, which interested me from a political point of view. I hated the business of Jamaica being a place where you had a tabernacle on every street corner and a murder, and I was politically interested in religion. I wasn't really interested in theatre, but that's why I wrote the play … it should have been gripping drama, but I wasn't that sort of writer … I think the Court did it because it was exotic and the language was poetic, and this is what they expect from Black people.[6]

Cleo Laine and Pearl Prescod in Barry Reckord's *Flesh to a Tiger* 1958. (Author's collection, courtesy of cast member Pearl Connor-Mogotsi)

In 1961, Reckord returned to the Royal Court with *You in Your Small Corner*. In this play, he examined the relationship between a young man from the Caribbean and his white working-class girlfriend. It transferred to the New Arts Theatre. Reckord then adapted it for ITV's *Play of the Week* television anthology series in 1962 and *The Times* (6 June 1962) said, 'Mr Reckord has devised a clear, lively play about believable individuals rather than skin-deep stereotypes.'

Reckord's experiences of teaching in a London secondary school provided him with material for his next play, *Skyvers*, directed by Ann Jellicoe. It premiered at the Royal Court on 7 April 1963 as a Sunday night production (a fully rehearsed play without décor or costumes and staged for one or two nights only). *Skyvers* then graduated to a proper run at the Royal Court on 23 July 1963. This was Reckord's crushing indictment of the secondary school system and what it was doing to aimless, restless working-class lads.

Said Irving Wardle in his biography of George Devine:

> This study of a school malcontent was one of the closest exercises in British social analysis ever to appear at the Court … The subject of *Skyvers* was one after Devine's heart, and he considered Reckord's play as by far his best; although at the time, in spite of a meteoric debut by David Hemmings (who instantly vanished into films), the production fared little better at the box office than the other new shows.'[7]

The theatre critic for *The Times* (8 April 1963) described this as Reckord's most accomplished work so far: 'It deserves a far wider audience … the impeccable cast could hardly be bettered.' The following year *Skyvers* was presented by students of RADA, directed by Lloyd Reckord. *The Stage* newspaper (2 July 1964) described the play as 'bitterly realistic'.

In 1968, Reckord took part in a Black playwrights' benefit at the Round House in Chalk Farm. Leroi Jones, Wole Soyinka and Obi Egbuna were the recipients of the benefit evening while they were facing imprisonment for alleged anti-government activities in England, Nigeria and the USA.

In 1969, Reckord's *Don't Gas the Blacks* was presented at the Open Space Theatre. It was revived at the Greenwich Theatre in 1971 with a new title, *A Liberated Woman*. *Skyvers* was revived in 1971 at the Theatre Upstairs and the Roundhouse and *X* was produced at the Theatre Upstairs in 1974.

In 1972, Reckord wrote *In the Beautiful Caribbean* for BBC Television's *Play for Today* anthology series. It was set in Jamaica and followed the events leading to a Black Power uprising. In 1997, when he reflected on the state of Black British drama, Reckord told David Johnson:

> Over the decades my writing got more rigid; it got more interested in ideas. I start a play … Shakespeare says hold a mirror up to nature; nature bores the arse off me. I cannot stand people's love lives or their struggles with money; they

> are too repetitive, and this is what soap opera is about. I don't give a shit about that. The only thing that worries me as a Black man is that we need better writers and better politicians than white people, and I want to push forward ideas. I like the theatre enough to want to push them forward … I'd like to see Black theatre in England carry the positive discrimination thing as far as it will go and pick up young Black writers who they can sense want to write about ideas, want to describe what it is like to be Black in England.[8]

When Reckord passed away in 2012, Margaret Busby wrote in *The Guardian* (17 January 2012), 'Reckord's ambitions to earn a living as a playwright went largely unfulfilled, partly due to his uncompromising espousal of unfashionable ideas – about religion and politics, especially sexual politics – which did not necessarily make for good drama.'

Black and Unknown Bards

On 5 October 1958, Cleo Laine, the star of Barry Reckord's *Flesh to a Tiger*, was invited back to the Royal Court to take part in a celebration of African American poets. The performance was called *Black and Unknown Bards*, and it also featured the actors Gordon Heath and Earle Hyman. In her autobiography, Laine described the performance as 'a remarkable evening of caustic, funny, hip and religious poetry, by Black American poets such as Margaret Walker, Countee Cullen, Sterling Brown, Langston Hughes and many more … I was deeply moved by the whole experience.'[9]

Errol John, Part 1

America's Earle Hyman had made his London stage debut in *Anna Lucasta* in 1947. When he joined Cleo Laine and Gordon

Heath on stage at the Royal Court, he was about to open there in Errol John's play *Moon on a Rainbow Shawl*. As an actor, the Trinidadian John had scaled the heights when he played Othello at the Old Vic in 1963. As a dramatist, he was best-known for *Moon on a Rainbow Shawl*.

After leaving school in Trinidad, John earned a living as a journalist and commercial artist. His ambition was to become an actor. To gain acting experience, he joined the Whitehall Players, an amateur group. For them, he acted, designed, directed and wrote three one-act plays. John arrived in Britain in 1951 and joined the BBC's West Indies play-reading group, which broadcast in the 'Caribbean Voices' literary segment of the series *Calling the West Indies*. It was here that he befriended Pauline Henriques, who remembered Errol with affection:

> I immediately recognised his lovely personality and tremendous voice. But he was a rather shy, reserved, retiring person who found it difficult to be with a group of actors who were taking the job of acting seriously, but also enjoying it and being very joyous about it. This wasn't Errol's scene. He found it quite hard to do that. I can remember encouraging him to come out of his shell and to enjoy acting – because Black actors have this ability to bring a sort of inner joy and vivacity to the roles that they play. I tried to encourage this in Errol. I was right there behind him, doing a good counselling job on him. I think it gave him a good start.[10]

Pauline did give him a good start, because John immediately began to find acting work on the stage as well as in films, television and radio. His earliest London stage appearances included Haemon in Sophocles' *Antigone* (1951) and the title role in Derek Walcott's *Henri Christophe* (1952), both directed by Errol Hill, at the Hans Crescent student centre. John then became a professional actor with *Cabaret Caribbean* (1952) at the Irving Theatre, directed by Edric Connor; *Cry, the Beloved Country* (1954) at St Martin-in-the-Fields; and *The Member of the Wedding* (1957) at the Royal Court, among others.

As a writer, he beat 2,000 competitors to win the 1956 *Observer* Drama Competition with *Moon on a Rainbow Shawl*. The judges included the well-known actors Alec Guinness and Peter Ustinov, the young director Peter Hall, and Michael Barry, the Head of BBC Television Drama. John had written the play in 1955 during a period when he felt dissatisfied with the roles he was expected to play. With *Moon on a Rainbow Shawl*, he intended to create work for Black British actors, especially those from the Caribbean. It focused on Ephraim, a young trolley bus driver who dreams of leaving Trinidad and coming to the 'mother country'. He knows that he is doomed if he cannot make his escape. With Ephraim, John brilliantly captured the feelings and ambitions of many Caribbean people in the immediate post-war world. They believed a new life in Britain would provide them with the standard of living denied to them in the repressive colonies.

One of the other competition judges was Kenneth Tynan, the drama critic who had cast Gordon Heath and Pauline Henriques in his production of *Othello* in 1950. Tynan loved John's play and later praised it in his preface to *The Observer Plays*:

> There was never much doubt that the first prize would go to *Moon on a Rainbow Shawl* ... its lyricism, compassion ... made it the obvious choice. The title alone presaged writing of uncommon quality, arousing hopes which the play more than fulfilled. It is a hauntingly, hot-climate, tragi-comedy about backyard life in Trinidad. The dreams and disasters of two coloured families are poignantly interwoven, and expressed in a stark, gay, ribald, sing-song idiom that our theatre has certainly never heard before ... Mr. John orchestrates his themes like a master.[11]

The play was first performed when John was invited by the BBC to adapt it for radio with a different title, *Small Island Moon*. It was broadcast on 27 May 1958 with a cast that included John (as Ephraim), Barbara Assoon, Sylvia Wynter, Andrew Salkey, Lionel Ngakane and the veteran Robert Adams. *Moon on a Rainbow Shawl* opened at the Royal Court on 4 December that same year. Most reviews were excellent. *Punch* (10 December 1958) described Errol as 'a writer of understanding, sensitive to the shades of human weakness'.

In the *Manchester Guardian* (6 December 1958), Philip Hope-Wallace described John's play as:

> Vivid and, on the whole, well-acted … it earns some respect for its sincerity, its language, which has a bumpy sing-song vitality of its own, and also for its loyalty to a certain idiom which derives ultimately from Sean O'Casey – i.e. naturalism, with lyrical overtones. But it does not, unfortunately, persuade us to take a deep interest in its characters.

In the *Observer* (7 December 1958), the novelist Doris Lessing enthused: 'It has a warmth and power which makes most of our indigenous products look thin. In spite of the obvious difficulties in casting an all-coloured play, it is consistently well acted.'

The 'obvious difficulties' in casting the play, as mentioned by Doris Lessing, concerned the Court's decision to invite three African Americans to play leading roles: Earle Hyman, Vinnette Carroll and John Bouie. By 1958, Edric and Pearl Connor's agency was established, and Pearl was convinced that Britain had enough African and Caribbean artistes to fill all the roles. She later said:

> This was a shock to us … we thought, 'What a loss of an opportunity. Here is a Caribbean play which we could do very well and yet this stereotypical practice is happening.' We were very disappointed … There was unfortunately,

> at that time, a bias about either using Black Americans, or casting Caribbean actors with American accents ... because the American media and the American projection was so enormous that British people were comatose under its influence.[12]

After *Moon on a Rainbow Shawl*, John continued his acting career, and in 1962 he appeared at the Old Vic as the Prince of Morocco in *The Merchant of Venice*. Though he played a small role, critics such as R.B. Marriott singled him out for praise, commenting that John's performance remained 'stamped on the memory because of his measured dignity and beauty of speech' (*The Stage*, 25 October 1962).

John was asked to remain at the OId Vic to play Othello in January 1963. He was a replacement for Mogens Wieth, a white Danish actor who had died of a heart attack in London in September 1962. However, John was subjected to harsh criticism. Gordon Heath felt that he was too 'lightweight' for the role. So did the director John Elliot, who had worked with Errol at the BBC: 'Errol was essentially a film and television actor, what I call a "close-up" actor. He didn't have the voice training to reach a large audience in the theatre. Perhaps that was one of the causes of his disquiet.'[13]

America's James Earl Jones, who had played Ephraim in the 1962 New York (off-Broadway) production of *Moon on a Rainbow Shawl* with Vinnette Carroll and Cicely Tyson, also saw John's *Othello*. Jones said it was 'lambasted' by the critics:

> Errol and I talked about the problem, about how the critics had dealt with him. He was convinced that the critics in England did not want to yield to an Othello who was a Black African. They were willing, though, for Othello to be a Moor, a Semitic, a North African, but not a Black African, sub-Sahara. Any purely Black-skinned human being playing Othello, Errol believed, went against the grain of British

> sensibility, although I must admit, he himself was one of the most uptight, defensive Othellos I had ever seen.[14]

The following year, those who lambasted John's Othello were the same critics who embraced Laurence Olivier's blackface Othello. If Jones's assessment of Errol John's portrayal is correct, surely it would have been preferable to see an 'uptight, defensive' Black African Othello than Olivier's crude minstrel show? Not, it appears, if you are a white, middle-class, male English theatre critic.

Other Black Playwrights at the Royal Court

In addition to Barry Reckord and Errol John, the Royal Court showed an interest in staging the work of other Black dramatists. In 1960, Lloyd Reckord directed Derek Walcott's one-act plays *Sea at Dauphin* and *Six in the Rain*.

In 1959, Wole Soyinka was studying at the University of Leeds when his play *The Lion and the Jewel* was read at the Court. It made an impression with 'the ease of transitions between song, dance and mime in a representation of real life, rich with ritual in an African village.'[15] Soyinka was invited to join the Writers' Group and in 1959 he directed the Sunday night production of his unpublished satirical play *The Invention*.

In 1966, Soyinka's *The Lion and the Jewel* was produced at the Court. The film director Lindsay Anderson praised the play's 'rich and poetic combination of primitivism and sophistication'.[16] *The Times* (16 December 1966) said:

> This is the third play by Wole Soyinka to appear in London since last year, and this work alone is enough to establish Nigeria as the most fertile new source of English-speaking drama since Synge's discovery of the Western Isles ... Even

> this comparison does Soyinka less than justice, for he is dealing not only with rich folk material, but with the impact of the modern on tribal custom: to find any parallel for his work in English drama, you have to go back to the Elizabethans.

Another innovative Royal Court production was Jean Genet's *The Blacks* (1961), which Oscar Lewenstein described as 'the best play in our season'. Following a successful run in Paris as *Les Negres*, Genet's 'Clown Show', as he described it, was staged by the Court with a Black British cast. Genet used the framework of a play within a play to expose racism and racial stereotypes while at the same time exploring Black identity. Lewenstein said it looked 'absolutely wonderful' and acknowledged in his autobiography that there were very few opportunities for Black actors to act in good plays with decent parts for them:

> The Court from quite early on had been in the forefront of those trying to change this situation and had presented several plays by Black writers, but it was hard to find an experienced Black cast to cope with the difficult language of Genet's play, and in fact we did not succeed in this. The cast looked wonderfully right. They came from the West Indies, all parts of Africa, and one actress from India, but the audience found their accents difficult to understand. When someone told Genet this, he said 'make it even more incomprehensible' … Despite its almost complete failure with the critics and the public this is one of the productions I look back upon with most pleasure.[17]

Three years after *Flesh to a Tiger*, Cleo Laine hoped to return to the Court in *The Blacks*, but following an audition she was told she was 'too white' for the role – even though the cast cover their faces with white masks.

In 1958 the Jamaican Sylvia Wynter completed *Under the Sun*, which was bought by the Royal Court, but it doesn't appear

Theatre programme for Jean Genet's *The Blacks* at the Royal Court Theatre, 1961. (Author's collection/Mary Evans Picture Library)

to have been produced there. Instead it was broadcast by BBC Radio on 5 October 1958 with a magnificent cast that included Laine, Elisabeth Welch, Pauline Henriques, Nadia Cattouse, Pearl Prescod and Sheila Clarke.

Another ten years would pass before a Black female writer would be given the opportunity to have her work produced at the Royal Court. This was an American, Adrienne Kennedy. In 1968 there was a double-bill of her plays *Funnyhouse of a Negro* and *A Lesson in a Dead Language*. Kennedy had been influenced by the work of the dramatist Edward Albee (who became her mentor) and the absurdist movement. 'My plays are meant to be states of mind,' she said.

Funnyhouse was first produced in Albee's workshop and then presented in 1964 in an off-Broadway production. On

10 December 1964 it was broadcast on BBC Radio in a landmark series called *The Negro in America*. In the play, the central character, a biracial woman called Sarah, struggles to come to terms with her identity as she splits into a number of characters, including Jesus, the Duchess of Hapsburg, Queen Victoria and the dynamic Congolese leader Patrice Lumumba. Kennedy transforms the stage into a manifestation of Sarah's mind and uses these historical figures to represent her both Black and white ancestry, and her inner self.

Richard E.T. White summed up her achievement in *Black Women in America: Theater Arts and Entertainment*:

> Few writers have been so successful at breaking the bonds of realism on the stage and challenging notions of personal, racial and historical identity. Her plays use masks, carnival images, magic, and poetic incantations to take us into a world where deeply personal dreams and nightmares become ceremonies of transformation and awakening consciousness.[18]

Errol John, Part 2

As far as Errol John was concerned, British theatregoers would have to wait until he was ready to direct a revival of *Moon on a Rainbow Shaw*. In 1986, almost thirty years later, Philip Hedley, the Theatre Director of the Theatre Royal in Stratford East, agreed to stage it, and asked John to direct it. One of the cast members was Joanne Campbell, who later gave an intriguing insight into his directing style:

> Errol John was a reserved, disciplined man. He was also a true gentleman. I loved working with him. For our production of *Moon on a Rainbow Shawl*, Errol insisted that we have Barbara Assoon and Errol Hill brought over from Trinidad to be in the cast. In rehearsal Errol encouraged the younger actors to

> learn about Trinidad from the older actors. He was interested in the younger actors and how we were growing and developing. Errol rehearsed the play like a film. For instance, he gave us, the actors, the kind of attention and detail of a film. He would come very close to us, like a camera. Directors soon have an intuition, and become technically proficient but, for me, a director who is also an actor has more intimate energy. They are 'in' the scene with you. But it was interesting working with a *Black* director who had acting experience. Errol brought the essence of film to theatre.[19]

Two years later, John granted London's Almeida Theatre permission to stage the play for Akintunde Productions. Over lunch, he told Joanne that he had only agreed 'on condition he direct': 'He was hurt and angry when the Almeida asked Maya Angelou instead. Errol never bad-mouthed people; he always found something positive to say. But it was difficult to know what he thought about Maya. He wasn't angry with her, just with the lack of respect shown to him.'[20] The Almeida production closed on 4 June 1988, and Errol John passed away in London just a few weeks later, on 10 July.

Philip Hedley described him in *The Independent* as a man who got a reputation for being 'difficult', 'which is often the case with actors who ask intelligent questions of directors, or who are prepared to take a stand on principle. He was a respected, highly professional artist and a very proud man, with many qualities which justified his pride.'[21]

The Trinidadian playwright Mustapha Matura also reflected on Errol:

> In the heat of the cultural and political explosion of the 1960s, we all thought he was an 'Uncle Tom'. It was only after I encountered obstacles myself that I realised that he was quite a remarkable man. He fought a lot of racism and shit which sent him round the bend. He simply refused to take

it lying down, uncompromising – more like a Jamaican than a Trinidadian. He was considered a trouble-maker, which meant that his work wasn't done.[22]

Pearl Connor-Mogotsi had the greatest respect for Errol, and expressed her regret that he did not receive the acclaim he deserved:

Errol became more and more frustrated about not achieving what he thought he would achieve … He was a very versatile man, a brilliant actor and a talented writer … He had the sort of achievements which, when they happen to a white actor, mean that person receives a great deal of recognition. But that didn't happen for Errol, and eventually he was brought down to his knees with the frustration of not getting things done. His talent was always there but the ability to project it wasn't. He virtually dropped out altogether … Isolated, lonely, feeling forgotten and dejected, he died alone in his bed. He was found by his landlady. It was a tragic end to one of our most talented artistes.[23]

Clockwise from top left: Cleo Laine in 1958 (Author's collection); *Valmouth* (1959) (Photo: David Sim); *A Midsummer Night's Dream* (1967); and *Show Boat* (1971) (Photo: Reg Wilson).

20

Cleo Laine: Shakespeare and All That Jazz

Cleo Laine is best known as a jazz singer and in this guise, since the 1950s, she has been a force to be reckoned with. As a singer, Cleo is up there with Frank Sinatra and Ella Fitzgerald. In spite of managing to overcome obstacles to stake a claim as an actress of natural talent and ability, she is not up there with Judi Dench and Maggie Smith. Too often this important aspect of her long and eventful career is overlooked or overshadowed by her jazz singing. In 1988 she said: 'I've a wide variety of acting experience. I can play tragic and dramatic roles, and over the years a comic streak has crept in which is developing nicely, so as I get older I'll be able to play funny old ladies!'[1]

Cleo was born in Southall, Middlesex, in 1927. She was the daughter of Alexander Campbell, a Jamaican, and Minnie Hitchen, who was born and brought up in Swindon in Wiltshire. Said Cleo:

> My father was Black and my mother white. You don't realise it at the time, you accept your mother and don't think of her as being different from anyone else. It's only later on in life

> you realise how heroic those women were in the 1920s and 1930s. In those days, depending on where they lived and their standing in society, it was pretty tough for white women with Black husbands. My mother's society was working class and I can remember her chasing people with a broom when anything unkind was said about her children.[2]

After leaving school, Cleo worked as an apprentice hairdresser, milliner, pawnbroker's assistant, librarian and shoe repair shop manageress before her singing career took off. Cleo had been singing professionally with John Dankworth and his band for several years before an opportunity came to take on the dramatic lead in a play. She once said: 'I couldn't have acted if I hadn't sung with John first and sung the kind of material that I'd been singing with him – I had to get something out of these songs instead of just singing them so when I did start acting, that was my marvellous background.'[3]

The play was Barry Reckord's *Flesh to a Tiger* and it was produced at the Royal Court in 1958. Cleo auditioned for the lead, a young Jamaican woman who has to choose between modern medicine and a voodoo practice called Obeah, to cure her sick child. Its director, Tony Richardson, was not aware of Cleo's singing career and chose her following an audition where she sang the torch song 'Stormy Weather' and expressed, he said, 'raw strength coupled with tremendous stage presence'.[4] Said Cleo:

> Learning the lines of a play is like learning thirteen difficult Cole Porter lyrics. I tried to learn them like a song but using my stage movements as a guiding framework instead of the melody of a song. It isn't really difficult to diversify. If you take what you're doing as a singer seriously then you become very aware of words. The feel of words. Then acting and poetry follow easily.[5]

Cleo said that she didn't have to work hard to affect a Jamaican accent: 'Although I had always thought my father never had one, I found my ear was suddenly picking up the musical sounds and nuances of his voice as I read and re-read the part.'[6] Theatre critics praised her. Said the critic for the *Daily Sketch* (22 May 1958): 'Cleo Laine made an astonishing debut as an actress last night ... she brought a beautiful speaking voice and genuine acting ability to the role.'

Most of the cast of *Flesh to a Tiger* were from the Caribbean and some of them became close friends of Cleo. They included Nadia Cattouse from Belize who, in addition to acting, became a central figure in the folk music revival of the 1960s. There was also Pearl Prescod, a Trinidadian with a larger-than-life personality. Cleo remembered her as an earth mother who possessed a most powerful voice. In 1964 Cleo, Nadia and Pearl were reunited for an award-winning television documentary with a concert format called *Freedom Road* which featured songs from slavery to the civil rights movement. Cleo sang Billie Holiday's 'Strange Fruit'. In 1966, not long after joining Laurence Olivier's National Theatre company at the Old Vic and playing Tituba for them in *The Crucible*, Pearl sadly died at the age of 46.

When Cleo was launched into the world of drama with *Flesh to a Tiger* she admitted it was a big challenge: 'I had been thrown into the deep end of a new world and I was learning to swim daily. Sometimes I felt I was on the verge of drowning, but my built-in survival kit always came to the rescue, and I'd get away without egg on my face.'[7]

Very little attention has been given to the work of the Black presence in BBC Radio and so it is worth noting that a host of African and Caribbean actors and writers worked in the medium in the post-war years. *Under the Sun* (1958) was written for BBC Radio by Sylvia Wynter, a Jamaican novelist, dramatist, critic and essayist. It was a powerful play about a mountain community in Jamaica and Wynter provided strong roles for an impressive cast of women including Cleo, Elisabeth Welch, Pearl Prescod, Pauline Henriques and Nadia Cattouse. Also in 1958, Wynter adapted Lorca's *Yerma* as *The Barren One* and transposed it to the Caribbean. Once again, Cleo played the lead role.

It was only a matter of time before Cleo was offered a role in a stage musical and the opportunity came when she was asked to replace the African American jazz singer Bertice Reading in Sandy Wilson's *Valmouth*. When it opened in October 1958 at the Lyric, Hammersmith, located a few miles away from the West End, it shocked some of its audiences and was understood by relatively few. Wilson had adapted it from the 'scandalous' works of the innovative gay novelist Ronald Firbank (1886–1926). The controversy was caused by some of its characters who behaved outrageously. Said Keith Howes in *Broadcasting It* (1993): 'No cause for alarm. What may at first appear as an Edwardian retelling of Sodom and Gomorrah is a captivating musical for innocents of all ages … where characters do what comes naturally, if not strictly within the bounds of convention.'[8]

Bertice Reading was cast as the excitable Mrs Yajnavalkya ('Mrs Yaj') the masseuse with 'magic fingers' who offers advice and her services to the inhabitants of a spa town. In spite of its strangeness, *Valmouth* had a great score and Reading stopped the show every night with the song 'Big Best Shoes'. By the time it transferred to the Saville Theatre in the West End on 27 January 1959, Reading had returned to the United States and Cleo stepped into the role of 'Mrs Yaj'. Its West End run lasted 102 performances to more confused and offended audiences, but they kept on coming. The critic for *Plays and Players* (March 1959) loved it: '*Valmouth*, in short, bewitches by its riches as the opening chorus swore it would.' Said Graham Collier: 'Cleo's performance on the original cast recording of *Valmouth* shows a warmth and vitality that is not as apparent on her previous more conventional recordings.'[9] Cleo had a great time and made friends with the cast, especially Fenella Fielding and Doris Hare:

> the company was a joy, each one giving me a lesson in stagecraft … The last week of *Valmouth* was very emotional for all of us, like the end of a mass love affair … Thank goodness there are those in the theatre who are keepers-in-touch who, once they experience that close relationship, like to hold on to the memory with constant friendship. I bless them.[10]

Cleo found herself a replacement for the second time when, in 1961, Lotte Lenya withdrew from an Edinburgh Festival production of Kurt Weill and Bertolt Brecht's opera *The Seven Deadly Sins*. It later transferred to the Sadlers Wells Theatre in London. The leading role of Anna had been created for Lenya in 1933 by her husband, Kurt Weill, and the playwright Bertolt Brecht. Lenya complained that the tone of the production was not in keeping with her style of playing. Graham Collier found Cleo's approach to Weill fresh and exciting:

> She once again shows her enormous awareness of lyrics – which are, as one might expect, several notches above those she is usually presented with. There is more meaning to them and there is characterisation within which she can act. She wanted to record *The Seven Deadly Sins* but [said Cleo] '… it's not allowed. Lotte Lenya loves the piece – it's her baby and she won't give permission to record it. Perhaps I'll do it when she dies!'[11]

The composer and jazz pianist Richard Rodney Bennett also enjoyed Cleo's interpretation of Anna: 'What I did love her doing was Kurt Weill's *The Seven Deadly Sins* – it was one of the best things I've ever heard her do. It wasn't basically a very complex piece so she was in her element. She could put her entire self into it.'[12]

In complete contrast to *The Seven Deadly Sins*, Cleo's next stage musical, *Cindy-Ella (or I Gotta Shoe)*, was a jazzed up version of the Cinderella story, by Caryl Brahms and Ned Sherrin who later recalled: 'We opened in that awful Winter of 1962–63 and the snow was high outside the Garrick Theatre. It was a potent combination with Cleo Laine, Elisabeth Welch, Cy Grant and dear George Browne, who had that wonderful deep voice. It was a very attractive production.[13]

The critic for *Theatre World* (February 1964) loved it:

> A quartet of immaculate artists acting out the Cinderella story provided an evening of remarkable charm which in spite of flashes of sophistication, was often touching in its very simplicity … Cleo Laine, possessor of just about the loveliest, most caressing voice in the land, which she uses to dazzling effect in the title role, was also seen as a skilled and incisive comedienne with impeccable timing.

While Cleo's stage career was developing nicely, her film career was restricted to brief appearances as a singer. However, in 1963, she made an important contribution to director Joseph Losey's intense psychological drama *The Servant*, starring Dirk Bogarde. The moody theme song, 'All Gone', written by Harold Pinter (who also wrote the film's screenplay) and sung by Cleo in various atmospheric John Dankworth arrangements, is possibly the first use of a song lyric as part of a script. It is not only the film's warning voice of the gathering darkness surrounding two of its main characters, Susan (Wendy Craig) and the spoilt, wealthy Tony (James Fox), but it also draws attention to Tony's growing emotional and possible sexual dependence on his man-servant, Barrett (Bogarde).

In 1964 Cleo took the leading role in a new adaptation of the ancient Greek comedy *Lysistrata* by Aristophanes which was presented at the Bath Festival. It was written for Cleo by her husband John Dankworth (they had married in 1958) and the jazz saxophonist Benny Green. In addition to being a production with an anti-war message and a women's rights theme, this ambitious version of *Lysistrata* also featured a ballet. Reviews were mixed. Said Edward Mason in the *Sunday Times* (14 June 1964): 'Only Cleo Laine, in the title role, emerged unscathed.' Cleo told the *Daily Mirror* (13 June 1964): 'This is a new adventure, some fresh field I have always longed to explore. Those who condemn it as sacrilege cannot look any farther than their classical whims. I think it's all rather fun myself.'

In 1966 Cleo extended her acting range even further with the role of Andromache in the Greek tragedy *The Trojan Women* by Euripides at the Edinburgh Festival. The cast also included Flora Robson as Hecuba. The production was made possible by the innovative theatre director Frank Dunlop who launched his Pop Theatre Company at that year's Festival with *The Trojan Women* and Shakespeare's *The Winter's Tale*. Cleo later said that Dunlop had a lot of faith in her as an actress.[14]

For her performance in *The Trojan Women*, Cleo received enthusiastic praise from a number of critics including Allen Wright who, in *The Scotsman* (30 August 1966), described her as 'one of the glories of this Festival':

> She recharged the faltering batteries of Frank Dunlop's production … She even seemed to give fresh inspiration to Flora Robson, whose remarkable performance as Hecuba grew in dignity and compassion … Cleo Laine's Andromache, with vibrant voice and majestic anguish, is so moving that anything which follows must be anti-climax. Her last moments with Astyanax are as beautiful and pitiable as anything I have experienced in the theatre … Pop Theatre's first enterprise at the Festival has been valuable – not least because it has discovered in Cleo Laine a considerable tragedienne.

It was only a matter of time before Cleo attempted her first Shakespearean role. Before that happened, in 1964 she made a television special with her husband called *Lyrics by Shakespeare*. Cleo sang the Bard's words and sonnets set to music by, amongst others, composers that included John Dankworth and Duke

Ellington. That same year she released a critically acclaimed record album *Shakespeare and All That Jazz*. Said Gerald Lascelles in *The Tatler* (24 June 1964): 'The fantastic range of her voice enables her to tackle with graceful ease the contrasting styles required of her.' Cleo said:

> It is one of my favourite albums, one that I am most proud of. My voice was coming together and feeling strong, and I had a feeling that I was able to tackle anything that was put in front of me. There was a lot of challenging music, some of which has never been surpassed in my repertoire, combined with some glorious settings of Shakespeare's great words and sonnets. They have never left my programme: they are timeless and a part of me.[15]

Three years later, Frank Dunlop invited Cleo to make her Shakespearean debut on stage in a Pop Theatre production of *A Midsummer Night's Dream* at the Edinburgh Festival. Said Cleo: 'Frank was the first director to ignore the fact that as far as classic plays were concerned, I was thought of as a Black actress.'[16] It is possible that Dunlop's production of *A Midsummer Night's Dream* was the first in Britain to have one person – Cleo – playing two roles: Titania and Hippolyta. Another member of the cast, Robin Bailey, doubled as Theseus and Oberon. With music by John Dankworth, it had an impressive cast that also included Jim Dale. In spite of mixed reviews, it later transferred to the Saville Theatre, London, where the critic for *What's on in London* (6 October 1967) singled out Cleo for praise: '[Her] sultry Titania is very engaging.'

Cleo's singing talents and versatility was clearly suited to musical theatre but since *Valmouth* she hadn't been offered anything. In 1968 John Dankworth and Benny Green joined forces again and wrote a new musical with a dual role for her. They called it *Boots with Strawberry Jam* and focused on the dramatist George Bernard Shaw and his relationships with two famous actresses: Ellen Terry and Mrs Patrick Campbell. The actor

John Neville was running the Nottingham Playhouse at the time and he happily agreed to stage the production and play Bernard Shaw. *Boots with Strawberry Jam* premiered on 28 February 1968 and some reviews were favourable. The critic for the *Birmingham Daily Post* (1 March 1968) described it as 'thoroughly enchanting' and added that Cleo 'as Mrs Campbell has a real part to play which she does with convincing passion'. Sadly, the production didn't do well enough to transfer to London's West End.

Another serious role awaited her at the Marlowe Theatre in Canterbury. In 1970 she played the lead in Henrik Ibsen's *Hedda Gabler*. This was a triumph. The critic for the *Herne Bay Press* (30 October 1970) enthused:

> It was not until the third act that Cleo Laine immersed herself into the part, and from then on she was magnificent. Her sheer personality power gave Hedda Gabler all the credence necessary, and her stagecraft did the rest … There is no doubt that Cleo Laine can be a very notable dramatic actress.

One of Cleo's greatest successes in British musical theatre came when she played the role of Julie in a revival of *Show Boat*. This was considered one of the greatest American musicals since its debut on Broadway in 1927. It never lost its original magic and this was mainly because Jerome Kern (music) and Oscar Hammerstein II (main lyricist) composed a magnificent score. Much publicity was made about the casting of Cleo, with claims being made that she was the first non-white actress to play the role of the tragic mixed-race Julie. Cleo welcomed the opportunity to break with that tradition. The character had always been played by white actresses on stage and in films, such as MGM's 1951 version with Ava Gardner in the role. The new version was lavish with elaborate sets and costumes and, when it opened at the Adelphi Theatre on 29 July 1971, it was a huge success. It ran for 910 performances, the longest production of *Show Boat* ever staged.

Before accepting the offer, Cleo expressed concern that Julie had only two songs in the show: 'Can't Help Lovin' That Man' and 'Bill'. Her request for a third song to be added was granted and 'Nobody Else But Me', the last song written by Jerome Kern before he died in 1945, was added. Cleo's singing of 'Bill' stopped the show every night and theatre critics praised her performance. Said John Higgins in *The Times* (30 July 1971): '[her] performance of "Bill", sung simply, regretfully and with great tenderness is alone worth the price of the Adelphi admission ticket.' In *The Stage* (5 August 1971), R.B. Marriott described her portrayal of Julie as 'memorable: natural, deeply moving'.

Cleo later said that her appearance in *Show Boat* had led to a 'disintegration of my out-and-out jazz image'.[17] However, she was neglected for a long time before she made a return to musical theatre. Her career as a jazz singer continued to soar, especially in America. Then, in 1980, John Dankworth wrote the music and lyrics for *Colette* which starred Cleo as Colette, the famous French author and woman of letters. It opened at London's Comedy Theatre to mixed reviews. Said Cleo:

> I suppose *Colette* was my worst failure. John wrote both the book and the music, but it was my idea. I researched Colette for a long, long time ... I always felt that Colette was right for me and I had this burning desire to play her. We had a lot in common: a Black relative – her grandfather, her love for her mother, and her mother as an influence. We also shared a love of words, for me not so much as a writer but as a singer and actress. Aspects of her philosophy of life appealed to me as well. John's music was marvellous. Eventually people will realise it was good regardless of the reviews it received ... But I'm a pick-yourself-up, dust-yourself-off person and that wasn't going to destroy me. If I'd taken it to heart I would have given up.[18]

The time frame of this book doesn't make it possible to include all of Cleo's post 1975 theatre appearances but it is worth noting that she did have successes in American musical theatre including Stephen Sondheim's *Into the Woods* and the acclaimed Broadway show *The Mystery of Edwin Drood* (1985), for which she was nominated for the coveted Tony award as Best Actress in a Musical.

After *Hedda Gabler* there were very few dramatic roles offered to Cleo, but one of the exceptions was a BBC Radio 4 version of *The Member of the Wedding*, broadcast on 5 March 1973. This was Carson McCullers's finely observed study of Frankie Adams, an adolescent white girl who experiences a painful growth to maturity in America's deep south. Cleo played the family cook Berenice, the complex 'earth mother' role created by Ethel Waters on Broadway and in the 1952 film. Berenice cares deeply for Frankie and her cousin, John Henry. They are her family of 'misfits'. In one memorable scene Berenice reveals her own tragic past. It was another acting triumph as David Wade commented in *The Times* (10 March 1973):

> The most remarkable performance came from Cleo Laine making a rare, too rare, radio appearance. This was superlative acting, every word alive. With her immense warmth and understanding of the part, Miss Laine establishes Berenice as the safe emotional focus of the children's lives. This was pointed up by Richard Wortley's production which put her very close to the microphone, a device to which she responded with an intimacy of voice proper to the born radio actress. Magnificent.

With no dramatic roles in films or television plays to show us what Cleo was capable of as a 'straight' actress, all we are left with are the outstanding reviews by theatre critics. These at least highlight what she brought to her on-stage performances. A recording of her superb portrayal of Berenice in BBC Radio 4's *The Member of the Wedding* has survived, and with a bit of digging on You Tube it is possible to see a handful of excerpts from *Show Boat*. These were recorded at the Adelphi Theatre for inclusion in the 1973 Tony Awards telecast in America. Cleo looks breathtakingly beautiful and one can understand why her magnificent interpretation of the torch song 'Bill' stopped the show every night. As for Cleo, there is a sense that she was disappointed with the lack of acting roles available to her. In 1976 she told Graham Collier: 'There are a lot of roles I would like to do but the one that I'd really like to have ago at is Mother Courage. I like that character: she's a lady that appeals to me … and then there's Lady Macbeth! I'd like to do a new musical – something that hasn't been done before.'[19]

In 1988, Cleo reflected: 'In the main, it's been singing that's been my glory. When I'm on stage singing well it's joyful and I'm happy. That's where I come alive.'[20]

In 1997 Cleo was created a Dame of the British Empire.

The statue of the playwright and actor Alfred Fagon in St Pauls, Bristol, after it had been attacked with bleach in 2020. (© Alamy)

21

Three Playwrights: Mustapha Matura, Michael Abbensetts and Alfred Fagon

The early 1970s witnessed an important shift in British theatre in which Black playwrights emerged to build upon the groundbreaking work of such African and Caribbean trailblazers as Barry Reckord, Errol John, Clifton Jones and Wole Soyinka. This followed just over a decade of plays in London theatres written by acclaimed and dynamic African American playwrights, including: Langston Hughes (*Simply Heavenly*, Adelphi, 1958 and *Black Nativity*, Criterion, 1962); Lorraine Hansberry (*A Raisin in the Sun*, Adelphi, 1959, starring Earle Hyman and Juanita Moore); James Baldwin (*Blues for Mr Charlie*, Aldwych, 1965 and *The Amen Corner*, Saville, 1965); Leroi Jones, later known as Amiri Baraka (*Dutchman*, Hampstead Theatre Club, 1967, starring Calvin Lockhart); Donald McKayle (*Black New World*, Strand, 1967); and Adrienne Kennedy (*A Lesson in a Dead Language* and *Funnyhouse of a Negro*, Theatre Upstairs, Royal Court, 1968).

The American civil rights campaign and the Black Power movement had reached a peak in the 1960s, raising the consciousness of and radicalising many African Americans. These political developments also inspired and influenced Black Britons, and some of them found ways to express themselves in a range of arts, including theatre. Consequently, the ICA, InterAction, Theatre Upstairs (Royal Court), Soho Poly and Open Space began to recognise and embrace a new generation of Black playwrights. There was also a succession of Black-run companies such as The Dark and Light Theatre (renamed the Black Theatre of Brixton in 1975), Temba Theatre, the Drum Centre and the Keskidee Centre.

All of this activity led to the emergence of Britain's modern Black theatre movement, and Mustapha Matura, Michael Abbensetts and Alfred Fagon were among the playwrights who were there at the beginning. Each of them made an impact in the early 1970s.

When George Devine was the Artistic Director of the English Stage Company, he opened doors for many Black actors, and some playwrights, at the Royal Court. His untimely death in 1966 at the age of 55 was a shock to everyone in the theatre world. To honour his memory, the George Devine Award was launched in 1967 and presented annually to creative artists in the theatre: playwrights, directors or designers. The 1972 award was shared between two Black playwrights who had made an impression: Mustapha Matura and Michael Abbensetts.

'I think it is tremendous that two Black writers should get an award like this,' Matura told the *Daily Telegraph* (18 July 1973). 'I am a racially-motivated writer, but in a human sense. I am not a Black Power writer. I want to write about Black people in every situation, not just in a political context.'

The Guardian (18 July 1973) noted that Matura and Abbensetts met for the first time at the reception in their honour at the Royal Court, where they were presented with their awards:

> They weren't indulging in any generalised chat about the upsurge of West Indian drama and culture in exile; and there was no talk of schools or movements either. The men could not

be more different: Matura, who is from Trinidad (best known for his ironic tales of West Indian life in London, and the efforts of Black and white to make social contact) has the appearance of a guru in denims; sleek hair, silver rings and sad eyes behind heavy tinted glasses. Abbensetts is from Guyana: a bulkier, nervously jaunty figure (his tinted specs have silver rims). He's very arrogant, he says, and kept joking about how hard it was to have to share the prize; what do you have to do to get it all?

Mustapha Matura

Mustapha Matura had ambitions when he arrived in Britain in 1961 but, as Naseem Khan explained in the *Radio Times* (12–18 October 1985), none of his ambitions were fulfilled. She said he worked in an assortment of jobs, such as part-time demolition worker or temporary sorter of Her Majesty's mail:

> He tried various college courses but couldn't cope, and the future seemed a choice of either dead-end jobs or the dole. It was while he was working in the stock-room of a garment factory that he started writing. It wasn't a novel … but a play: a play in dialect about West Indians living in Britain. Other pieces followed, none written with any idea at all of production or publication. It was only by chance that Ed Berman of InterAction heard about them. Berman was trying to set up a series of plays that would demonstrate Black feeling in Britain. Matura's *Black Pieces* marked his beginnings as a playwright.

Black Pieces comprised three short plays, *Dialogue*, *Indian* and *Party*, and featured the actors Alfred Fagon and T-Bone Wilson. It was directed by Roland Rees, a leading fringe and touring theatre director, and it was staged in 1970 during the ICA's series on Black and White Power Plays.

Afterwards, Matura was commissioned to write *As Time Goes By*. It was first performed at the Traverse Theatre Club, Edinburgh, on 13 July 1971 before transferring to the Theatre Upstairs at the Royal Court. Once again, Roland Rees directed, and Matura's marvellously rich and witty play featured a great cast of Caribbean actors, all based in Britain. Each of them brought his characters to life. They included Alfred Fagon, Mona Hammond, Oscar James, Stefan Kalipha, Corinne Skinner-Carter, T-Bone Wilson and the veteran Frank Singuineau.

Some of the actors who appeared in Matura's plays have commented on how much they appreciated working together as a group of performers who all had Caribbean backgrounds. In 1998, Skinner-Carter reflected on how it felt in the early 1970s to work in the stage productions of Caribbean playwrights:

> I felt so proud and uplifted … If they'd told me to stand on my head, I would have done so! That's how thrilled I was. You see, in those days, when Black actors appeared, we were often isolated from each other … in these plays we were together, and we could relax. It was fantastic. We were like a family. We all knew each other, and supported each other. There was no jealousy or competition. And we kept those friendships going. Most of the friends I have today started from those early productions.[1]

In an interview with Michael McMillan, Matura described *As Time Goes By* as 'a folksy conventional Caribbean play. The female character, Batee [Mona Hammond], hated England. That was so unusual for people then. The myth was that immigrants didn't say things like that.'[2] At the end of the play, Batee's disillusionment is complete and McMillan suggested to Matura that, by the late 1970s, this disillusionment had become quite widespread in Britain's Caribbean community. McMillan then asked Matura if he felt vindicated. He replied:

> No. By that time I had moved on but personally I had also come to the conclusion, and as impractical as it may sound, that this country was a prison and that Caribbean people should return home. I don't think English culture is particularly helpful to Black people from the Caribbean. That is a tragedy. We seem to be stranded here. We came here to improve our lives but I feel that the Caribbean spirit is stifled here.[3]

Matura's early work also included the one-act monologue *Nice* with Stefan Kalipha, which was first staged at the Almost Free Theatre on 12 February 1973, and the satirical *Play Mas* – its title is roughly translatable as 'do your own thing' – which looked at post-independence Trinidad. *Play Mas* was written after Matura returned to Trinidad in 1972. He had been away for twelve years, and in 1962, not long after he had left home, the island gained its independence from Great Britain:

> Post-independence Trinidad was in a world of its own … As an exile, it was quite a wonderful journey to make. I was particularly fascinated by how multi-layered the place was – all the cultures and peoples. *Play Mas* explored the social and political vacuum left by the transition from the white colonial power to the Black bourgeoise, and how they were fucking things up. It also explored the significance of carnival and its influence on the people. After that, I wrote *Meetings* and *Independence*. They further explored the ironies and contradictions of independent nationhood. These plays were important to me because hitherto all my plays had been located in England.[4]

When *Play Mas* opened at the Royal Court on 10 July 1974 (later transferring to the Phoenix Theatre), cast members included Norman Beaton, Stefan Kalipha, Rudolph Walker, Tommy Eytle, Lucita Lijertwood, Frank Singuineau, Trevor Thomas and Mona Hammond. Michael Billington later described the

Theatre programme for Mustapha Matura's *Play Mas*. (Author's collection)

Royal Court as Matura's 'spiritual home' and described *Play Mas* as an ambitious play: 'a sharp-edged satire that depicts how a tailor's apprentice rises to the post of a police chief in post-independence Trinidad and uses the love of the island's annual carnival for political ends. Under its ebullient surface the play shows how the movement towards independence contained an element of masquerade.'[5]

Reviews were outstanding. Milton Schulman in the *Evening Standard* (17 July 1974) said:

> From the moment the curtain first rises on *Play Mas* it is evident we are in for a very special treat … If Mr Matura can be credited with something so pompous as a message, he is probably trying to say that simple people … are corrupted by the temptations of economic growth and the trappings of political power. But less important than the message is the kindliness and humour with which he examines these characters so that we can but laugh and forgive them even when they are behaving in the most crass and violent manner. As the bewildered tailor, Stefan Kalipha gives the most endearing performance seen on the English stage for a long time.

'S.F.' in *Miss London* (23 September 1974) considered *Play Mas:*

> Quite the funniest and most intelligent play I've seen for at least two years … Although the theme of the play is serious, Matura has a light touch. Each character is humorously observed, and although the setting is Trinidad … it's as recognisable a cross-section of humanity as you'd find in any London district.

When Antonia Fraser commented on Mustapha Matura receiving the *Evening Standard* award for Most Promising Playwright of 1974 in the *Evening Standard* (17 January 1975), she described his play as 'the next best thing to Trinidad carnival'.

When Matura passed away on 29 October 2019, Michael Billington described him in his obituary in *The Guardian* (1 November 2019) as:

> a proud Trinidadian who argued time and time again that British colonialism had robbed his people of their sense of history. He was also a genuine pathfinder who not only paved the way for a new generation but who co-founded, with Charlie Hanson, the Black Theatre Co-operative, to commission and support work by Black writers in Britain. If those

plays are now widely produced on British stages, it is because of Matura's heroic example and practical encouragement.

Michael Abbensetts

Michael Abbensetts came from a middle-class Guyanese family of mixed African and European heritage. Inspired by a performance of John Osborne's ground-breaking *Look Back in Anger*, he moved to Britain in 1963 to begin his writing career in the theatre. Ten years later he made a successful move to television. Meanwhile, he supported himself by working as a security officer at the Tower of London. After arriving in Britain, Abbensetts became a regular theatregoer, but it was the Royal Court in Sloane Square that opened his eyes to ambitious and experimental stage productions. His ambition was to have his first play produced there.

Sweet Talk was Abbensetts's first stage play and to his delight it opened at the Royal Court's Theatre Upstairs on 31 July 1973. The cast included Allister Bain, Mona Hammond, Don Warrington and Joan-Ann Maynard. *Sweet Talk* depicted the tensions in the lives of Caribbean settlers living in cramped conditions in a London bedsit.

In 1978, Mike Phillips described Abbensetts as probably the Black playwright who is most accessible to British people:

> The plays are carefully and traditionally constructed and any social issues which arise are always seen through the development and response of the characters. He confesses to admiring John Osborne and David Mercer and suitably the key to his heroes is that they are all in the grip of an obsession with the past. The dominant mood in *Sweet Talk* is nostalgia, defeat and fierce longing for the almost mythical joys of the Caribbean. The hero of *Sweet Talk* is a betting shop gambler whose ambition is to win enough money to go back home to

the Caribbean, and like Abbensetts's other heroes, his obsession is a destructive one, as much to the people around him, like his wife, as to himself.[6]

Abbensetts told Mike Phillips:

> Currently a lot of people are concerned with writing about race and racial issues, but that happened in the States and now it's changed. The thing is that Black people don't think about white people twenty-four hours a day. Most of the time they think about themselves or other Black people or their taxes even.[7]

Sweet Talk opened in the same week that *The Museum Attendant*, his first television drama – based on his experiences at the Tower of London – was shown on BBC2. The following year he was appointed writer in residence at the Royal Court.

The next decade was Abbensetts's busiest, moving between theatre, television and radio. He later explained that he was offered a variety of work because he included Black and white characters together. He said, 'they thought "oh he can write white characters as well" so people began to take more notice of my work.'[8]

As Michael Coveney later observed, 'The legacy of the colonial experience in the Caribbean, with its confusions of racial identity and mixed-blessing migration to Britain in the 1960s, was a potent theme in [his] stage and television work.'[9]

Throughout his writing career, Abbensetts explored issues of race and power, but he was determined to avoid being categorised as a one-theme dramatist. Consequently, his plays were much broader and more multilayered in their scope. On many occasions he challenged racial stereotypes by creating strong, believable Black characters, sometimes based on people he knew in Britain's Caribbean community. In doing so, he provided memorable roles for an entire generation of Britain's established

Black actors, among them Norman Beaton, Mona Hammond, Rudolph Walker and Carmen Munroe.

He later explained to Michele Stoby:

> I try to write about people as I know them ... I suppose I find it easier to write about people who are born in the Caribbean. They don't have to be my age, but I do think if you're born in the Caribbean, and in my case if you're Guyanese, you have a certain way of looking at life.[10]

Abbensetts's final public appearance was on 9 December 2012 at a tribute organised in his honour at the Tricycle Theatre. It featured a reading of his first stage success, *Sweet Talk*. He died on 24 November 2016.

Alfred Fagon

On his arrival in Britain from Jamaica in 1955, Alfred Fagon worked for British Rail in Nottingham. After a stint in the army, he spent time travelling while earning a living as a calypso singer. Settling in the St Paul's area of Bristol, he worked as a welder before pursuing an acting and writing career.

In 1970, Fagon's role in Mustapha Matura's play *Black Pieces* brought him to London for his professional acting debut. It was a turning point for Fagon because Matura broke new ground by encouraging his actors to use the dialect of the Caribbean islands. As Roland Rees explained in his introduction to Fagon's *Plays*, the language Fagon was being asked to speak amazed him: 'He had never before seen patois, an oral tradition, written down on paper. This was a clarifying moment for him and one which was to have far-reaching repercussions.'[11]

Matura's writing had an enormous influence on Fagon, as Rees witnessed:

> It persuaded him that he could write plays with characters that could tell his stories, culled from his own experience, in a language natural to them. He was convinced that this would lead him to write plays entirely different in style and emotional content to Matura. He knew he had a very different voice. But the one lesson he had learnt along with the rest of the cast was … they now knew they did not have to try to be English anymore.[12]

Inspired by Matura's writing and the other Caribbean actors in *Black Pieces*, Fagon's first production as a dramatist was *11 Josephine House*, presented by Foco Novo with InterAction in 1972 at the Almost Free Theatre. It focused on the life of a Jamaican family living in Bristol and the cast included Fagon, T-Bone Wilson, Mona Hammond, Oscar James and Horace James. It was directed by Roland Rees. A review in *The Stage* (30 November 1972) praised Fagon's work: 'The play is brilliantly entertaining, well written, and beautifully performed.' One of the cast members, Oscar James, later reflected, 'It was about West Indians bringing their own culture and community here, into England, into the English culture … There is unity in that life, whereas the whole English system was tearing them apart. It is about exile.'[13]

Fagon played a crucial role in the development of a new kind of Black theatre in Britain. In 1974, when he directed his stage play *No Soldiers* at the Metro Club, off Westbourne Grove in London, he took his work into the heart of the Black community. His other plays at this time included *The Death of a Black Man* at the Hampstead Theatre as a Foco Novo production in 1975, directed by Roland Rees. For television Fagon wrote and starred in *Shakespeare Country* (1973), for BBC2's *Thirty-Minute Theatre* series. In this semi-autobiographical drama he explored the difficulties faced by a struggling Black actor trying to make his way in a profession dominated by the language of William Shakespeare.

Fagon continued acting and writing into the 1980s. The dramatist Howard Brenton remembered him as:

> A really interesting man. He was a self-taught scholar, a street scholar, how the British working class used to be. Alfred's knowledge of Milton was fantastic. He could quote reams of it. I loved talking to him about Milton. He was a boxer, had been in jail for a while, and an excellent actor.[14]

Roland Rees said, 'He could be demure, motionless and silent one minute, gargantuan, life-enhancing and loud the next, qualities that always permeated the characters in his plays as did the streak of poetic invention that interfused his own conversation.'[15]

On 29 August 1986, Fagon suffered a fatal heart attack while jogging near his home. He was declared dead on arrival at King's College Hospital, Denmark Hill, Lambeth. Afterwards the police claimed that an officer had visited his home and could not find any contacts for him. However, it was later established that the officer had overlooked a great deal of information about him including his diary with phone numbers, Equity union card, passport, and a BBC script next to his bed. Consequently, it was two weeks before his family and friends were made aware that he had died and been given a pauper's funeral. Rees later said that the young police officer who searched Alfred's flat 'made assumptions – that this man was a loner, a Black man who nobody would miss.'[16]

In 1987, on the first anniversary of his death, a bronze bust of Fagon on a black marble pedestal was erected on the Ashley Road/Grosvenor Road Triangle in the St Paul's area of Bristol. Fagon became the first Black person to be honoured with a statue in Bristol. Paul Stephenson, who chaired the committee that raised funds for the memorial, acknowledged that Fagon had been very popular in Bristol's African Caribbean community because of his warmth and sensitivity. Ten years later, with support from the Royal Court Theatre, the Arts Council of England, the Peggy Ramsay Foundation and the Talawa Theatre Company, the annual Alfred Fagon Award was inaugurated, for a play by a writer from the Caribbean or of Caribbean descent.

On 7 June 2020, a statue of the slave trader Edward Colston was pulled down and thrown into Bristol Harbour during the Black Lives Matter protests. This was sparked by the death of an African American, George Floyd, while in the custody of Minneapolis police in the USA. Just nine days after the toppling of the Edward Colston statue, the bust of Alfred Fagon was covered in bleach by vandals.

Norman Beaton. (Author's collection, courtesy of Norman Beaton)

Postscript

Norman Beaton

Trailblazers of Black British Theatre is dedicated to the memory of Norman Beaton, one of the finest actors we ever had and a great Black Briton. Norman was the Guyanese actor most loved and cherished by the playwright Michael Abbensetts. They worked together on a number of productions, including *Home Again* (BBC Radio, 1975), *Black Christmas* (BBC TV, 1977), *Empire Road* (BBC TV series, 1978–79), *Samba* (Tricycle Theatre, 1980), *Alterations* (BBC Radio, 1980), *In the Mood* (Hampstead Theatre, 1981), *Easy Money* (BBC TV, 1981), *Big George is Dead* (Channel 4 TV, 1987) and *Little Napoleons* (Channel 4 TV, 1994).

When Beaton died on 13 December 1994 at the age of 60, Abbensetts felt he had lost the charismatic and 'larger than life' actor who gave his work a voice. He wrote very little thereafter.

Beaton left Guyana for Britain in 1960 and originally worked as a teacher. The success of *Jack of Spades*, his first stage production at Liverpool's Everyman Theatre, encouraged him to give up teaching and become a full-time actor. His reputation grew steadily and his stage career 'bridges' the period covered by this book (1825–1975) and contemporary Black British theatre.

Beaton progressed from regional theatre to leading roles at the Old Vic, the National Theatre (where he played the villainous Angelo in a Black-cast version of Shakespeare's *Measure for Measure* in 1981), and the Royal Court Theatre. Apart from Shakespeare, his stage roles also encompassed Pinter, Beckett, Gilbert and Sullivan, Brecht, Molière, and pantomime. In 1974 he started the Black Theatre of Brixton, which was instrumental in developing contemporary Black theatre in Britain. For years he acted in plays by a range of Black dramatists, including Michael Abbensetts, C.L.R. James, Derek Walcott and Edgar White.

In his autobiography, *Beaton But Unbowed* (1986), Beaton stated that Mustapha Matura was:

> easily the most lyrical of the playwrights to come from the West Indies. His speeches and situations develop in elliptical rhythms, seeming to come back to the original statement but expressed in a permutation of the first. He develops speeches or situations in a series of ever increasing circles. It is beautiful writing, easy on the ear and extremely funny.

Beaton starred in three of Matura's plays: *Play Mas* (1974), *Rum and Coca Cola* (1976) and *Nice* (1979).

One of Beaton's most successful West End productions was *The Black Mikado* (1975), a modern version of Gilbert and Sullivan's *The Mikado* in which he played Nanki Poo. In his autobiography, Beaton recalled the 'stupendous' opening night at the Cambridge Theatre:

> That large auditorium of 1,200 red velvet seats, gilt adornments, chandeliers and discreet wall lighting had not seen such an enthusiastic gathering for ages. Listening on the tannoy in my dressing-room, the first round of applause deafened the eardrums as the curtain went up and the Titipu stage was revealed. I knew we were away. At the end of the show

> we took maybe a dozen curtain calls to a thunderous standing ovation. We were ecstatic. *The Black Mikado* received some of the best notices any West End musical has ever received.

In addition to his stage work, Beaton became one of Britain's leading film and television actors. His most memorable on-screen role was Desmond Ambrose, the manic barber's shop owner in the long-running situation comedy series *Desmond's*. He starred in over seventy episodes. With sharply observed

Theatre programme cover for *The Black Mikado* starring Norman Beaton at the Cambridge Theatre in 1975. (Author's collection, courtesy of Norman Beaton)

scripts by a young Black writer called Trix Worrell, and many others, *Desmond's* ran from 1989 to 1994 on Channel 4.

Towards the end of his life, when he was interviewed in the BBC Television documentary *Black and White in Colour* (1992), Beaton reflected on the roles available to Black actors and actresses:

> My own view is that what you've seen me in are the only roles that are available for Black men in this country, and they don't really reflect our views, our understanding of life, our intelligence, or where we are coming from. In that respect I would say that Caryl Phillips' scenario for [the 1986 film] *Playing Away* did get around that particular hurdle. It lived up to nearly all the expectations that Black people ought to be living up to ... But what I find difficult to come to terms with is the absence of a heroic figure like Paul Robeson in all the work I've done. There is no writer on that scale, or in those grand, magnificent terms about a Black figure who we all admire or aspire to be like. And I don't know when our people are going to actually start saying 'We are terrific!' and start writing something wonderful about just being us.

When he passed away, Carmen Munroe, who played Beaton's wife Shirley in *Desmond's*, told *The Voice* (20 December 1994):

> He put his whole life and soul into any part he was asked to play and never spared himself. He worked at his craft and produced brilliance. His particular blend of comic energy and professional application will be missed most keenly in the future when excellence is sought.

Appendix

Database of Stage Productions from 1825 to 1975

The following database is an extension of the list that I researched for *Black and Asian Performance at the Theatre Museum: A User's Guide*, published by the Theatre Museum in 2003. For this new list I revisited the cast lists that were printed in twelve volumes of *Who's Who in the Theatre*, which cover the years 1922 to 1975. However, the volumes only include productions from London's West End. Where possible I have added some titles performed off West End and in other parts of the country, but this is not exhaustive. It is intended to be a starting point for others who wish to continue researching this subject. The names of Black lead actors, authors, producers and directors are highlighted in bold.

Year	Production title	Theatre	Key black personnel
Late 1700s	*Romeo and Juliet/The Beggar's Opera*	Unknown (Lancashire)	Unidentified actress as Juliet/Polly
1825	*Revolt of Surinam or A Slave's Revenge*	Royal Coburg	
1833	*Othello*	Theatre Royal, Covent Garden	
	The Padlock	Surrey	
1841	*The Black Doctor*	City of London	**Ira Aldridge**
1852	*Titus Andronicus*	Britannia, Hoxton	
1858	*Othello*	Lyceum	
1865		Theatre Royal Haymarket	
1866	*Othello*	Royal Olympic	**Morgan Smith**
1883	*Othello/Richard III*	Kilburn Town Hall	**Paul Molyneaux**
1900	*Uncle Tom's Cabin*	Elephant and Castle	J.G. Johnston, Lizzie Allen
	Madame Delphine	Wyndham	Amy Height
1903	*In Dahomey*	Shaftesbury	**Bert Williams, George Walker, Aida Overton Walker**
1906	*Nero*	His Majesty's	**Samuel Coleridge-Taylor** (music)
1912	*Othello*		
1914	*Mameena*	Globe	Kuamina Alexander
1915	*Honi Soit … !*	London Pavilion	Louis Douglas
1916	*Chu Chin Chow*	His Majesty's	Napoleon Florent
	Pick-a-Dilly	London Pavilion	Louis Douglas
1917	*Cheerio*		
1921	*The Edge O'Beyond*	The Garrick	Napoleon Florent
	Welcome Stranger	The Lyric	Ernest Trimmingham
1922	*The Dippers*	Criterion	
1923	*The Rainbow (Plantation Days)*	Empire	Leonard Harper, James P. Johnson
	Dover Street to Dixie	London Pavilion	**Florence Mills**
	Down South	Hammersmith Palais	Will Garland
1924	*Elsie Janis at Home*	Queen's	**Layton & Johnstone**
	White Cargo	The Playhouse	Chief Luale

Year	Production title	Theatre	Key black personnel
	The Blue Peter	Prince's	Harry Quashie
1925	*South of the Line*	'Q'	Irene Howe
	The Emperor Jones	Ambassadors	**Paul Robeson**, Irene Howe
	In Walked Jimmy	'Q'	Ernest Trimmingham
1926	*Bongola*	'Q'	Napoleon Florent, Donald Walcott
	And So to Bed	Queen's	Emma Williams
	Blackbirds	London Pavilion	**Florence Mills**
1927	*White Cargo*	Strand	Chief Luale
	Might-Have-Beens	Prince's	Ernest Trimmingham
	The Girl Friend	Palace	
	When Blue Hills Laughed	Criterion	Donald Walcott
	Simoun	'Q'	Kuamina Alexander
1928	*Back to Methuselah (The Thing Happens)*	Court	Emma Williams
	Show Boat	Drury Lane	**Paul Robeson**, Alberta Hunter, Norris Smith
	Virginia	Palace	Ernest Trimmingham, Cora La Redd
1929	*Porgy*	His Majesty's	**Frank Wilson, Evelyn Ellis**, Georgette Harvey, Jack Carter, Leigh Whipper
	Coquette	Apollo	Eva Hudson
	All God's Chillun Got Wings	Court	**Frank Wilson**, Emma Williams, Henry Brown (aka Ray Ellington)
	Brown Birds	(Tour)	Will Garland, Evelyn Dove, Stanley Coleman, Arthur Dibbin, Lily Jemmott
1930	*Othello*	Savoy	**Paul Robeson**
	Ever Green	Adelphi	Buddy Bradley (choreographer)
1931	*The Improper Duchess*	Globe	James Solomon
	The Hairy Ape	Ambassadors	**Paul Robeson**
	Salome	Savoy	James Rich

Year	Production title	Theatre	Key black personnel
	Cavalcade	Drury Lane	Jack London, Leslie Thompson
	And So to Bed	Globe	Emma Williams
	Peter Pan	Palladium	Ernest Trimmingham
1932	*The Green Pack*	Wyndham's	Napoleon Florent
	Lovely Lady	Phoenix	Eva Hudson
	The Cat and the Fiddle	Palace	Buddy Bradley (choreographer)
1933	*Once in a Lifetime*	Queen's	Napoleon Florent
	All God's Chillun Got Wings	Embassy	**Paul Robeson**
	Dark Doings	Leicester Square	Elisabeth Welch
	Nymph Errant	Adelphi	
	Night Club Queen	Playhouse	Jack London
	The Colour Bar	Grand, Fulham	Napoleon Florent
	At What a Price	YWCA/Scala	**Una Marson** (author)
1934	*Spring, 1600*	Shaftesbury	James Rich
	Magnolia Street	Adelphi	Ernest Trimmingham
	The Pursuit of Happiness	Vaudeville	Oscar Polk
	They Shall Not Die	Holborn Empire	Harry Quashie, Amy Barbour-James, Una Marson, Viola Thompson, Orlando Martins
	Blackbirds of 1934	Coliseum	**Valaida**, Peg Leg Bates, Edith Wilson
	Sweet Aloes	Wyndham's	Ernest Trimmingham
	Blackbirds of 1935	Coliseum	**Valaida**, Peg Leg Bates, Edith Wilson
	Robinson Crusoe	Lewisham Hippodrome	**Alberta Hunter**, John Payne, Rita Stevens
1935	*Anything Goes*	Palace	Buddy Bradley (choreographer)
	Between Us Two	Criterion	Eva Hudson
	Basalik	Arts	**Paul Robeson**
	Glamorous Night	Drury Lane	Elisabeth Welch

Year	Production title	Theatre	Key black personnel
	Stevedore	Embassy	**Paul Robeson**, Eva Hudson, Lawrence Brown, John Payne, Robert Adams
	The Miracle Man	Victoria Palace	Ernest Trimmingham
	The Mysterious Universe	Arts	Johnny Nit
	These Mortals	Aldwych	John Payne
1936	*Follow the Sun*	Adelphi	Jeni LeGon
	At the Silver Swan	Palace	Johnny Nit
	Toussaint L'Ouverture	Westminster	**C.L.R. James** (author), **Paul Robeson**, Robert Adams, Orlando Martins, Lawrence Brown, John Ahuma
	Chastity, My Brother	Embassy	Robert Adams
	Blackbirds of 1936	Gaiety	**Jules Bledsoe**, Lavaida Carter, Eunice Wilson, Fela Sowande, The Nicholas Brothers
	Let's Raise the Curtain	Victoria Palace	**Elisabeth Welch**
	Transatlantic Rhythm	Adelphi	Buck and Bubbles
	Blackbirds of 1936 (second edition)		**The Nicholas Brothers**, Lavaida Carter, Eunice Wilson, Fela Sowande
	Adventure	Victoria Palace	John Ahuma, Napoleon Florent, James Solomon, Kathleen Davis, Kuamina Alexander, Harry Crossman
1937	*No Sleep for the Wicked*	Streatham Hill/ Daly's	Ernest Trimmingham
	Charlot's Non-Stop Revue No. 3	Vaudeville	Una Mae Carlisle
	The Fight's On	Richmond	James Solomon, Irene Howe
	It's in the Bag	Saville	**Elisabeth Welch**
	You Can't Take it With You	St James's	Robert Adams

Year	Production title	Theatre	Key black personnel
1938	*Welcome Stranger*	Saville	Ernest Trimmingham
	Plant in the Sun	Unity	**Paul Robeson**
	The Sun Never Sets	Drury Lane	**Todd Duncan**, **Adelaide Hall**, Robert Adams, Harry Quashie, Mako Hlubi
1939	*Colony*	Unity	Robert Adams, Orlando Martins
	Of Mice and Men	Gate/Apollo	Edward Wallace
1941	*No Time for Comedy*	Haymarket	Elisabeth Welch
	Room V	Garrick	Ernest Trimmingham
	Chu Chin Chow	Palace	Harry Crossman, Napoleon Florent, Tunji Williams, Earl Cameron
	Get a Load of This	Hippodrome	Chick Alexander
	Peter Pan	Adelphi	Harry Crossman
1942	*Happidrome*	Prince of Wales's	Leslie 'Hutch' Hutchinson
	Full Swing	Palace	Buddy Bradley (choreographer)
	Watch on the Rhine	Aldwych	Norris Smith
	Big Top	His Majesty's	Buddy Bradley (choreographer)
	Sky High	Phoenix	**Elisabeth Welch**
	The Little Foxes	Piccadilly	Connie Smith, Robert Adams
	The Old Town Hall	Winter Garden	**Adelaide Hall**
	The House of Jeffreys	Playhouse	Robert Adams
	The Petrified Forest	Globe	Earl Cameron
	Peter Pan	Winter Garden	Harry Crossman
1943	*Something in the Air*	Palace	Buddy Bradley (choreographer)
	Show Boat	Stoll	Rita Stevens, Sadie Hopkins
	The Judgement of Dr Johnson	Arts	Robert Adams
	It's Time to Dance	Winter Garden	Buddy Bradley
	Sunny River	Piccadilly	James Rich
	He Signed His Name	'Q'	Robert Adams

<table>
<tr><th>Year</th><th>Production title</th><th>Theatre</th><th>Key black personnel</th></tr>
<tr><td></td><td>Arc de Triomphe</td><td>Phoenix</td><td>Elisabeth Welch</td></tr>
<tr><td></td><td>Panama Hattie</td><td>Piccadilly</td><td>Chick Alexander</td></tr>
<tr><td></td><td>Peter Pan</td><td>Cambridge</td><td>Harry Crossman</td></tr>
<tr><td>1944</td><td>Three's a Family</td><td>Saville</td><td>Connie Smith</td></tr>
<tr><td></td><td>Happy and Glorious</td><td>Palladium</td><td>Elisabeth Welch</td></tr>
<tr><td></td><td>Daughter Janie</td><td>Apollo</td><td>James Rich</td></tr>
<tr><td></td><td>Peter Pan</td><td>Stoll</td><td>Harry Crossman</td></tr>
<tr><td></td><td>Robinson Crusoe</td><td>Wimbledon</td><td>Uriel Porter</td></tr>
<tr><td>1945</td><td>Panama Hattie</td><td>Adelphi</td><td>Chick Alexander</td></tr>
<tr><td></td><td>The Night and the Music</td><td>Coliseum</td><td>Worthy and Jarrett</td></tr>
<tr><td></td><td>The Hasty Heart</td><td>Aldwych</td><td>Orlando Martins</td></tr>
<tr><td></td><td>To-Morrow Will Be Different</td><td>Lindsay</td><td>Eva Hudson</td></tr>
<tr><td></td><td>Peter Pan</td><td>Scala</td><td>Harry Crossman</td></tr>
<tr><td></td><td>Aladdin</td><td>Cambridge</td><td>James Rich</td></tr>
<tr><td>1946</td><td>All God's Chillun Got Wings</td><td>Unity</td><td>Robert Adams, Ida Shepley</td></tr>
<tr><td></td><td>Stage Door</td><td>Saville</td><td>Connie Smith</td></tr>
<tr><td></td><td>Les Ballets Nègres</td><td rowspan="3">Granville</td><td>Berto Pasuka</td></tr>
<tr><td></td><td>Cellar</td><td>Robert Adams</td></tr>
<tr><td></td><td>G. I. Brides at Sea</td><td rowspan="2">Uriel Porter</td></tr>
<tr><td></td><td>The Eagle Has Two Heads</td><td rowspan="2">Lyric Hammersmith</td></tr>
<tr><td></td><td>The Assassin</td><td>Harry Quashie</td></tr>
<tr><td></td><td>Peter Pan</td><td>Scala</td><td>Harry Crossman</td></tr>
<tr><td>1947</td><td>Caviar to the General</td><td>New Lindsey</td><td>Robert Adams, Pauline Henriques</td></tr>
<tr><td></td><td>Hattie Stowe</td><td>Embassy</td><td>Connie Smith, Augustus Newton, Susan Hudson</td></tr>
<tr><td></td><td>Now Barabbas …</td><td>The Boltons/ Vaudeville</td><td>Harry Quashie</td></tr>
<tr><td></td><td>Cry Havoc</td><td>Alexandra, Stoke Newington</td><td>Sadie Hopkins</td></tr>
<tr><td></td><td>Caviar to the General</td><td>Whitehall</td><td>Robert Adams, Ida Shepley</td></tr>
<tr><td></td><td>Here, There and Everywhere</td><td>Palladium</td><td>Mable Lee</td></tr>
</table>

Year	Production title	Theatre	Key black personnel
	Annie Get Your Gun	Coliseum	Don Johnson, James Clark
	S. S. Glencairn	Mercury	Connie Smith, Pauline Henriques, Sadie Hopkins, Susan Hudson
	Deep Are the Roots	Wyndham's	**Gordon Heath**, Evelyn Ellis, Helen Martin
	The Respectable Prostitute	Lyric Hammersmith	Orlando Martins
	The Coral Snake	'Q'	Connie Smith, Norris Smith
	Point Valaine	Embassy	Pauline Henriques, Louise Toummavoh
	Tuppence Coloured	Lyric Hammersmith/ Globe	**Elisabeth Welch**
	Finian's Rainbow	Palace	John Bouie
	Anna Lucasta	His Majesty's	**Hilda Simms**, Fredrick O'Neal, Georgia Burke, Frank Silvera, Earle Hyman
	Peter Pan	Scala	Harry Crossman
1948	*The Vigil*	Embassy/Prince of Wales's	Ida Shepley
	Native Son	Boltons	**Richard Wright** (author), **Robert Adams**, Viola Thompson, Harry Scott, Frank Singuineau, Augustus Newton, Carmen Manley
	Dark Eyes	Strand	Norris Smith, Gladys Taylor
	Hellzapoppin'	Prince's	The Clark Brothers
	Calypso	Wimbledon/ Playhouse	**Edric Connor, Evelyn Dove, Mable Lee,** Cherry Adele
	A Caribbean Rhapsody	Prince of Wales's	**Katherine Dunham**
	Georgia Story	New Lindsey	Edric Connor, Louise Toummavoh

Year	Production title	Theatre	Key black personnel
	Something Different	Maccabi House, West Hampstead, London	**The Negro Theatre Company**, Pauline Henriques (producer), Edric Connor, Ida Shepley, Neville Crabbe, Rudy Evans, Rita Stevens, Earl Cameron, Frank Silvera
	These Mortals	People's Palace	Harry Quashie
	Oranges and Lemons	Lyric Hammersmith/ Globe	**Elisabeth Welch**
	Peter Pan	Scala	Harry Crossman
	Jason	New Lindsey	Connie Smith
1949	*Jail-Break*	'Q'	Earl Cameron
	Primrose and the Peanuts	Playhouse	Orlando Martins
	Foxhole in the Parlor	New Lindsey	Earl Cameron
	The Male Animal	Arts/New	Pauline Henriques
	Sauce Tartare	Cambridge	Buddy Bradley (choreographer), **Muriel Smith**
	The Golden Door	Embassy	Connie Smith
	Peter Pan	Scala	Harry Crossman
1950	*Othello*	(Tour)	**Gordon Heath**, Pauline Henriques
	Primrose and the Peanuts	Bedford	Orlando Martins
	How I Wonder	Unity	Errol Hill
	Latin Quarter	Casino	The Clark Brothers
	Detective Story	Prince's	Neville Crabbe
	Sauce Piquante	Cambridge	**Muriel Smith, Buddy Bradley** (choreographer)
	How I Wonder	Fortune	Orlando Martins
	Golden City	Adelphi	Mako Hlubi
	Desire Caught by the Tail	Watergate	Louise Toummavoh
	Longitude 49	Unity	Errol Hill
	Peter Pan	Scala	Chick Alexander

Year	Production title	Theatre	Key black personnel
1951	*Kiss Me, Kate*	Coliseum	Adelaide Hall, Archie Savage
	Hassan	Cambridge	**Hilda Simms**, Orlando Martins
	Tiger Bay	New Lindsey	**Earl Cameron**, Mona Baptiste, Dan Jackson
	Penny Plain	St Martin's	**Elisabeth Welch**
	The Silent Inn	'Q'	Frank Singuineau
	The Peep Show	Palladium	**Edmundo Ros** and his Rumba Band
	Pearl Primus and her Negro Dancers	Prince's	**Pearl Primus**
	South Pacific	Drury Lane	**Muriel Smith**, Evelyn Dove, Archie Savage, Neville Crabbe
	Peter Pan	Scala	Dan Jackson
1952	*Katherine Dunham and her Negro Dancers*	Cambridge	**Katherine Dunham**
	The Golden Door	Embassy	Connie Smith
	First Time Here	Watergate	**Archie Savage**
	Love From Judy	Saville	Adelaide Hall
	Porgy and Bess	Stoll	**William Warfield, Leontyne Price, Cab Calloway,** Georgia Burke
	The Respectable Prostitute	Royal Artillery, Woolwich	Earl Cameron
	The Sky is Red	Irving	Frank Singuineau
	Remains to be Seen	Her Majesty's	Harry Quashie
	Peter Pan	Scala	Astley Harvey
1953	*The Shrike*	Prince's	Edric Connor, Frank Singuineau, John Harrison
	Before the Deluge	Boltons	Lionel Ngakane
	The Man with Expensive Tastes	'Q'/Vaudeville	Dan Jackson
	High Spirits	Hippodrome	**Marie Bryant**
	Caribbean Cruise	Irving	**Donald Heywood** (producer)

Year	Production title	Theatre	Key black personnel
	Anna Lucasta	Prince of Wales's/London Hippodrome	**Isabelle Cooley**, Neville Crabbe, Rita Stevens, Errol John
	Pardon My French	Prince of Wales's	**Winifred Atwell**
	Fun and the Fair	Palladium	**Deep River Boys**
	The King and I	Drury Lane	**Muriel Smith**
	The Big Knife	Wimbledon/ Duke of York's	John Harrison
	Peter Pan	Scala	Joseph Layode
1954	*Cry, the Beloved Country*	St Martin-in-the-Fields	**Orlando Martins, Edric Connor, Evelyn Dove**, John Akar, Kathleen Davis, Errol John, Lionel Ngakane
	Mislike Me Not	Royal Artillery, Woolwich	Frank Singuineau
	Local Colour	'Q'	Errol John
	Hot from Harlem	tour including Chiswick Empire	**Woods and Jarrett, Shirley Bassey**, Cyril Lagey, Astley Harvey
	Cockles and Champagne	Saville	Mildred Joanne Smith
	Salome	'Q'	Frank Singuineau, K.A. Medas (Ayton Medas)
	The Respectable Prostitute		Frank Singuineau
	Salome	St Martin's	Errol John, Ayton Medas
	The Respectable Prostitute		Errol John
	The Love Game	Richmond	Harry Quashie
	The Immoralist	Arts	Gladys Taylor
	Pay the Piper	Saville	**Elisabeth Welch**
	Peter Pan	Scala	Ayton Medas
1955	*Night Returns in Africa*	'Q'	Harry Quashie, Lionel Ngakane, Dan Jackson
	Chestnuts in Soho	Rudolf Steiner	Frank Singuineau
	South	Arts	Errol John, John Harrison, Rita Stevens
	Kismet	Stoll	Harry Baird

Year	Production title	Theatre	Key black personnel
	The Jazz Train	Piccadilly	**Edric Connor, Uriel Porter**, Boscoe Holder, Bertice Reading, Lucille Mapp, Sheila Clarke, Cyril Lagey
	Strangers' Wharf	New Lindsey	Harcourt Curacao
	Anniversary Waltz	Streatham Hill/ Lyric	Pauline Henriques
	Junction Village	Irving	**Edric Connor** (producer), **Douglas Archbald** (author), Nadia Cattouse, John Harrison, Mark Heath, Pearl Prescod
	Caribbean Revue	Irving	**Edric Connor** (producer and author), Pearl Prescod, John Harrison, West African Rhythm Brothers
	Such is Life	Adelphi	**Shirley Bassey**
	Cranks	New Watergate	**Gordon Heath**
	Peter Pan	Scala	Ayton Medas
1956	*The End Begins*	'Q'	**Earl Cameron**
	Summer Song	Prince's	**Edric Connor**, Thomas Baptiste
	The Good Sailor	Lyric Hammersmith	Clifton Jones
	The Crucible	Royal Court	**Connie Smith**
	Rocking the Town	Palladium	**Winifred Atwell**
	Someone To Talk To	Duchess	Adelaide Hall
	Nude With Violin	Globe	Thomas Baptiste
1957	*The Member of the Wedding*	Royal Court	**Bertice Reading**, Connie Smith, Orlando Martins, Errol John
	Camino Real	Phoenix	Elroy Josephs
	Tropical Heatwave	New Lindsey/ Lyric Hammersmith	Pearl Prescod
	The Best Damn Lie	Winter Garden	Ida Shepley
	The Last Hero	Strand	Thomas Baptiste
	We're Having a Ball	Palladium	**Clark Brothers**

Year	Production title	Theatre	Key black personnel
	The Waters of Babylon	Royal Court	Lucille Mapp
	Requiem for a Nun	Royal Court	**Bertice Reading**
	Robinson Crusoe	Palladium	Joseph Layode
1958	*Lady at the Wheel*	Lyric Hammersmith/ Westminster	Lucille Mapp
	The Iceman Cometh	Arts	Robert Adams
	Cat on a Hot Tin Roof	Comedy	Don Johnson, Mark Heath
	Simply Heavenly	Adelphi	**Langston Hughes** (author), Rita Stevens, Earl Cameron, Evelyn Dove, Marpessa Dawn, Bertice Reading, Bari Johnson, John Bouie, Don Johnson, Isabelle Lucas, Harry Baird
	Flesh to a Tiger	Royal Court	**Barry Reckord** (author), **Cleo Laine**, Tamba Allen, Pearl Prescod, Lloyd Reckord, Johnny Sekka, Nadia Cattouse, Connie Smith
	Pericles	Shakespeare Memorial Theatre, Stratford-upon-Avon	**Edric Connor**
	A Taste of Honey	Theatre Royal, Stratford East	Jimmie Moore
	The Joshua Tree	Duke of York's	Rita Stevens
	Valmouth	Lyric Hammersmith	**Bertice Reading**, Maxine Daniels
	The Hostage	Theatre Royal, Stratford East	Roy Barnett
	Hot Summer Night	New	**Lloyd Reckord**
	Moon on a Rainbow Shawl	Royal Court	**Errol John** (author), **Earle Hyman**, Barbara Assoon, Vinnette Carroll, Lionel Ngakane, Johnny Sekka, John Bouie, Clifton Jones

Year	Production title	Theatre	Key black personnel
1959	*A Taste of Honey*	Theatre Royal, Stratford East/ Wyndham's	**Clifton Jones**
	Valmouth	Saville	**Cleo Laine**
	Blue Magic	Prince of Wales	**Shirley Bassey**
	Orpheus Descending	Royal Court	John Harrison
	The Hostage	Theatre Royal, Stratford East/ Wyndham's	Roy Barnett
	Swinging Down the Lane	Palladium	**The Peters Sisters**
	Dark Halo	Arts	Andre Dakar
	The Sunset Gun	Aldwych	Frank Singuineau
	Othello	Shakespeare Memorial Theatre, Stratford-upon-Avon	**Paul Robeson**
	Anne Marie	National Film Theatre	**Douglas Archibald** (author), **Edric Connor, Pearl Connor**
	A Raisin in the Sun	Adelphi	**Lorraine Hansberry** (author), **Lloyd Richards** (director), **Earle Hyman, Juanita Moore**, Kim Hamilton, Olga James, Lionel Ngakane, Bari Johnson
	The Crooked Mile	Cambridge	**Elisabeth Welch,** Isabelle Lucas, George Webb
	Cock-a-Doodle-Dandy	Royal Court	Berto Pasuka
	One More River	Duke of York's	Tommy Eytle
1960	*The Room*	Royal Court	Thomas Baptiste
	Flower Drum Song	Palace	**Ida Shepley**

Year	Production title	Theatre	Key black personnel
	Hello, Out There	Theatre Royal, Stratford East	**New Negro Theatre Company, Clifton Jones** (director), Johnny Sekka, Gloria Higdon, Mark Heath, Neville Munroe, Clifton Jones, Carmen Munroe
	No Count Boy		**New Negro Theatre Company, Clifton Jones** (director), Gloria Higdon, Mark Heath, Tamba Allen, Carmen Munroe
	The Comedy of Errors	Bristol Old Vic	**Cy Grant**
	Innocent as Hell	Lyric Hammersmith	Richardena Jackson
	Sea at Dauphin	Royal Court	**Derek Walcott** (author), **Lloyd Reckord** (director), Leo Carrera, Lionel Ngakane, Dudley Hunte
	Six in the Rain		**Derek Walcott** (author), **Lloyd Reckord** (director), Lionel Ngakane, Leo Carrera, Barbara Assoon, Lloyd Reckord
	Mister Johnson	Lyric Hammersmith	**Johnny Sekka**, Lionel Ngakane, Gladys Taylor, Joseph Layode, Connie Smith, Leo Carrera, Dudley Hunte, Yemi Ajibade, George Webb
	This Way to the Tomb	Arts	Cy Grant
	Toys in the Attic	Piccadilly	William Marshall, George Webb, Tommy Eytle

Year	Production title	Theatre	Key black personnel
	La Mere	Theatre Royal, Stratford East	**New Negro Theatre Company, Clifton Jones** (author/director), Carmen Munroe, Dudley Hunte
	The S Bend	Theatre Royal, Stratford East	**New Negro Theatre Company, Clifton Jones** (author/director), **Clifton Jones,** Tamba Allen, Neville Munroe, Carmen Munroe, Gladys Taylor
	The Maimed	Royal Court	Nadia Cattouse, Tommy Eytle
	The Tinker	Comedy	Mark Heath
1961	*The Connection*	Duke of York's	**Carl Lee**, Mark Heath
	King Kong	Prince's	**Nathan Mdledle, Peggy Phango, Joe Mogotsi**, Alton Kumalo
	The Miracle Worker	Royalty	Pearl Prescod, Rosita Yarboi
	You in Your Small Corner	Arts	**Barry Reckord** (author), Pearl Nunez, Gordon Woolford, Neville Munroe
	South	Lyric Hammersmith	Tommy Eytle, Randolph Mackenzie, Nadia Cattouse, Clifton Jones
	The Irregular Verb to Love	Criterion	Gladys Taylor
	The Blacks	Royal Court	Neville Munroe, Harry Baird, Bloke Modisane, Joan Hooley, Lloyd Reckord, Joseph Layode
	Tresper Revolution	Arts	Christopher Carlos, Sheila Clarke, Mark Heath

Year	Production title	Theatre	Key black personnel
	Empress With Teapot	Royal Court	Bloke Modisane
	The Kitchen		Tommy Eytle
	Humphrey, Armand and the Artichoke		Willie Payne
	August for the People		**Edric Connor**, Yemi Ajibade
	The Death of Bessie Smith		Tommy Eytle, Neville Monroe
	The Hurricane	Westminster	**Muriel Smith**
	A Wreath for Udomo	Lyric Hammersmith	**William Branch** (author), **Earl Cameron**, **Edric Connor**, **Lloyd Reckord**, **Evelyn Dove**, Horace James, Harry Baird, Andre Dakar, Willie Payne, Joan Hooley
1962	*A Gazelle in Park Lane*	Streatham Hill	Joan Hooley
	A Time to Laugh	Piccadilly	**Cleo Laine**
	Blitz!	Adelphi	Mark Heath
	Period of Adjustment	Royal Court/ Wyndham's	Carmen Munroe
	Jungle of the Cities	Theatre Royal, Stratford East	Joan Hooley
	The Genius and the Goddess	Comedy	Isabelle Lucas
	The Captain's Hero	Royal Court	Tommy Eytle
	Black Nativity	Criterion	**Vinnette Carroll** (director), **Langston Hughes** (author), Vinnette Carroll, Alex Bradford, Marion Williams, Madeleine Bell
	Do Somethin' Addy Man!	Theatre Royal, Stratford East	Horace James, Joan Hooley, George Webb, Charles Hyatt, Tommy Eytle, Pearl Prescod
	Day of the Prince	Royal Court	Bari Johnson
	Talking to You	Duke of York's	Johnny Sekka

Year	Production title	Theatre	Key black personnel
	The Merchant of Venice	Old Vic	Errol John
	Cindy-Ella or I Gotta Shoe	Garrick	**Cleo Laine, Elisabeth Welch, Cy Grant, George Browne**
1963	*Othello*	Old Vic	**Errol John**
	The Blood Knot	New Arts	**Zakes Mokae**
	Black Nativity	Piccadilly	
	Measure for Measure	Old Vic	**Errol John**
	Skyvers	Royal Court	**Barry Reckord** (author)
	Day of the Prince		Bari Johnson
	Wiley		Charles Hyatt
	Behan Bein' Behan	Prince Charles	Nadia Cattouse
	A Funny Thing Happened on the Way to the Forum	Strand	Fay Craig
	Pocahontas	Lyric	Isabelle Lucas
	Cindy-Ella	New Arts	**Cleo Laine, Elisabeth Welch, Cy Grant, George Browne**
	No Strings	Her Majesty's	**Beverley Todd**
1964	*Mr. Brown Comes Down the Hill*	Westminster	Mark Heath, Astley Harvey
	The Raft	Hampstead Theatre Club	Willie Jonah
	Saint Joan of the Stockyards	Queen's	Dudley Hunte
	The Man on the Stairs	New Lyric Hammersmith	**Gordon Heath**
	Maggie May	Adelphi	Diana Quiseekay
	Black Nativity	Vaudeville	**Vinnette Carroll** (director), **Langston Hughes** (author), **Ida Shepley**, Marion Williams
	Every Other Evening	Phoenix	Dolores Mantez
	In White America	New Arts	**Earl Cameron, Gordon Heath**, Fitzroy Coleman

Year	Production title	Theatre	Key black personnel
1965	*The Crucible*	Old Vic (National Theatre)	Pearl Prescod
	Blues for Mister Charlie	Aldwych	**James Baldwin** (author), Al Freeman Jr, Hilda Haynes, Beverley Todd, Percy Rodriguez and the Actors Studio Theatre Company of New York
	Man Better Man	Scala (The Commonwealth Arts Festival)	**Errol Hill** (author), Trinidad Theatre Company
	The Road	Theatre Royal, Stratford East (The Commonwealth Arts Festival)	**Wole Soyinka** (author), Bari Johnson, Willie Jonah, Rudolph Walker, Horace James, Alton Kumalo, Harcourt Curacao
	Song of the Goat/ The Masquerade	Scala (The Commonwealth Arts Festival)	**John Pepper Clark** (author), **John Ekwere** (director), Eastern Nigerian Theatre Company
	The Amen Corner	Saville	**James Baldwin** (author), **Lloyd Richards** (director), **Claudia McNeil**, Helen Martin, Georgia Burke
	Othello	Phoenix Theatre Company (Leicester)	**Cy Grant**
1966	*Othello*	Malvern Festival Theatre	**Rudolph Walker**
	The Owl and the Pussycat	Criterion	**Diana Sands**
	Santa Cruz	New Lyric Hammersmith	Frank Singuineau
	Funny Girl	Prince of Wales	Isabelle Lucas
	The Trials of Brother Jero	Hampstead Theatre Club	**Wole Soyinka** (author), **Zakes Mokae**, Jumoke Debayo, Femi Euba

Year	Production title	Theatre	Key black personnel
	The Blood Knot	Hampstead Theatre Club	**Zakes Mokae**
	A Share in the Sun	Cambridge	Charles Hyatt, Frank Singuineau
	Macbeth	Royal Court	Jumoke Debayo, Zakes Mokae, Femi Euba
	The Lion and the Jewel		**Wole Soyinka** (author), Lionel Ngakane, Jumoke Debayo, Femi Euba
	Hutch-Builder to Her Majesty	Mercury	Louis Mahoney, Charles Hyatt, Rosita Yarboi
1967	*Happy Deathday*	Westminster	Clifton Jones
	Benito Cereno	Mermaid	Rudolph Walker, Danny Daniels
	Coriolanus	Royal Shakespeare Theatre, Stratford-upon-Avon	Louis Mahoney
	Neighbours/Dutchman	Hampstead Theatre Club	**Leroi Jones** (author, *Dutchman*), **Calvin Lockhart**
	All's Well That Ends Well	Royal Shakespeare Theatre, Stratford-upon-Avon	Alton Kumalo
	Ogodiveleftthegason	Royal Court	Harry Baird
	Black New World	Strand	**Donald McKayle** (author, director)
	Romeo and Juliet	Royal Shakespeare Theatre, Stratford-upon-Avon	Oscar James, Louis Mahoney, Alton Kumalo
	A Midsummer Night's Dream	Saville	**Cleo Laine**
	Wise Child	Wyndham's	**Cleo Sylvestre**
	Sweet Charity	Prince of Wales	Paula Kelly
	Number Ten	Strand	Dennis Alaba Peters

Year	Production title	Theatre	Key black personnel
1968	*All's Well That Ends Well*	Aldwych	Alton Kumalo
	Bakke's Night of Fame	Hampstead Theatre Club	**Johnny Sekka**
	The Adventures of the Black Girl in Her Search for God	Mermaid	Mona Hammond
	Julius Caesar	Royal Shakespeare Theatre, Stratford-upon-Avon	Alton Kumalo, Oscar James
	A Lesson in a Dead Language	Theatre Upstairs (Royal Court)	**Adrienne Kennedy** (author), Nina Baden-Semper, Elizabeth Adare, Stefan Kalipha, Sheila Scott Wilkinson
	Funnyhouse of a Negro		
	In His Own Write	Old Vic	**Adrienne Kennedy** (co-author)
	Janie Jackson	New	**Marlene Warfield, Earl Cameron, Adelaide Hall**, Horace James, Calvin Butler, Rudolph Walker
	Hair	Shaftesbury	**Peter Straker, Marsha Hunt**
	Johnny So Long	Arts	Rudolph Walker
	God Bless	Aldwych	Ram John Holder
	Julius Caesar		Alton Kumalo, Oscar James
1969	*The Boys in the Band*	Wyndham's	Reuben Greene
	Pericles	Royal Shakespeare Theatre, Stratford-upon-Avon	Alton Kumalo

Year	Production title	Theatre	Key black personnel
	Song of the Lusitanian Bogey	Aldwych	**Michael Schultz** (director), Negro Ensemble Company from New York including Rosalind Cash, Esther Rolle, Clarice Taylor
	God is a (Guess What?)	Aldwych	**Michael Schultz** (director), **Ray McIver** (author), Negro Ensemble Company from New York including Rosalind Cash
	High Diplomacy	Westminster	**Muriel Smith**
	Women Beware Women	Royal Shakespeare Theatre, Stratford-upon-Avon	Alton Kumalo
	Back to Methuselah Part I (The Thing Happens)	Old Vic (National Theatre)	Isabelle Lucas
	The Body Builders	Open Space	Sheila Scott-Wilkinson
	4 Dimensional Me	Hampstead Theatre Club	**Bari Jonson** (director), **Rudolph Walker**, **Sheila Scott-Wilkinson**
	There'll Be Some Changes Made	Fortune	**Carmen Munroe**
	The National Health, or Nurse Norton's Affair	Old Vic (National Theatre)	**Cleo Sylvestre**, **Isabelle Lucas**, George Browne
	Martin Luther King	Greenwich Theatre	**Bari Johnson**, Nina Baden-Semper, Frank Cousins, Jumoke Debayo, Mark Heath, Harcourt Curacao, Derek Griffiths
	Insideout	Royal Court	Femi Euba
	Don't Gas the Blacks	Open Space	**Barry Reckord** (writer), **Lloyd Reckord** (director), Rudolph Walker

Year	Production title	Theatre	Key black personnel
	The Electronic Nigger	Ambiance Theatre, Westbourne Grove	**Ed Bullins** (author), **Stefan Kalipha, Charles Hyatt, Sheila Scott-Wilkinson**
	A Minor Piece		**Ed Bullins** (author), **Stefan Kalipha, Sheila Scott-Wilkinson**
1970	*The Blacks*	Round House	Jason Rose, Harry Baird, Frank Cousins, Bloke Modisane, Glenna Forster-Jones, Nina Baden-Semper, Nadia Cattouse, Carmen Munroe, Jumoke Debayo, Horace James, Charles Hyatt
	The Hallelujah Boy	Duchess	Thomas Baptiste
	Sing a Rude Song	Greenwich/ Garrick	Derek Griffiths
	The Apple Cart	Mermaid	**Carmen Munroe**
	The Dictator's Slippers/ The Ladder	Westminster	Mark Heath
	Rats Mass	Royal Court	**Adrienne Kennedy** (author)
	The Tempest	Mermaid	**Rudolph Walker, Norman Beaton**
	The Winter's Tale	Aldwych	Alton Kumalo
	The Plebeians Rehearse the Uprising		
	Oh! Calcutta	Round House	Brenda Arnau
	Twelfth Night	Aldwych	Alton Kumalo
	Cyrano	Cambridge	Willie Jonah, Isabelle Lucas
	Down the Arches	Greenwich	Derek Griffiths
	AC/DC	Royal Court	Sheila Scott-Wilkinson
	Give a Dog a Bone	Westminster	Lon Satton
	Pirates	Royal Court	Bloke Modisane, Alfred Fagon, Norman Beaton, Corinne Skinner-Carter
	Catch My Soul	Round House	P.P. Arnold, Totlyn Jackson

Year	Production title	Theatre	Key black personnel
	The High Bid	Criterion	**Eartha Kitt**
1971	*The Duchess of Malfi*	Royal Court	Sheila Scott-Wilkinson
	After Haggerty	Criterion	Merdelle Jordine
	Mister	Duchess	Oscar James
	The Merchant of Venice	Royal Shakespeare Theatre, Stratford-upon-Avon	Alton Kumalo
	Twelfth Night		
	Passion	Alexandra Park Racecourse	Norman Beaton
	One at Night	Royal Court	Rudolph Walker
	No Sex Please – We're British	Strand	Vicki Richards
	Skyvers	Theatre Upstairs	**Barry Reckord** (author)
	Caesar and Cleopatra	Chichester Festival	Elroy Josephs
	Boseman and Lena	Theatre Upstairs	**Zakes Mokae, Bloke Modisane**
	Tyger	New (National Theatre)	Isabelle Lucas, Norman Beaton
	Showboat	Adelphi	**Cleo Laine, Thomas Carey**, Ena Cabayo, Eddie Tagoe
	Danton's Death	New (National Theatre)	Elizabeth Adare
	Jump	Queen's	Sheila Scott-Wilkinson
	As Time Goes By	Theatre Upstairs	**Mustapha Matura** (author), Alfred Fagon, Stefan Kalipha, Corinne Skinner, Mona Hammond, Oscar James, Frank Singuineau, T-Bone Wilson
	A Liberated Woman	Greenwich	**Barry Reckord** (author), Barry Reckord, Rudolph Walker
	Cato Street	Young Vic	Norman Beaton, Louis Mahoney

Year	Production title	Theatre	Key black personnel
	Pirates	Theatre Upstairs	Bloke Modisane, Alfred Fagon, Norman Beaton, Corinne Skinner
1972	*The Slave*	Dark and Light Theatre	**Amiri Baraka** (author)
	The Threepenny Opera	Prince of Wales/ Piccadilly	Lon Satton
	The Black Macbeth	Round House	**Oscar James, Mona Hammond,** Jeffrey Kissoon, Christopher Asante, Neville Aurelius, Merdelle Jordine, Charles Hyatt, Kwesi Kay
	Quetzalcoatl		Charles Hyatt
	Umabatha	Aldwych	**Welcome Msomi** (author), **Natal Theatre Workshop Company**
	Coriolanus	Royal Shakespeare Theatre, Stratford-upon-Avon	Tony Osoba
	Julius Caesar		Joseph Marcell, Jason Rose
	Gone with the Wind	Drury Lane	**Isabelle Lucas,** Marion Ramsey, Anni Domingo
	An Othello	Open Space	**Rudolph Walker, Anton Phillips**
	The Merchant of Venice	Aldwych (Royal Shakespeare Company)	Kwesi Kay
	Po' Miss Julie	Hampstead Theatre Club	Joan Ann Maynard, Lon Satton
	Cowardy Custard	Mermaid	**Elaine Delmar**
	Liberty Ranch	Greenwich	Derek Griffiths
	Jesus Christ Superstar	Palace	Paul Barber, Larrington Walker, Sally Sagoe, George Harris, Esther Byrd, Floella Benjamin

Year	Production title	Theatre	Key black personnel
	Caesar and Cleopatra	Royal Shakespeare Theatre, Stratford-upon-Avon	Joseph Marcell, Jason Rose, Calvin Lockhart
	Richard's Cork Leg	Royal Court	Olu Jacobs
	Mother Earth	Roundhouse	Peter Straker
	Titus Andronicus	Royal Shakespeare Theatre, Stratford-upon-Avon	**Calvin Lockhart**
	Bunny	Criterion	**Eartha Kitt**
	Raas	Dark and Light Theatre	**Anton Phillips**
	Anansi and Brer Englishman		**Yvonne Brewster** (director)
1973	*Savages*	Royal Court	Frank Singuineau
	Born Yesterday	Greenwich	Elroy Josephs
	Two Gentlemen of Verona	Phoenix	Derek Griffiths, Brenda Arnau, Keefe West, Patricia Ebigwei (aka Patti Boulaye), Johnny Worthy
	The Banana Box	Hampstead Theatre Club/ Apollo	Don Warrington, Elizabeth Adare
	The Me Nobody Knows	Shaw	Reg Tsiboe, Joan Ann Maynard, Peter Straker, Angela Bruce
	Umabatha	Aldwych	**Welcome Msomi** (author and director), Zulu Company from South Africa
	Signs of the Times	Vaudeville	Norman Beaton
	Voices from the Frontline (Babylon Ghetto, Voices of the Living and the Dead, The Bus Rebel)	Keskidee Centre	**Dam-X (Steve Hall)** (author), **Linton Kwesi Johnson** (author), **Eseoghene** (author)
	Antony and Cleopatra	Aldwych (Royal Shakespeare Company)	Tony Osoba
	Julius Caesar		Joseph Marcell

Year	Production title	Theatre	Key black personnel
	Sweet Talk	Theatre Upstairs (Royal Court)	**Michael Abbensetts** (author), Mona Hammond, Allister Bain, Don Warrington, Joan Ann Maynard, Lee Davis
	The Bacchae	Old Vic (National Theatre)	**Wole Soyinka** (author, adapted from Euripides), Isabelle Lucas, Ram John Holder
	Decameron '73	Roundhouse	Miquel Brown
	Sizwe Bansi is Dead	Theatre Upstairs (Royal Court)/ Royal Court (1974)	**John Kani** (author), **Winston Ntshona** (author), **John Kani, Winston Ntshona**
	Section Nine	The Place (Royal Shakespeare Company)	Joseph Marcell
	Coriolanus	Aldwych (Royal Shakespeare Company)	Tony Osoba, Oscar James, Joseph Marcell
	Pippin	Her Majesty's	**Elisabeth Welch, Northern J. Calloway**
	Design for Living	Phoenix	Willie Jonah
	The Party	Old Vic (National Theatre)	Ram John Holder
	Black Feet in the Snow	Keskidee Centre	**Jamal Ali** (author and director)
	The Emperor Jones	Dark and Light Theatre	**Thomas Baptiste**
	The Trials of Brother Jero		**Wole Soyinka** (author)
1974	*The Island*	Royal Court (English Stage Company)	**John Kani** (author), **Winston Ntshona** (author), **John Kani, Winston Ntshona**
	The Black and White Minstrels	Hampstead Theatre Club	Taiwo Ajai
	Mind Your Head	Shaw	Norman Beaton
	A Streetcar Named Desire	Piccadilly	Louise Nelson

Year	Production title	Theatre	Key black personnel
	Bird Child	Theatre Upstairs	Jumoke Debayo
	The Bewitched	Aldwych (Royal Shakespeare Company)	Joseph Marcell
	Birds of Paradise	Garrick	Pauline Peart
	Hair	Queen's	Miquel Brown
	Play Mas	Royal Court (English Stage Company)/ Phoenix	**Mustapha Matura** (author), Stefan Kalipha, Rudolph Walker, Norman Beaton, Tommy Eytle, Lucita Lijertwood, Frank Singuineau, Trevor Thomas, Mona Hammond
	X	Theatre Upstairs	**Barry Reckord** (author)
	Let My People Come	Regent	Johnny Worthy
	Measure for Measure	Royal Shakespeare Theatre, Stratford-upon-Avon	Jeffery Kissoon
	Body and Soul	Keskidee Centre	**T-Bone Wilson** (author), **Yemi Ajibade** (director)
	The Connection	Hampstead Theatre Club	Mark Heath
	The Little Hut	Duke of York's	Olu Jacobs
	Marching Song	Greenwich	**Cleo Sylvestre**
1975	*Renga Moi*	Aldwych (Royal Shakespeare Company)	**Robert Serumaga** (author/director), **Abafumi Company of Kampala, Uganda**
	The Jumble Street March	Keskidee Centre	**T-Bone Wilson** (author)
	The Black Mikado	Cambridge	**Norman Beaton, Vernon Nesbeth, Derek Griffiths,** Patricia Ebigwei (aka Patti Boulaye), Floella Benjamin, Val Pringle
	The Sunshine Boys	Piccadilly	Isabelle Lucas

Year	Production title	Theatre	Key black personnel
	The Death of a Black Man	Hampstead Theatre Club	**Alfred Fagon** (author), Gregory Munroe, Mona Hammond, Anton Phillips
	Kwa Zulu	New London/ Piccadilly	Victor Ntoni (music and lyrics), Kwa Zulu company
	Sex and Kinship in a Savage Society	Theatre Upstairs	Lucita Lijertwood
	Black Slaves, White Chains		**Mustapha Matura** (author), **Rufus Collins** (director), Olu Jacobs, Eddy Grant, Mark Heath
	Othello	Young Vic	Cleo Sylvestre
	All Walks of Leg		
	Betzi	Haymarket	Peggy Phango
	A Man's Man	Hampstead Theatre Club	Stefan Kalipha
	The Time of Your Life	Victoria Palace	Rosita Yarboy
	Macbeth	Young Vic	Cleo Sylvestre
	Ipi Tombi	Her Majesty's	Ipi Tombi company
	The Swamp Dwellers	Keskidee Centre	**Wole Soyinka** (author), **Howard Johnson** (director), **Imruh Caesar, Willie Payne**

Notes

Introduction

1 John Jackson, *The History of the Scottish Stage* (Peter Hill, 1783), p. 350.

Chapter 1

1 Kwesi Owusu, *The Struggle for Black Arts in Britain* (Comedia, 1986), p. 97.
2 *Ibid.*, p. 98.

Chapter 2

1 Winsome Hines, '*The Voice* Interview: Rudolph Walker', *The Voice* (19 July 1994).
2 Hugh Quarshie, 'Conventional Folly: A Discussion of English Classical Theatre' in Kwesi Owusu (ed.), *Black British Culture and Society: A Text Reader* (Routledge, 2000), p. 289.
3 John Cottrell, *Laurence Olivier* (Weidenfeld & Nicolson, 1975), p. 337.
4 *Ibid.*, p. 341.
5 Donald Spoto, *Laurence Olivier: A Biography* (HarperCollins, 1991), p. 283.
6 Roger Lewis, *The Real Life of Laurence Olivier* (Arrow, 1996), p. 115.
7 Philip Ziegler, *Olivier* (Maclehose Press, 2013), pp. 282–3.
8 Anthony Holden, *Olivier* (Little Books, 2007), p. 379.
9 *Ibid.*

10 Logan Gourlay (ed.), *Olivier* (Weidenfeld & Nicolson, 1973), p. 43.
11 Holden, p. 379.
12 Gourlay, p. 162.
13 *Ibid.*, p. 153.
14 Edric Connor, interview with Lewis Nkosi, 1964. Transcribed by Ray Funk from a sound recording in Indiana University. Courtesy of Ray Funk.
15 Gordon Heath, *Deep Are the Roots: Memoirs of a Black Expatriate* (University of Massachusetts Press, 1992), pp. 146–7.
16 Cy Grant, *Blackness and the Dreaming Soul: Race, Identity and the Materialistic Paradigm* (Shoving Leopard, 2007), p. 38.
17 *Ibid.*
18 Owusu, p. 90.
19 Allan Lord Thompson, *Paul Robeson: Artist and Activist on Records, Radio and Television* (Allan Lord Thompson, 2004), X.11.1953.
20 Ziegler, pp. 121–2.
21 Lindsey R. Swindall, *The Politics of Paul Robeson's Othello* (University Press of Mississippi, 2011), pp. 172–3.

Chapter 3

1 Bernardine Evaristo, email to Stephen Bourne, 7 November 2020.
2 Kat Hopps, 'West End trailblazer Cleo Sylvestre still has "unfinished business" at 75', *Express* (25 November 2020).
3 Cleo Sylvestre, interview with Stephen Bourne, 12 January 1976.
4 *Ibid.*
5 Hopps, *Express*.
6 Sylvestre, interview with Stephen Bourne, 1976.
7 Lanre Bakare, 'Being an actor was like being a hamster on a wheel', *The Guardian* (15 October 2020).
8 Cleo Sylvestre, interview with Brian Kamm, British Library's Theatre Archive Project, 15 December 2008.
9 *Ibid.*
10 Thomas Baptiste, interview with Stephen Bourne, 8 July 1991; see also Jim Pines (ed.), *Black and White in Colour: Black People in British Television Since 1936* (British Film Institute, 1992).
11 Baptiste, interview with Stephen Bourne, 1991.
12 Bakare, *The Guardian*.

Chapter 4

1 Herbert Marshall and Mildred Stock, *Ira Aldridge: The Negro Tragedian* (Macmillan, 1958), p. 335.

2 Folarin Shyllon, *Black People in Britain 1555–1833* (Oxford University Press, 1977), p. 204.
3 *Ibid.*, p. 205.
4 *Ibid.*, p. 206.
5 Edward Scobie, *Black Britannia: A History of Blacks in Britain* (Johnson, 1972), p. 129.
6 Shyllon, p. 208.
7 Scobie, p. 131.
8 Heidi J. Holder, 'Ira Aldridge (1807–1867)' in *Oxford Dictionary of National Biography* (Oxford University Press, 2004).
9 Peter Fryer, *Staying Power: The History of Black People in Britain* (Pluto Press, 1984), p. 255.
10 *Ibid.*, p. 256.
11 *Ibid.*
12 Corporal John Lovell Jr, 'Shakespeare's American Play' in *Theatre Arts* Vol. xxviii, No. 6 (June 1944).
13 *Ibid.*
14 Rose Collis, 'Ira Aldridge' in *The New Encyclopedia of Brighton* (Brighton and Hove Libraries/Brighton and Hove City Council, 2010), p. 26.
15 Errol Hill, *Shakespeare in Sable: A History of Black Shakespearean Actors* (University of Massachusetts Press, 1984), p. 19.

Chapter 5

1 Hill, p. 39.

Chapter 6

1 Ziggi Alexander, 'Black entertainers of the Edwardian era', *Weekend Voice* (21–27 December 1987).
2 Henry T. Sampson, *The Ghost Walks: A Chronological History of Blacks in Show Business, 1865–1910* (Scarecrow Press, 1988), p. 43.
3 Jeffrey Green and Rainer E. Lotz, 'James Douglas Bohee (1844–1897)' in *Oxford Dictionary of National Biography* (Oxford University Press, 2011).
4 Stephen Bourne, 'Amy Height (1866–1913)' in *Oxford Dictionary of National Biography* (Oxford University Press, 2012).
5 Stephen Bourne, 'Edward Peter [Eddie] Whaley (1877x80–1960)' in *Oxford Dictionary of National Biography* (Oxford University Press, 2013).
6 Jeffrey Green, interview with Stephen Bourne, 19 July 1994.
7 Eric Ledell Smith, *Bert Williams: A Biography of the Pioneer Black Comedian* (McFarland, 1992), pp. 72–3.
8 *Ibid.*, pp. 73–4.

9 Colin Grant, *The Essay (Thinking Black)*, BBC Radio 3 (7 October 2020).
10 Jeffrey Green, 'High Society and Black Entertainers in the 1920s and 1930s' *New Community* Vol. 13, No. 3 (Spring 1987).

Chapter 7

1 Scobie, p. 177.
2 Pauline Henriques, interview with Stephen Bourne, 4 August 1989.
3 Stephen Bourne, 'Connie Smith (1875–1970), music-hall entertainer and actress' in *Oxford Dictionary of National Biography* (Oxford University Press, 2011).
4 Henriques, interview with Stephen Bourne, 1989.
5 Edward Scobie, 'A Little Old Lady With a Big Heart', *Flamingo*, (April 1962).
6 Henriques, interview with Stephen Bourne, 1989.

Chapter 8

1 Marie Seton, *Paul Robeson* (Dennis Dobson, 1958), p. 34.
2 C.L.R. James, 'Paul Robeson', *Race Today*, 16, No. 4 (May/June 1985).
3 *Paul Robeson: Portraits of the Artist*, DVD box set (Criterion Collection, 2007).
4 Paul Robeson, BBC Radio Light Programme (6 September 1959).
5 Martin Bauml Duberman, *Paul Robeson* (The Bodley Head, 1989), p. 49.
6 Seton, p. 10.
7 Paul Robeson and Lloyd L. Brown, *Here I Stand* (Beacon Press, 1958), p. 49.
8 Stephen Bourne, 'Lawrence Brown (1893–1972)' in *Oxford Dictionary of National Biography* (Oxford University Press, 2015).
9 Seton, pp. 232–3.
10 Eslanda Goode Robeson, *Paul Robeson: Negro* (Victor Gollancz, 1930), pp. 96–7.
11 Seton, p. 43.
12 *Ibid.*, pp. 49–50.
13 Stephen Bourne, 'At home with Amanda Ira Aldridge', *The Historian* (Autumn 2020).
14 Pauline Henriques, interview with Stephen Bourne, 24 July 1991.
15 Seton, p. 54.
16 Kenneth Barrow, *Flora: An Appreciation of the Life and Work of Dame Flora Robson* (Heinemann, 1981), p. 25.
17 Seton, pp. 61–2.
18 Eslanda Robeson, *African Journey* (Victor Gollancz, 1946), p. 49.
19 Marcus Garvey, *Black Man*, Vol. 1, No. 7 (June 1935).

20 Rupert Lewis, *Marcus Garvey: Anti-Colonial Champion* (Karia Press, 1987), p. 250.
21 Seton, pp. 102–3.
22 *Ibid.*, p. 100.
23 C.L.R. James, 'Paul Robeson: Black Star', *Black World* (November 1970).
24 Sean Creighton, *Politics and Culture: Paul Robeson in the UK* (Agenda Services, 1998), p. 4.
25 Peter Noble, *Reflected Glory* (Jarrolds, 1958), p. 37.
26 Lloyd L. Brown, *The Young Paul Robeson* (Westview Press, 1997), p. 160.
27 Paul Robeson Jr, *The Undiscovered Paul Robeson: Quest for Freedom, 1939–1976* (John Wiley, 2010), p. 293.
28 *Ibid.*, p. 294.
29 *Ibid.*
30 Tony Richardson, *Long Distance Runner: A Memoir* (Faber and Faber, 1993), p. 101.
31 Swindall, p. 177.
32 Brown, p. 160.
33 *Ibid.*
34 Seton, p. 121.
35 Paul Robeson, *Here I Stand* (Beacon Press, 1958), p. 48.

Chapter 9

1 The others are John Boyega, Marianne Jean-Baptiste, John Primero, Dr Harold Moody, Belle Davis, George A. Roberts and Sam King.
2 Hakim Adi, *Black and Asian Studies Newsletter*, No. 24, April 1999, pp. 32–3.
3 Delia Jarrett-Macauley, *The Life of Una Marson 1905–65* (Manchester University Press, 1998), p. 43.
4 *Ibid.*
5 *Daily Gleaner*, 13 June 1932, p. 6.
6 Jarrett-Macauley, p. 51.
7 Colin Chambers, *Black and Asian Theatre in Britain: A History* (Routledge, 2011), p. 99.
8 Una Marson: Race and Censorship in 1930sTheatre/Collection in Focus/British Library (YouTube, 2023).
9 Hakim Adi, *West Africans in Britain 1900–1960* (Lawrence and Wishart, 1988), p. 55.
10 Chambers, p. 102.
11 Susan Croft, *She Also Wrote Plays* (Faber and Faber, 2001), pp. 171–2.
12 Una Marson, *Pocomania and London Calling* (Blouse and Skirt Books and National Library of Jamaica, 2016). See also Alison Donnell, *Una Marson: Selected Poems* (Peepal Tree, 2011).

13 For more information about Una's wartime work at the BBC see Stephen Bourne, *Under Fire: Black Britain in Wartime 1939–45* (The History Press, 2020). For an overview of Una's work in Britain see Marc Matera, *Black London* (University of California Press, 2015).

Chapter 10

1 Lena Horne, *Lena* (André Deutsch, 1966), p. 93.
2 James Weldon Johnson, *Black Manhattan* (Alfred A. Knopf, 1930), p. 199.
3 Elisabeth Welch, interview with Stephen Bourne, 15 August 1993.
4 Langston Hughes, *The Big Sea* (Alfred A. Knopf, 1940), p. 223.
5 Claude McKay, *A Long Way From Home* (L. Furman, 1937), p. 141.
6 Horne, pp. 92–3.
7 Charles B. Cochran, *Secrets of a Showman* (Heinemann, 1925), p. 415.
8 Charles Graves, *The Cochran Story* (W.H. Allen, 1951), p. 111.
9 Charles B. Cochran, *Cock-A-Doodle-Doo* (J.M. Dent, 1941), p. 116.
10 Frances Rust, *Dance in Society* (Routledge, 1969), p. 90.
11 Welch, interview with Stephen Bourne, 1993.
12 Frank C. Taylor with Gerald Cook, *Alberta: A Celebration in Blues* (McGraw-Hill, 1987), p. 95.
13 Welch, interview with Stephen Bourne, 1993.

Chapter 11

1 Cleo Laine, interview with Stephen Bourne, London, 2 June 1994.

Chapter 12

1 Marshall and Jean Stearns, *Jazz Dance: The Story of American Vernacular Dance* (Macmillan, 1968), p. 162.
2 *Ibid.*
3 Julie Kavanagh, *Secret Muses: A Life of Frederick Ashton* (Faber and Faber, 1996), p. 151.
4 Herbert Harris, 'Our Busby Berkeley', *Film Weekly* (25 January 1935).
5 Dorothy Bradley, letter to Stephen Bourne, 12 January 1991.
6 Peter Noble, *British Ballet* (Skelton Robinson, 1950), pp. 102–3.
7 Fred Isaac, 'Speaks for his race with ballet', *The Evening Chronicle, Manchester* (9 July 1949).
8 Eric Johns, 'Negro Ballet – the story of an interesting new venture', *Theatre World* (April 1946).
9 Glyn Kelsall, 'Negro Ballet: Berto Pasuka on coming London season', *The Stage* (7 February 1946).
10 Johns, *Theatre World.*
11 Noel Vaz, *West African Review* (Spring 1947).

Chapter 13

1 Henriques, interview with Stephen Bourne, 1989.
2 Peter Fiddick, *Miss Lou at RADA*, BBC Radio 4 (9 September 2005).
3 Pearl Connor-Mogotsi, interview with Stephen Bourne, 26 July 1993.
4 Mervyn Morris, *Miss Lou: Louise Bennett and Jamaican Culture* (Signal Books, 2014), p. 15.
5 *Ibid.*
6 Leonie Forbes, *Miss Lou at RADA*.
7 Linton Kwesi Johnson, *Miss Lou at RADA*.
8 Leonie Forbes as told to Mervyn Morris, *Leonie: Her Autobiography* (LMH Publishing, 2012), p. 41.
9 *Ibid.*
10 *Ibid.*, p. 28.
11 Edric Connor, *Horizons: The Life and Times of Edric Connor* (Ian Randle, 2007), p. 67.
12 Earl Cameron, interview with Stephen Bourne for Bourne, *Black in the British Frame: The Black Experience in British Film and Television* (Continuum, 2001), p. 106.
13 Stephen Bourne, Errol Hill obituary, *The Independent* (18 October 2013).
14 Hill, p. xix.
15 *Ibid.*
16 Yvonne Brewster, *Desert Island Discs*, BBC Radio 4 (27 March 2005).
17 *Ibid.*
18 Allister Harry, '*The Voice* Interview: Enter, stage left!', *The Voice* (7 November 1995).

Chapter 14

1 Ida Shepley File, 1938–1962, BBC Written Archives.

Chapter 15

1 Peter Noble, letter to Stephen Bourne, 27 October 1982.
2 Thelma Singh, letter to Stephen Bourne, 11 March 1983.
3 Robert Adams, 'Colour Prejudice in Art', *Film Reel Review* (1948). The 'continental' actor referred to by Adams was Frederick Valk, a German-born Jewish stage and screen actor of Czech Jewish descent who fled to Britain in the late 1930s to escape Nazi persecution and subsequently became a naturalised British citizen.
4 Robert Adams, letter to Mr Greenidge, 28 November 1948. Courtesy of Val Wilmer.
5 Henriques, interview with Stephen Bourne, 1991. See also Jim Pines (ed.), *Black and White in Colour: Black People in British Television Since 1936* (British Film Institute, 1992).

6 Henriques, interview with Stephen Bourne, 1991.
7 *Ibid.*
8 Henriques, interview with Stephen Bourne, 1989.
9 *Ibid.*

Chapter 16

1 Henriques, interview with Stephen Bourne, 1991. See also Pines (ed.).
2 Leslie Schenk, in conversation with Stephen Bourne, 20 September 1995.
3 Heath, pp. 123–4.
4 *Ibid.*, p. 120.
5 Schenk, in conversation with Stephen Bourne, 1995.
6 Paul Breman, *The Independent*, 13 September 1991.
7 Schenk, in conversation with Stephen Bourne, 1995.

Chapter 17

1 Carmen Munroe, interview with Stephen Bourne, 25 July 1991. See also Pines (ed.).
2 Pearl Connor-Mogotsi, interview with Stephen Bourne, 13 July 1989.
3 Connor-Mogotsi, interview with Stephen Bourne, 1993
4 *Ibid.*
5 *Ibid.*
6 *Ibid.*
7 Thomas Baptiste, interview with Stephen Bourne, 17 August 1993.
8 *Ibid.*
9 Connor-Mogotsi, interview with Stephen Bourne, 1989.
10 *Ibid.*
11 'Coloured Actors Meet Equity', *The Stage* (4 September 1958).
12 For further information about the Negro Theatre Workshop see www.georgepadmoreinstitute.org/collection/negro-theatre-workshop.
13 Rudolph Walker, interview with Stephen Bourne, 29 July 1991. See also Pines (ed.).
14 Lloyd Reckord, interview with Stephen Bourne, 1 August 1991. See also Pines (ed.).
15 *Ibid.*
16 Connor-Mogotsi, interview with Stephen Bourne, 1993
17 *Ibid.*

Chapter 18

1 Stephen Bourne, *Black in the British Frame: The Black Experience in British Film and Television* (Continuum, 2001), p. 136.
2 *Ibid.*

3 Louis Mahoney, 'Racist Beliefs Endemic Amongst White Population', *The Stage* (2 October 1975). See also 'Creating a Black Theatre in Britain' in Charles Husband (ed.), *White Media and Black Britain: A Critical Look at the Role of the Media in Race Relations Today* (Arrow Books, 1975).
4 Cy Grant, interview with Isaac Julien, 26 July 1991. See also Pines, (ed.).
5 www.longfieldhall.org.uk

Chapter 19

1 Connor-Mogotsi, interview with Stephen Bourne, 1991. See also Jim Pines (ed.).
2 Ruth Little and Emily McLaughlin, *The Royal Court Theatre: Inside Out* (Oberon Books, 2007), p. 9.
3 Amanda Bidnall, *The West Indian Generation: Remaking British Culture in London, 1945–1965* (Liverpool University Press, 2017), p. 205.
4 Barry Reckord in conversation with David Johnson, 22 April 1997, for Talawa's *Blackgrounds* oral history project; Talawa Theatre Company Archive, Ref. TTC/10/1/4/8; Department of Theatre and Performance, Victoria and Albert Museum.
5 Richardson, p. 98.
6 Barry Reckord in conversation with David Johnson, 1997.
7 Irving Wardle, *The Theatres of George Devine* (Jonathan Cape, 1978), pp. 251–2.
8 Barry Reckord in conversation with David Johnson, 1997.
9 Cleo Laine, *Cleo* (Simon and Schuster, 1994), p. 149.
10 Henriques, interview with Stephen Bourne, 1991. See also Pines (ed.).
11 Kenneth Tynan, *The Observer Plays* (Faber and Faber, 1958), p. 9.
12 Connor-Mogotsi, interview with Stephen Bourne, 1991.
13 John Elliot, letter to Stephen Bourne, 11 February 1996.
14 James Earl Jones and Penelope Niven, *James Earl Jones: Voices and Silences* (Charles Scribner's Sons, 1993), pp. 165–6.
15 Little and McLaughlin, p. 101.
16 *Ibid.*
17 Oscar Lewenstein, *Kicking Against the Pricks – A Theater Producer Looks Back: The Memoirs of Oscar Lewenstein* (Nick Hern Books, 1994), p. 102.
18 Darlene Clark Hine (ed.), Richard E.T. White, *Black Women in America: Theater Arts and Entertainment* (Facts on File, 1997), p. 127.
19 Joanne Campbell, interview with Stephen Bourne, 4 January 1997.
20 *Ibid.*
21 Philip Hedley, *The Independent* (19 July 1988).

22 Michael McMillan, 'Ter speak in yer mudder tongue: An interview with playwright Mustapha Matura', in Kwesi Owusu (ed.), *Black British Culture and Society: A Text Reader* (Routledge, 2000), p. 259.
23 Connor-Mogotsi, interview with Stephen Bourne, 1991.

Chapter 20

1 Nikki Henriques, *Inspirational Women* (Grapevine, 1988), p. 32.
2 *Ibid.*, p. 26.
3 Graham Collier, *Cleo and John: A Biography of the Dankworths* (Quartet Books, 1976), p. 60.
4 *Ibid.*
5 *Ibid.*, p. 61.
6 Cleo Laine, *Cleo* (Simon and Schuster, 1994), p. 145.
7 *Ibid.*, p. 148.
8 Keith Howes, *Broadcasting It: An Encyclopaedia of Homosexuality on Film, Radio and TV in the UK 1923–1993* (Cassell, 1993), p. 879.
9 Collier, p. 63.
10 Laine, p. 166.
11 Collier, p. 84.
12 Collier, p. 153.
13 Ned Sherrin, interview with Stephen Bourne, London, 12 August 1993.
14 Henriques, p. 31.
15 Laine, p. 209.
16 Laine, p. 210.
17 Laine, p. 237.
18 Henriques, p. 34.
19 Collier, p. 146.
20 Henriques, p. 37.

Chapter 21

1 Corinne Skinner-Carter, interview with Stephen Bourne, 24 August 1998.
2 McMillan in Owusu (ed.), p. 259.
3 *Ibid.*
4 *Ibid.* p. 260.
5 Michael Billington, 'Mustapha Matura obituary', *The Guardian* (1 November 2019).
6 Mike Phillips, *The Guardian* (5 June 1978).
7 *Ibid.*
8 Michelle Stoby, 'Black British Drama After *Empire Road*: an interview with Michael Abbensetts', *Wasafiri*, Issue 35 (Spring 2002).

9 Michael Coveney, 'Michael Abbensetts obituary', *The Guardian* (30 November 2016).
10 Stoby, 2002.
11 Roland Rees, *Alfred Fagon: Plays* (Oberon Books, 1999), p. 9.
12 *Ibid.*
13 *Ibid.*, p. 12.
14 Roland Rees, *Fringe First: Pioneers of Fringe Theatre on Record* (Oberon Books, 1992), p. 211.
15 Rees, *Plays*, p. 11.
16 *Ibid.*, p. 20.

Further Reading

Plays

Abbensetts, Michael, *Four Plays* (Oberon Books, 2001)

Brewster, Yvonne (ed.), *For the Reckord: A Collection of Three Plays by Barry Reckord* (Oberon Books, 2010)

Fagon, Alfred, *Alfred Fagon: Plays* (Oberon Books, 1999)

Hogsbjerg, Christian (ed.), C.L.R. James, *Toussaint L'ouverture* (Duke University Press, 2013)

Marson, Una, *Pocomania and London Calling* (Blouse and Skirt Books, National Library of Jamaica, 2016)

Matura, Mustapha, *Matura: Six Plays* (Methuen, 1992)

Criticism

Banham, Martin, Errol Hill and George Woodyard (eds), *The Cambridge Guide to African and Caribbean Theatre* (Cambridge University Press, 1994)

Bidnall, Amanda, *The West Indian Generation: Remaking British Culture in London, 1945–1965* (Liverpool University Press, 2017)

Goddard, Lynette, *Errol John's Moon on a Rainbow Shawl* (Routledge, 2018)

Husband, Charles (ed.), *White Media and Black Britain: A Critical Look at the Role of the Media in Race Relations Today* (Arrow Books, 1975)

Johnson, David Vivian, *Talawa Theatre Company: A Theatrical History and the Brewster Era* (Bloomsbury, 2021)

Owusu, Kwesi, *The Struggle for Black Arts in Britain* (Comedia, 1986)
Owusu, Kwesi (ed.), *Black British Culture and Society: A Text Reader* (Routledge, 2000)
Swindall, Lindsey R., *The Politics of Paul Robeson's Othello* (University Press of Mississippi, 2011)
Walmsley, Anne, *The Caribbean Artists Movement 1966–1972: A Literary and Cultural History* (New Beacon Books, 1992)

History

Bourne, Stephen, *Black in the British Frame: The Black Experience in British Film and Television* (Continuum, 2001)
Chambers, Colin, *Black and Asian Theatre in Britain: A History* (Routledge, 2011)
Croft, Susan, with Stephen Bourne and Dr Alda Terracciano, *Black and Asian Performance at the Theatre Museum: A User's Guide* (Theatre Museum, 2003)
Fryer, Peter, *Staying Power: The History of Black People in Britain* (Pluto Press, 1984)
Hill, Errol, *Shakespeare in Sable: A History of Black Shakespearean Actors* (The University of Massachusetts Press, 1984)
Pines, Jim (ed.), *Black and White in Colour: Black People in British Television Since 1936* (British Film Institute, 1992)
Rees, Roland, *Fringe First: Pioneers of Fringe Theatre on Record* (Oberon Books, 1992)
Scobie, Edward, *Black Britannia: A History of Blacks in Britain* (Johnson, 1972)
Shyllon, Folarin, *Black People in Britain 1555–1833* (Oxford University Press, 1977)
Vernon, Patrick and Angelina Osborne, *100 Great Black Britons* (Robinson, 2020)

Autobiographies and Biographies

Beaton, Norman, *Beaton But Unbowed* (Methuen, 1986)
Bourne, Stephen, *Elisabeth Welch: Soft Lights and Sweet Music* (Scarecrow Press, 2005)
Brewster, Yvonne, *The Undertaker's Daughter: The Colourful Life of a Theatre Director* (Black Amber Books, 2004)
Connor, Edric, *Horizons: The Life and Times of Edric Connor* (Ian Randle, 2007)
Duberman, Martin Bauml, *Paul Robeson* (The Bodley Head, 1989)
Egan, Bill, *Florence Mills: Harlem Jazz Queen* (Scarecrow Press, 2004)
Forbes, Leonie, *Leonie: Her Autobiography* (LMH, 2012)
Grant, Cy, *Blackness and the Dreaming Soul: Race, Identity and the Materialistic Paradigm* (Shoving Leopard, 2007)

Heath, Gordon, *Deep Are the Roots: Memoirs of a Black Expatriate* (The University of Massachusetts Press, 1992)
Laine, Cleo, *Cleo* (Simon & Schuster, 1994)
Lindfors, Bernth (ed.), *Ira Aldridge: The African Roscius* (University of Rochester Press, 2007)
Lindfors, Bernth, *Ira Aldridge: The Early Years 1807–1833* (University of Rochester Press, 2011)
Lindfors, Bernth, *The Theatrical Career of Samuel Morgan Smith* (Africa Word Press, 2018)
Marshall, Herbert and Mildred Stock, *Ira Aldridge: The Negro Tragedian* (Rockliff, 1958)
Robeson Jr, Paul, *The Undiscovered Paul Robeson: An Artist's Journey, 1898–1939* (John Wiley, 2001)
Robeson Jr, Paul, *The Undiscovered Paul Robeson: Quest for Freedom, 1939–1976* (John Wiley, 2010)
Robeson, Paul, with Brown, Lloyd L., *Here I Stand* (Beacon Press, 1958)
Robeson, Susan, *The Whole World in His Hands: A Pictorial Biography of Paul Robeson* (Citadel Press, 1981)
Seton, Marie, *Paul Robeson* (Dennis Dobson, 1958)
Skinner-Carter, Corinne with Nia Reynolds, Z., *Why Not Me? A Memoir* (Black Stock Books, 2011)

Actors and Playwrights

For further information about the following actors and playwrights who are included in *Trailblazers of Black British Theatre*, please refer to Stephen Bourne's biographical essays in the *Oxford Dictionary of National Biography:* (www.oxforddnb.com):

Michael Abbensetts (1938–2016)
Robert Adams (*c.* 1900–65)
Thomas Baptiste (1929–2018)
Norman Beaton (1934–94)
Buddy Bradley (1905–72)
Edric Connor (1913–68)
Pearl Connor-Mogotsi (1924–2005)
Alfred Fagon (1937–86)
Cy Grant (1919–2010)
Gordon Heath (1918–91)
Amy Height (*c.* 1866–1913)
Pauline Henriques (1914–98)
Isabelle Lucas (1927–97)
Florence Mills (1896–1927)
Lionel Ngakane (1928–2003)
Berto Pasuka (1917–63)
Barry Reckord (1926–2011)
Lloyd Reckord (1929–2015)
Ida Shepley (1909–75)
Frank Singuineau (1913–92)
Connie Smith (1875–1970)
Elisabeth Welch (1904–2003)
Eddie Whaley (1877–1960)

Index

Names

Stage Productions

Theatre Companies

About the Author

Stephen Bourne is the author of *Black Poppies*, *Under Fire* and several other books about Black history. He is a graduate of the London College of Printing and received a MPhil from De Montfort University. He is also an honorary fellow of London South Bank University. Stephen has been the recipient of research grants for Black British theatre from The Society for Theatre Research and the Harold Hyam Wingate Foundation. In 1991, he became a founder member of the Black and Asian Studies Association.

www.stephenbourne.co.uk